W9-BUG-241

DRUMS
FOR EVERYONE

Flossmoor Public Library
1000 Sterling Avenue
Flossmoor, IL 60422-1295
Phone: (708) 798-3600

KNACK

DRUMS
FOR EVERYONE

A Step-by-Step Guide to Equipment, Beats, and Basics

Carmine Appice

Photographs by John Klicker

KNACK
MAKE IT EASY

Guilford, Connecticut
An imprint of Globe Pequot Press

To buy books in quantity for corporate use
or incentives, call **(800) 962-0973**
or e-mail **premiums@GlobePequot.com.**

Copyright © 2010 by Morris Book Publishing, LLC

ALL RIGHTS RESERVED. No part of this book may be reproduced or transmitted in any form by any means, electronic or mechanical, including photocopying and recording, or by any information storage and retrieval system, except as may be expressly permitted in writing from the publisher. Requests for permission should be addressed to Globe Pequot Press, Attn: Rights and Permissions Department, P.O. Box 480, Guilford, CT 06437.

Knack is a registered trademark of Morris Book Publishing, LLC, and is used with express permission.

Editor: Katie Benoit
Cover Design: Paul Beatrice, Bret Kerr
Interior Design: Paul Beatrice
Layout: Kevin Mak
Music Engraving by Richard Gratton
Cover photos © Shutterstock
Back cover photo by Alex Solca
Interior photos by John Klicker with the exception of photo page 32 by Charles Stewart, page 107 left by Dmitry Vinogradov/ Shutterstock

Library of Congress Cataloging-in-Publication Data is available on file.

ISBN 978-1-59921-777-2

Printed in China

10 9 8 7 6 5 4 3 2 1

The information in this book is true and complete to the best of our knowledge. All recommendations are made without guarantee on the part of the author or Globe Pequot Press. The author and Globe Pequot Press disclaim any liability in connection with the use of this information.

For Mary and Charlie Appice

Acknowledgments

Thanks to Leslie Gold for her help in this project and to all my endorsement companies for helping out, especially DDRUM. Special thanks to:
  Aquarian Heads
  Calzone/Anvil Cases
  DDRUM
  DW Pedals
  Rhythm Tech Products
  Sabian Cymbals
  Shure Mics
  Vic Firth Sticks
  Zoom Products

CONTENTS

INTRODUCTION

Before you even pick up your sticks, there are two questions I'd like you to think about. First, what makes a great drummer? And second (and more important), what are your personal goals as a drummer-to-be?

I can answer the first question for you. To me a great drummer is somebody who's got great timing, can power a band without overpowering it, understands melody, and has the technique and facility to play whatever comes to mind

As for the second question, only you can answer that. Only you know what you want to accomplish as a drummer. Maybe you just want to be able to play along with your favorite CDs. Maybe you want to get good enough to play gigs and make some extra cash. And maybe you want to become the next Gene Krupa, or Buddy Rich, or Yoshiki Hayashi or—OK—Carmine Appice.

Whatever your goals, this book can start you on the path to realizing them. But you'll have to take it from there. You'll have to make the commitment and set aside the time that's required to be good at anything.

I started playing drums when I was around twelve. I went for lessons, and I was so into it that I learned five years of music in three. Yeah, I caught on quick—but I also worked at it. I'd practice an hour a day with my books and an hour with the stereo. I also learned chords and harmonies on the piano and got pretty good on the guitar, which came in really handy when I decided to write songs. So I always recommend that a drummer learn to play something besides drums too, because otherwise the guitarist or vocalist has the big hits and the drummer ends up driving the VW!

Drums have always provided the means for me to both express and support myself. As a kid I didn't care about becoming a great drummer. I just wanted to be like my teacher, who made a great living. He pulled in $500 a week on gigs and $150 teaching. Now, $650 a week in 1961 was big money, let me tell you. So, as a teenager I started playing weddings and bar mitzvahs, and by the time I was seventeen, I was making $200 a weekend and bought myself a new car.

The idea of Carmine Appice playing society do's might seem just a little incongruous today, but don't knock it. In one weekend I'd play all sorts of music. My typical weekend consisted of a bar mitzvah, a wedding, a jazz gig, and a rock show. As a result I became very versatile and later, when I

or warn of danger. The "talking drums" of Ghana and Nigeria became a highly sophisticated means of communication between villoges; tuned to pitches approximating spoken language, they actually create dialogue that can be transmitted from as far as twenty miles away, like a walkie-talkie.

Drums have long played an essential role in the military. In the European infantry they coded commands to the soldiers in battle. The marching band contained the marching snare, the predecessor of today's snare drum; the larger and deeper toned bass drum; and hand cymbals, whose familiar "crash" was achieved, in the days before the cymbal stand, by hitting the cymbals together.

Until the late nineteenth century, band musicians carried their instruments, and the only way the drums and cymbals

toured with everybody from Vanilla Fudge and Pink Floyd to Bo Diddley, Rod Stewart, and Ozzy Osbourne, it wasn't hard for me to adjust to different groups and artists.

So the better and more well rounded you get with the drums, the wider the music world becomes for you. But let's begin by taking a look at the wide world of drums.

The Wide World of Drums

Although the concept of the modern drum set has only been around since the early twentieth century, drums have been part of the human experience since cave men used a combination of hollowed out wood, skins, and sticks to communicate with each other, both as a form of ritual and the first—sort of—telephone.

In Africa tribes still use drums to send messages to each other from miles away, to signal meetings, announce events,

could be played was individually, by hand. Then came the "big bang" that revolutionized the drum world—the drum set.

The Drum Set

The invention of the bass drum pedal in the late 1800s was the first breakthrough. This indispensable item made it possible for one person to play several percussion instruments (snare drum, bass drum, and cymbals) simultaneously. The mechanical pedal allowed the drummer to hit the bass drum with his foot instead of playing it by hand, and the cymbals could be placed on stands and played with sticks. With the bass drum on the floor and the snare drum and cymbals on stands, the drum set was born. With the addition of the low hat, a two-cymbal instrument that was operated by the foot opposite the bass drum and eventually raised up on a stand to become today's hi-hat, the basic drum set was complete.

By the 1920s the hot jazz scene of New Orleans led to the addition of exotic percussion instruments like the African-inspired tom-tom and the Turkish and Chinese cymbals. In the 1930s the great jazz drummer Gene Krupa, one of my all-time idols, put the toms on the map when he featured them in his playing. The drums really acquired status when Krupa brought them to the front of the stage and set the house on fire with his wild solos.

The drum set continued to evolve in the 1940s, when another great jazz drummer, Max Roach, began making more use of the cymbals for rhythmic emphasis, freeing up the bass drum for more creative experimentation. In the 1950s the marvelous Louie Bellson made history when he

used two bass drums, an innovation that would influence Cream's Ginger Baker, The Who's Keith Moon, and other great drummers of the Love Generation of music.

By the late 1960s rock music had attained the status of an art form and many drummers developed their own unique styles that involved more volume and energy. Drummers no longer played just with the hands and wrists; their entire bodies became part of the act, putting the drums to the endurance test. Since the drum sets of those days were still being made for light jazz, society, and show drummers and weren't intended for high-voltage treatment, the result was often disastrous. When I was with the rock group Vanilla Fudge, I used to do a good amount of damage to my drum set. This led me to get together with the legendary Ludwig Drum Company in experimenting with bigger and stronger drums.

Eventually, Ludwig created extremely sturdy drums and hardware. Meanwhile new drumhead companies started popping up with concepts that would change the drumhead forever. It was a great day when a rock drummer could get a drumhead that would not break easily, stayed in tune, and could be used for more than one show at a time.

In the 1970s the one and only John Bonham of Led Zeppelin was credited with taking the modern drum set to new heights, which included his signature gong. Not too many people know that it was yours truly who got John his first drum set and gong—a copy of my own drum set—and that Vanilla Fudge took Zeppelin on their very first tour.

Drums and You

OK. That's drum history in a nutshell. Now, where do you come in? Well, this book is for you. You'll learn about the drum set in detail so you can tune and maintain your drums. You'll learn some quick methods of hand development, and how to hold the sticks properly. I've also created "Red Lights"—things to avoid—and "Green Lights" and "Yellow Lights"—tips, trivia, and good ideas to remember. As you learn the rudiments of drumming, think of it as basic training for drummers—a combination of music lesson and cardiac exercise. It's like going to the gym without having to pay the membership.

I'll also be giving you some basic music theory. You'll learn the value of quarter notes, eighth notes, sixteenth notes, and their equivalent rest values. You will know what they look like, how to count them, and then how to play them. When you've got those basics down, I'll show you how to play some famous songs. When you're playing along with the music, well that is when the fun really begins, Trust me—you'll love it and never want to stop.

So, ready, set—drum set!

> Note: There are two signs we will use to count 8th notes
> 1) + symbol
> 2) &
> These are inserted so you can see variations for this count.

ACOUSTIC DRUMS

Today's acoustic drums: The different woods and finishes influence your instrument's color and tone

The acoustic drum is the one you are most familiar with. Hitting a drum with a stick or by hand produces the sound. The drums we will concentrate on in this book are the ones you strike with drumsticks: the snare drum, tom-toms, bass drums, and another percussion instrument, the cymbals. These make up your basic acoustic drum set.

Acoustic drums come in a variety of sizes and colors. Different woods produce different sounds. The most popular wood for drums is maple, which produces a warm sound with plenty of tone and bottom end. It also has a good amount of top end crack. Drummers today have been experimenting with other woods like babinga, walnut, and birch, each

The Log Drum

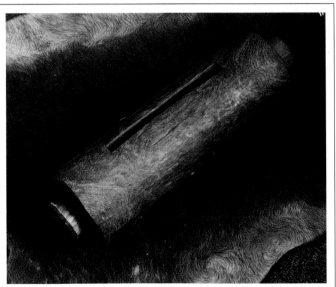

- Log drums were probably the first drums.

- Usually the middle piece of the log is cut out for sound.

- Log drums are still played on some islands in the

South Pacific. Visit the Cook Islands, if you have a chance, and take in a log drum show.

- Log drums are handmade, and played with large sticks made of tree branches.

The Modern Drum Set

- 1. Snare drum

- 2. Bass drum

- 3. Tom

- 4. Tom

- 5. Floor tom

- 6. Hi-hat (cymbal)

- 7. Cymbal

- 8. Cymbal

of which has a different sound and response. Drums have their own unique possibilities and personalities, all of which are affected by the materials from which they're created. The drum finishes are made with a plastic covering that is glued to the round drum shell. The thinner the shell, the better it can vibrate, and the better the sound will be. A second finish is a lacquer finish. Acquiring this finish is similar to painting a car, sanding down and applying numerous coats of enamel the paint. Finally, a clear sealer coat is applied for a beautiful final finish.

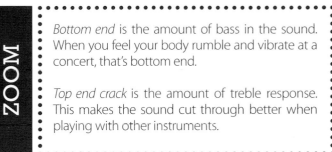

ZOOM

Bottom end is the amount of bass in the sound. When you feel your body rumble and vibrate at a concert, that's bottom end.

Top end crack is the amount of treble response. This makes the sound cut through better when playing with other instruments.

Wood or Lacquered Floor Tom

- Thin shelled floor toms weigh less than their thicker shelled counterparts and are thus easier to carry, especially when you start playing shows.

- Floor toms can be covered with plastic wraps that come in pearl or sparkle finishes. Be aware, however, that these wraps may change the sound. Toms also come in lacquer finishes (pictured here).

- I love the tribal sound of the floor tom.

Sparkle Finish Tom-Tom

- There are pros and cons to thin shells. On the plus side, they produce a better sound. On the minus, the shell can be so thin that strength and durability are compromised.

- Here is a 12 x 8-inch tom with a sparkle wrap finish.

- Think of the tom-toms as the drum set's "melody." With three or four toms tuned to different notes, you can come up with recognizable melodies.

DRUM STANDS & MORE

Tighten up and tune—the drum key, throw-off switch, and tom stand

A drum set is as much a mechanical apparatus as it is a musical instrument. So you'll need a tool box. The most important tool is the drum key. Think of it as your kit's ignition key. Shaped like a T, it fits all the drum set's tuning screws to tighten and loosen the drum parts.

The drum key is actually three kinds of keys: the regular key, the spinning key, and the ratchet key. The regular key works by putting the key on the drum accessory and tuning the drum by loosening or tightening it. The spinner is a key you put on the drum and turn from the top. As it spins around, it tightens or loosens the drum. The ratchet key works like a ratchet and performs the same function as the spinner.

KNACK DRUMS FOR EVERYONE

Snare Throw-off

Three Kinds of Keys

- The arrow shows how to turn the snares on and off and how the knob turns left or right to adjust the snare tension on the bottom head, allowing you to achieve the sound you want.

- There are the three primary drum keys: regular, spinner, and ratchet. Although more keys are available, these are all you need to set up and tune your set and get started.

- There's also a drum key that fits into an electric drill, making changing drumheads a breeze.

- Don't lose the drum key! Life is hard without it.

Always keep a few keys on hand, as they are easily lost and without a drum key, believe me, life is hard.

Then there's the snare throw-off. It allows you to change the sound from a tom to a snare by pushing a rod up or down.

The double tom stand can be either attached to the bass drum or on the floor.

When the bass drum is in position to hit the floor, spurs come down. These spurs stop the drum from moving forward when you hit it. A wing nut holds each spur in place. There is a height adjustment as well.

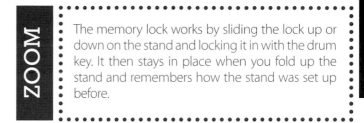

ZOOM

The memory lock works by sliding the lock up or down on the stand and locking it in with the drum key. It then stays in place when you fold up the stand and remembers how the stand was set up before.

Double Tom Stand

- The double tom can stand on the bass drum or on the floor stand. Both do the job, but in my opinion the floor stand is preferable because it's more flexible.

- You can adjust each stand at a variety of angles. There are also adjustments on the bracket part of the stand where the ball is.

Bass Drum Spurs

- This split close-up shot illustrates how a bass drum spur works in the up and down positions.

- Turn the spur clockwise or counterclockwise to adjust height. Bass drums need these spurs to function properly.

- In 1968 Ludwig created spurs that would retract into the shell and disappear when not in use. Some bass drums had four spurs instead of two—they actually worked better.

- Today's spurs came from a Japanese design that's been around for about 25 years.

THE SNARE DRUM
In the "choir" of the drum set, snare drums are the main voice

The snare drum is the main voice of your drum set. Its distinctive sharp sound has been an essential part of the percussion family for over two hundred years. It has two calfskin or plastic drumheads stretched tightly over a hollow metal frame. The top head, or batter head, is struck with wooden drumsticks, while the bottom head, or snare head, has catgut or metal wires called snares stretched tightly across it. When the

top head is struck, the snares produce a characteristic sharp rattling sound as they vibrate against the bottom head.

You need to know about the snare drum—how it works and its parts—so that you can play it and maintain it properly.

Snare drums are made of two types of material: wood and metal. In general wood snares have a deeper sound than metal snares, which have a crisper sound with more

Snare Drum

- Snare drums can be made of either metal or wood. The metal used is bronze, brass, or steel. The wood includes maple, birch, and mahogany.

- String or plastic belts hold snares onto the drum snare terminal and connect the snares to the drum. I recommend the plastic belts—they hardly ever break.

- Throw-off switches have become very hi-tech and can provide the classic snare with three different sounds. They even come in different colors!

Snare Top and Bottom

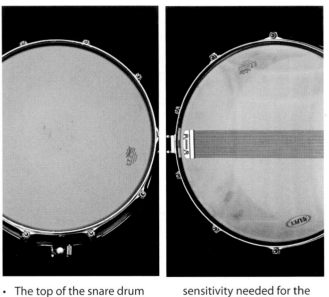

- The top of the snare drum is the batter head. The wire snares on the bottom head are where the sound comes from.

- The bottom head is made thinner, so that the snare wires can vibrate against it. If this head were thicker, it would not have the

sensitivity needed for the distinctive snare vibrations.

- The cut out in the bottom rim allows the snares to go across the bottom of the drum and keeps the snare wires close to the head.

crack—treble. The depth of the snare varies from three inches to eight inches, with each depth, of course, creating a different sound. Snares are tuned with single tension drum lugs, which allow for tuning the top and bottom heads individually, giving the drummer ample control of his sound.

ZOOM

Drumheads were originally made of calfskin, which was very much affected by weather. In the early 1960s plastic began replacing the calfskin. Originally the snares were made from catgut, which, like calfskin, was weather sensitive. Today "snare wires"—thin wires that look like squiggled lines—have replaced the catgut snares.

Tuning Lug

- The tuning lug is a very important part of the snare drum. The tuning screw twists into the lug, changing the head tension to tune the drum.

- Individual tuning lugs for top and bottom heads make it easy to tune each head individually. Keep the lug tuning rods greased for easier turning.

- Tuning rods come in different lengths for different drums. The snare and the small rack toms are about the same length. But the bass drum and floor toms are bigger.

Throw-off Switch on Snare

- The throw-off switch operation is demonstrated here, with arrows showing how the switch works.

- Turning the knob changes the tension of the snare wires on the bottom head.

- The plastic belt or snare string attaches to the throw-off switch.

- A little secret: I love to keep the tuning knob loose because it gives the snares a loose sound.

THE BASS DRUM
The bass drum provides the bottom, the big sound of today's music

After the snare drum, the bass drum is definitely the second in command. Known as the "bottom," the bass drum is actually used more than the snare. In most songs today, the snare drum plays what we call the back beat, on the two and four count. But the bass drum plays many different patterns that complete the drum groove. Listen to any hip hop or rock song and you'll hear the versatility of the bass drum.

The bass drum is usually made of wood, and in rare cases, metal, and comes in both plastic wrap and lacquer finish. As far as size goes, I recommend a 22 x 16-inch bass drum, which is good for most musical styles. You have full control over the tuning of the bass drum with single tension tuning screws or rods. Some bass drums come with a rack tom holder, mounted on the bass drum. All bass drums have what

KNACK DRUMS FOR EVERYONE

Bass Drum

Bass Drum Tuning Rods

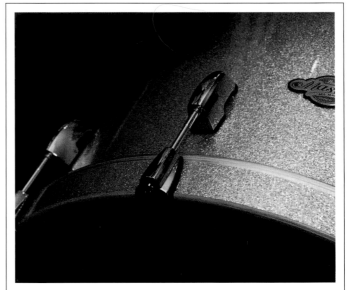

- Bass drums are the bottom on the drum set.

- Some drum sets have more than one bass drum. The great Louie Bellson made the dual-bass drum set popular.

- Bass drumheads come with or without a "porthole." You can choose either one, based on the sound you prefer.

- If you put a kick pad on the bass drum batter head, the head will last longer.

- Originally bass drums were carried and hit with a hand beater and the tuning was done with ropes.

- Today bass drums have individual tuning rods and lugs. The result is much better tuning.

- Chrome or brass? Tuning rods and lugs come in many different finishes.

- Bass drums have T-shape rods, or rods that require a drum key.

we call bass drum spurs. Today, there are bass drums that are made of plastic. These plastic drums come in many colors and have a different sound than the wood drums.

MAKE IT EASY

Metal drum sets are very heavy and can be a real pain to transport. Buy wood drums! Wood sounds good. Maple produces a warm, round sound, and birch a pleasant sound with more punch and not as much bottom end. Babinga wood sounds very punchy with the warmth of maple. Geez, you'd think we were at a wine tasting!

Rack Tom Bass Drum Mount

- Mounted toms, or rack toms, have been around for at least sixty years. The first rack tom held just one tom-tom.

- Today you can have one or two toms on one stand.

- The stand has many adjustments.

- Clip-on tom holders were popular in the early 1970s. The tom would clip onto the holder. The advantage was that it was a simple mount; the disadvantage was that it had limited adjustments.

Bass Drum Spurs

- At first spurs were made to clip onto the bass drum. Today they are cut into the shell to prevent the bass drum from moving when hit.

- Spurs have rubber tips to protect the floor.

- They also have a point at the end that digs into rugs, assuring the drum's stability.

- Even spurs can look hot, with chrome, brass, or black finishes.

TOM-TOM (RACK TOM)

The tom-tom is the melody of the drum set; thin shells vibrate better and offer a tribal sound

After the log drum, the tom-tom has to be the oldest of all drums. The Vikings used the beat of the tom-tom to keep rowers in synch and Native American powwows featured the tom-tom as an instrument of ceremony and communication.

Today's toms are very different from their early predecessors. Like the snare and bass drums, modern day toms have single tension tuning and come in wrap or lacquer finishes. They can be mounted on all sorts of stands—on the bass drum, on floor stands that hold two toms, or hung from cymbal stands. Some have legs and can stand on the floor—hence the name "floor toms."

Like all the drums in the drum set, the hanging toms, or

KNACK DRUMS FOR EVERYONE

Ancient Drums

- Ancient drums had a tom-tom quality to them. Animal skins stretched out over a shell produced the sound.

- These ancient drums were not tunable and the heads were difficult to change.

- They were hit with bigger sticks than those we use today.

- Viking ships employed drums like these to keep the pace for the rowers.

Rack Tom on Bass Drum Holder

- Rack toms date from the big band era. They were hooked onto the bass drum.

- Some rack tom holders have a tube that disappears into the bass drum and goes as low as the drum's depth.

- Some rack toms were deepened by one inch and were called power toms. By the 1960s tom holders were on a sliding tube system.

"rack toms," have an air hole in the shell. When the drum is hit, the hole lets out the air that is misplaced inside the drum, resulting in better drumhead action.

It was the legendary Gene Krupa who brought the tom-tom to modern prominence. He featured it in his drum set and became famous for his tom-tom solos—explosions of fantastic technique and raw energy that gave the drums a whole new identity as a solo instrument. Just listen to Krupa in the Benny Goodman numbers "Jungle Madness" and "Sing, Sing, Sing," and you'll understand how he mesmerized audiences.

ZOOM

Krupa would drive everyone crazy with his rhythms and his twirling. He was the first drummer to make a drum set "sexy." His body language was amazing—he was so into it. I was totally inspired by the 1959 movie, *The Gene Krupa Story*. I know every note of the soundtrack, and I got a lot of my twirling ideas from Krupa.

Rack Tom Floor Stand

- Some floor tom stands are attached to the cymbal stand with a bracket.

- The tom does not have as much bottom with these stands.

- When the tom is hanging from this stand, it's sometimes hard to get the correct angles on the cymbal stand and the drum.

Tom Air Hole

- Air holes revolutionized the drum. When you hit the drum, the pressure is released, taking pressure off the drumhead.

- This gives the drummer better stick action.

- Most drum companies use the air hole to display their logo, model, and serial numbers.

- Some drums come with as many as four air holes.

FLOOR TOM-TOM

The only tom-tom that stands on its own legs; you'll appreciate its distinctive deep sound

The floor tom is the biggest tom on the drum set. It has the lowest tom note—not as low as the bass drum, but pretty low. The bigger the tom, the deeper the sound.

The floor tom should be made of wood, preferably maple.

Again, some of these drums can be made of different woods to give you different kinds of attack and tone. They can be

made to have deeper length on the shells for a deeper tone. For example a 16 x 20-inch drum (20 inches being deeper) will have a deeper tone than one that is 16 x 16 inches.

The floor tom sits on the floor atop three legs, which can be adjusted to the best angle for you. Some floor toms are mounted on what we call floor stands, actually hanging from

Three-Legged Floor Tom

- Brackets allow you to position the three-legged floor tom at many possible angles. The one shown here is positioned at a severe angle.

- Some of the bigger floor toms have four legs.

Floor Tom Leg Bracket

- In this close up, you can see how the leg brackets work.

- Once you've found the proper angle for the floor tom, tighten the wing nuts.

- Note the hole in the middle of the leg bracket. It allows the leg to move freely up and down.

- Because every drum company makes different leg brackets, some brackets are bigger than others.

a bracket on the stand. This arrangement makes setting up more efficient, but without the tom standing directly on the ground, the sound suffers and, to me, anyway, seems to lose some bottom end.

Many drummers, myself included, use two floor toms. Sizes vary. The most common are 16 x 16 inches and 16 x 18 inches. I've had floor toms as large as 22 x 14 and 18 x 18 inches—big boys with a sound all their own. Your standard four-, five-, or six-piece drum kit includes one floor tom. The eight-piece set generally has one floor and two extra rack toms.

· · · · · · · · · · · · · · RED ● LIGHT · · · · · · · · · · · · · ·

Weight distribution is critical with the floor tom. If the legs are too high on one side, it can tip over. Play around with the angle of the legs until you find the proper position. Don't tighten the nuts until you feel comfortable with the height and angle.

Floor Tom Stand

- The legless floor tom rests on a floor stand.

- I prefer the legged toms because they have a deeper sound that comes from the legs touching the floor.

- Like the drums themselves, these stands also come in different finishes.

- Because these drums do not touch the floor, the toms lose some bottom end.

Two Floor Toms

- Two of the greatest drummers in history, Gene Krupa and Buddy Rich, used two floor toms.

- The 16 x 16-inch and the 16 x 18-inch floor toms are my favorites.

- An 18 x 18-inch floor tom sounds great, but these drums must be custom made.

- DDRUM drum company makes a nice-sounding 14 x 14-inch floor drum with legs.

HARDWARE, PLUS

Let's talk cymbal stands: the straight stand, boom stand, and cymbal boom arm

Buying a cymbal stand sounds easy enough, but guess what? An inferior quality cymbal stand can not only be an impediment, but can also ruin a great cymbal. Here's what to look for when you're choosing one.

Let's start off with the straight cymbal stand. This is a two-level floor stand that goes up and down by adjusting the

wing nuts. On the top is a cymbal tilt, which allows the cymbal to tilt up or down—a great leap forward for the drum set.

Then there's the boom stand. This stand has a long arm positioned at something like a seventy-five degree angle between the up and down adjustment on the cymbal stand

Cymbal Floor Stand

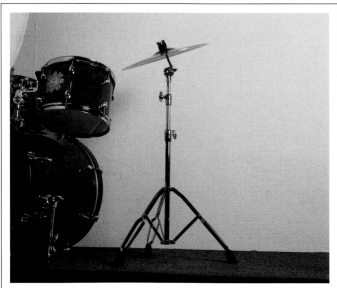

- In the 1930s and 1940s, there were no cymbal tilts. The cymbal sat flat on the stand.

- This stand gave the drummer a new way to place cymbals.

- The legs fold for easy packing. And the tubes go

- down, making the stand fairly small. This innovation led to more height being available for the cymbals.

- The drummer can also move the stand around for better placement, and can add as many cymbals as he likes to the set up.

Boom Stand

- When the Ludwig Drum Company introduced the boom stand in 1978, most drummers were ecstatic. What a great idea! With the boom, cymbals could now be placed at any angle and height. I've used two boom stands since 1978. I put my two china cymbals upside down on them.

- The boom stand is very heavy so that it doesn't move around when you're playing. It was specifically designed for rock drummers.

and the boom arm with the tilt on it. With the boom arm you're able to put a bracket onto any available stand and put a cymbal arm into it. This gives the drummer another way to add cymbals without having to use a cymbal stand base.

The top of each stand consists of the plastic collar, the felt where the cymbal is placed, and the second felt. I like to use a metal cymbal washer. When you tighten the wing nut, the cymbal is tight and doesn't over ring.

•••••••••••••• RED ● LIGHT ••••••••••••••
Avoid stands with hard plastic feet that are narrow and small. You want big, wide feet with angled floor contact surfaces made of soft, floor-gripping rubber. And beware of single-bar legs, which can bend under the weight of bigger cymbals. Make sure there's a counterweight on the end of the boom; otherwise it might topple over during heavy playing and you'll end up with a cracked cymbal.

Cymbal Tilt

- The cymbal tilt was another great innovation. Before the tilt came along, the cymbal sat flat on the stand, making it impossible to get a down angle on it unless you lowered the stand. With the tilt you could now even hang a cymbal from a boom stand.

- The first cymbal tilts were not very strong. I broke quite a few of them until Ludwig came out with the heavy-duty Atlas stand in 1969.

Cymbal Boom Arm

- The boom arm is the top part of the boom stand. The boom made the use of universal brackets very practical, making possible many different set ups.

- Some people put a second closed set of hi-hat cymbals on these arms for a different sound and to have a set of hi-hats near the ride cymbal.

13

SNARE DRUM STANDS

The ins and outs of the snare stand—setting up and adjustments

The snare stand is the most complicated of all the stands in your drum set. It requires side-to-side and up-and-down angles in order to move it up and down, and the drum must be clamped to the stand to remain stable. Originally it wasn't a very strong piece of equipment, but today rock drummers can be as brutal as they want and the snare stand can take it.

You have many stands to choose from. Some of the cheaper stands are not as strong as the more expensive ones, but they will do the job and hold the snare drum. What they will not do is adjust to any angle. The cheap stand usually only adjusts straight back and forth. The more expensive stand is on a swivel and can pretty much go anywhere you want it to go.

KNACK DRUMS FOR EVERYONE

Snare Stand

- Parts of the stand:

1. Up-down adjustment

2. Ball swivel mechanism

- Other parts include the base tightening wing screw, claw mechanism, rubber ends of the claw, claw tightening mechanism, and memory lock.

- The arrows indicate the direction of the swivel and the up-down direction.

Ball Swivel Up Close

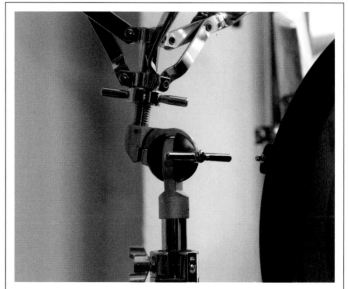

- The ball swivel was a wonderful invention that enabled the drummer to get virtually any playing angle.

- The ball swivel sits on top of the tube that gives you the up-and-down adjustment.

- The ball is made of rubber that grips the screw securely.

- Swivel adjustments are usually only available on snare stands that are higher priced. Cheap stands don't come with many adjustments.

The cheaper stands have much thinner legs. They also have very small rubber grips on the end of the legs to keep the stand steady. I need to use the more expensive stand as the legs are stronger and the rubber grips are bigger and hold the stand in place better.

Each snare stand has a claw that grips the drum. Open the claw by turning the knob on the stand. Put the drum on. Then tighten the claw until the drum is secure. Thanks to the claws, you can adjust the drum on the snare to an almost ninety degree angle and it won't fall off.

There's a memory lock on the stand for height adjustment, and the ball allows for swivel action, letting you position the drum at almost any angle.

The rubber ends on the claws, give a better grip on the drum. You can also adjust the base of the stand for spread.

Cheap Snare Stand

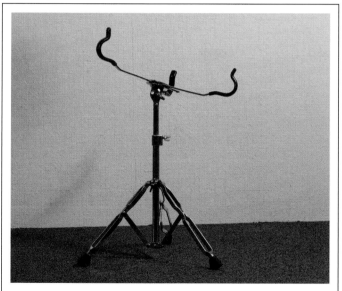

- Cheaper snares are fine for beginners. Just make sure you get one with a swivel.

- Lower-end stands are limited to the up-and-down motion on the tube. The up-and-down motion on the snare itself is limited to a nut that tightens over some lines on the metal to lock it in and only goes in one direction.

- The less expensive snare includes the up-and-down snare adjustment, up-and-down tube adjustment, claw grip, and legs and rubber stoppers.

Closing the Snare Stand

- The snare stand closes by turning the screw nut on the base to the left until the legs become loose and can be folded into the base.

- Next, loosen the nut at the top of the middle tube and push the tube down into the stand base. Try not to loosen the memory lock.

- Loosen the adjustment screw under the claw. Fold in the claws and push everything down, folding up the stand.

SEATS & THRONES

Cushions, bicycle seats, hydraulic seats, and how to make those easy, fast adjustments

A drummer's seat—or throne—is a very personal thing. Some drummers go all out for the perfect seat, while others are perfectly happy with cheaper models. Some seats are adjusted manually, with a screw; others run by hydraulics. And you can get any cushion you want—big or small, hard or soft. The bottom line is what you find most comfortable.

I personally like a smaller-sized hard cushion with a screw to adjust seat height. This type of adjustment uses a large screw instead of a middle bar. The seat turns to the right or left and goes up or down easily, and the screw nut is tightened to keep it in place.

The hydraulic seat, on the other hand, is a big lever-operated

All-Around Seat

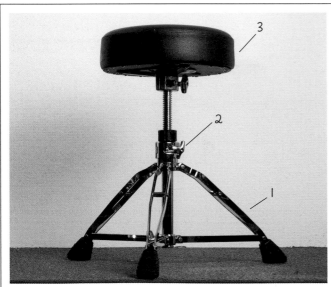

- Here are all the parts and features of a good seat.

1. Base stand

2. Middle screw rod

3. Cushion

- Turning the top of the seat counterclockwise raises it.

- Turning the seat top clockwise lowers it.

Cushions

- A cushion that's too big can affect your performance. Your thighs must be clear of the seat in order to play the bass drum properly.

- I like a small to medium cushion. It gives my thighs room to move and gives me a better performance on my feet.

- I don't like the bicycle seat. It might just be me, but I find it uncomfortable.

bicycle seat. When you pull up on the lever, the seat rises or falls to the desired height. It's quick and easy, but I prefer the screw seat because I get finer tuning and more of a choice of seat style.

The regular seats are easy to set up and take down. To set up, just open the base with the legs. Tighten the screw nut to keep it from closing. Put the seat onto the top of the big screw mechanism. Fasten the seat to the screw pole and tighten the screw to secure the seat to the stand. Use the memory lock on the stand for the repeat set up.

ZOOM

In the 1940s drummers like Gene Krupa and Buddy Rich had custom-made seats that consisted of a drum shell with a cushion on top. For a little extra oomph, the drum set and seat had a matching pearl finish.

EQUIPMENT

Hydraulic Seat

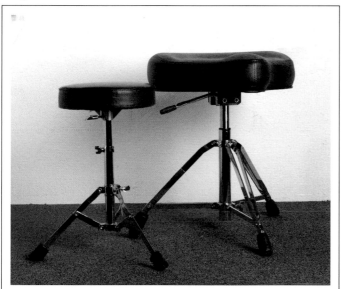

- The hydraulic seat is a newer concept in seat design.

- This seat adjusts very quickly. Just pull the lever up or down and you're in position.

- Many hydraulic seats have the bicycle seat. Just remember: Your thighs should be off, not on, the seat.

- Allow a little extra time to fold up the hydraulic seat when packing your gear.

Animal Seats

- Animal seats are a fashion statement and nothing more. They have no effect on your playing, nor do they make you an animal drummer! These seats come in many styles—leopard, tiger, zebra, to name a few. I own a few leopard seats because I think they're cool!

- The most commonly used drum seat cover is a simple black cloth. Leather is a possibility, provided you're not a "sweater." If you tend to perspire, you'll slide all over the slippery surface.

17

THE HI-HAT STAND

Setting up your hi-hat stand, mounting the cymbals, and making pedal adjustments

The hi-hat is a really cool part of the drum kit. It can be played with just the foot or hand, or a combination of both. The operation is simple. You push your foot down on the pedal and the two cymbals on the stand close.

Most hi-hat stands have three legs. Some of the new stands have only two legs and use the pedal part of the stand as a third leg for balance. This is very effective and also gives you more room for a second pedal when using a double-pedal set up. We'll get into the double pedal later in the book. There is also a spring adjustment near the pedal on the hi-hat.

Upper Part of the Hi-Hat Stand

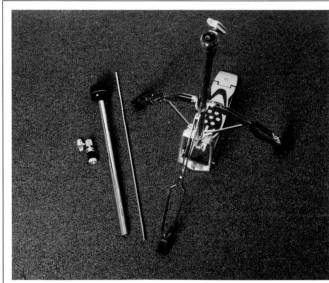

- The upper tube is made up of a metal tube going through the big tube shaft that fits into the base.

- At the bottom of the shaft is a nut-and-bolt mechanism that, when screwed together, attaches the upper tube to the base.

- The clutch can be set to make the cymbal tight or loose.

Base of the Hi-Hat Stand

- The hi-hat base usually has three legs, but some have two.

- Little pointed things near the pedal are called hi-hat spurs and their job is to keep the stand from moving on a hard surface.

- The moving parts of the hi-hat base include: the pedal, spring inside the tube, spring tension adjustment, folding legs, metal rod attaching to upper tube, spurs, and guide bars for the pedal.

Operating the hi-hat stand: The pedal is attached to a long skinny solid bar made of metal. The two cymbals sit opposite each other with the bell (curved part that looks like the top of a flying saucer) facing out. When the pedal is depressed, the cymbals clash.

MAKE IT EASY

Setting up the clutch, which holds the cymbals: Unscrew the two metal washers. Remove one of the felt washers. Put the top cymbal on the clutch (the threaded part) with the bell on top. Put the other felt washer on. Finally, screw in the metal washer until it is snug against the felt. The bottom cymbal goes on the top of the hi-hat tube with the bell underneath.

The Clutch

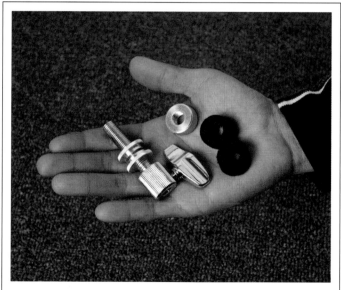

- The bottom cymbal sits upside down on top of the tube and is attached to the solid metal shaft. The clutch is hooked to the middle of the cymbal.

- A bottom cymbal screw adjustment under the cymbal moves the cymbal up and down, changing the sound accordingly.

- Tightening the screw turning key at the top of the clutch lets the top cymbal down on the bottom, creating a big, splashy sound.

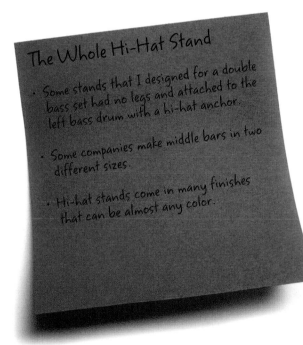

The Whole Hi-Hat Stand

- Some stands that I designed for a double bass set had no legs and attached to the left bass drum with a hi-hat anchor.

- Some companies make middle bars in two different sizes.

- Hi-hat stands come in many finishes that can be almost any color.

19

CARE OF THE DRUMS

Giving your drums, cymbals, and hardware the care they deserve pays off in performance

Caring for your drum set is like caring for your car. It needs to be cleaned and oiled, just like your vehicle, and if you perform this service regularly, it will reward you with top performance.

Fortunately maintaining your drum set is very simple. All it takes is a little Endust or Pledge and a soft rag for the finish,

chrome cleaner for the hardware, and a can of 3 in One Oil, for the pedals and tuning rods.

When cleaning the drum finish, make sure to go all over the lugs to get all the dirt and dust. Put some Endust or Pledge on a soft rag. Then put a drop—no more—of 3 in One Oil on the tuning rods, using a drum key to work it in. This will

Drum Cleaners

- You'll find cleaners available at any grocery or family mart. Generics are just as good as brand name products.

- The snare drum is the hardest drum to clean and oil because it has the most moving parts.

- Once the drums are cleaned, they will look and sound great. They'll be happy, and that'll make you happy!

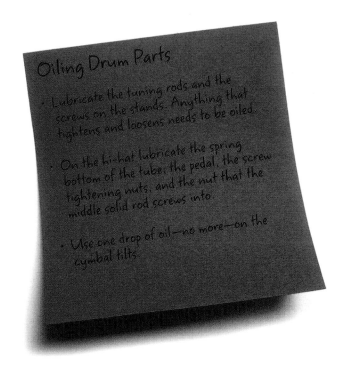

Oiling Drum Parts

- Lubricate the tuning rods and the screws on the stands. Anything that tightens and loosens needs to be oiled

- On the hi-hat lubricate the spring bottom of the tube; the pedal, the screw tightening nuts, and the nut that the middle solid rod screws into.

- Use one drop of oil—no more—on the cymbal tilts

oil it up well. Use any chrome cleaner on the hardware. Rub it on, wait for the film to form, and wipe it off. Remember to oil all the screws and nuts—again, all this takes is one drop of 3 in One.

The cymbals require a special cymbal cleaner, which you can find at any music store. I recommend the cleaner put out by Sabian cymbal company. Put some cymbal cleaner on a rag, rub it on the cymbal, and wipe it off after the film appears. Repeat the process until all marks and dirt are gone. The cymbals should come out looking great.

Oiling the Pedal

- The numerous moving parts of the drum pedal need oil on a regular basis using 3 in One Oil.

- Oil the clutch that goes across the top of the pedal and attaches to the spring. Use a drop or two.

- Oil the chain drive. Again only a drop or two does the trick.

- Where the pedal board and chain connect also needs oil.

- When you buy a pedal, look at the instructions. They tell you how to care for your pedal.

Like the oil change and lube job on your car, you should give your drum set a good cleaning every three to six months.

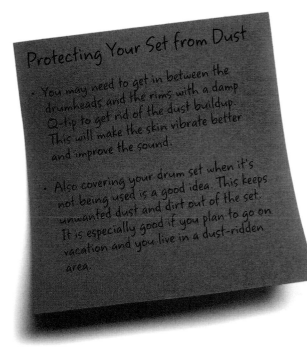

Protecting Your Set from Dust

- You may need to get in between the drumheads and the rims with a damp Q-tip to get rid of the dust buildup. This will make the skin vibrate better and improve the sound.

- Also covering your drum set when it's not being used is a good idea. This keeps unwanted dust and dirt out of the set. It is especially good if you plan to go on vacation and you live in a dust-ridden area.

CASES & COVERS
When buying drum cases, consider your needs and the protection your set requires

Once you start taking your drums to rehearsals or shows, you'll need something to protect your set from getting damaged. This is where drum cases come in.

Cases are made of cloth, molded plastic, or wood. Cloth is best for a beginner set. It provides inexpensive protection. But, if your drums collide with a hard object, they can get damaged with a cloth case. Plastic cases offer better protection, but they have two drawbacks: they're expensive and they're heavy. And weight is definitely a factor when you're toting your drums around.

Choose a case to fit your personal needs. If you're transporting your own drums and are very careful, you can go with a

Soft Cloth Cases

- Soft cases are the best way to go for the beginner. They're lightweight, less expensive, and do the job.

- The cloth cases are lined with a soft material that looks like wool and protects the drum. Cases with shoulder straps are recommended.

- So are zippers. You just pop the drum into the case, zip it up, and bingo—you're done.

- As far as brands go, DDRUMs makes a pretty nice soft case.

Molded Plastic Cases

- Many professional drummers use molded plastic cases because they are stronger than the cloth cases and protect the drums better during travel.

- The molded drums have flat or large square trap cases that roll. You can get tall cases on wheels that house two or three snare drums plus a seat, stick bag, and more.

soft cover. If you're playing gigs and hauling your set around in a truck or trailer, you'll need more protection.

When buying cases, you first need to know the sizes of each drum for proper fit. Then, check out the drum cases at a music store online or in person. You'll want one with a lining of fur or cotton to protect the drums. Since hardware is generally heavy, you want the hardware bags on wheels. Consider getting two of them, which distributes the weight.

······· GREEN ● LIGHT ··············

Buy your drum bags or cases at a discount music store where there are no shipping charges.

EQUIPMENT

The Ultimate Cases

- The ultimate cases are the Calzone and Anvil cases. They're expensive, but they'll last for years.

- These cases house the snare, toms, and hardware, making them indispensable when you are using truck or other transport.

- They're made of plywood with a plastic covering. The edges have metal strips riveted to the case and corners for extra durability.

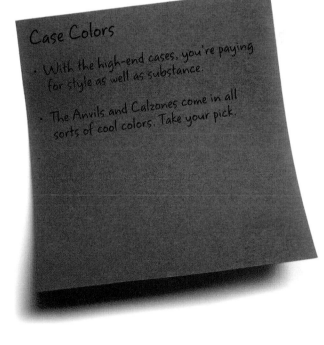

Case Colors

- With the high-end cases, you're paying for style as well as substance.

- The Anvils and Calzones come in all sorts of cool colors. Take your pick.

23

ELECTRONIC DRUM SETS

Exploring e-drumming—how you can use the "brain" to create drum sounds

Let's talk a little about electronic drums. E-drums are artificial drums. With e-drums you only hear sound through a set of earphones. When you hit an electronic drum without the earphones, acoustically it sounds like a drumstick hitting a book. But in your earphones, you can create whatever sound you want. You can also add some e-drums to an acoustic setup—an interesting concept.

The electronic kit comes in a box that contains all the different drums and the "brain." Each kit has its own kind of stand, pads, and brain. E-kit drums have what we call triggers inside of them. When you hit the drums, the triggers send the signal to the brain module, which contains all the sounds and

E-drum Kit

- The e-drum kit setup includes a five-pad system with two cymbals, hi-hat, bass drum pedal, and the brain, the module that produces all the sounds.

- The drum pads are set up on their own stands, some of which resemble stands in an acoustic kit.

- The hi-hat also works on a trigger but has a pedal so that it looks and feels like a real drum set.

The Brain

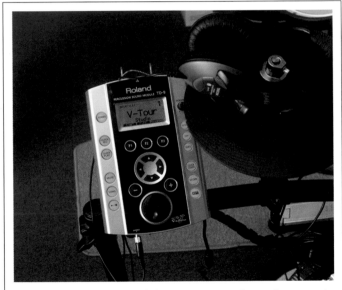

- The brain, or sound module, is the core of the e-kit. It's a computer that controls all the sounds of each drum or cymbal pad.

- You can choose from a variety of brain modules. The ones that have more features are more expensive.

produces them digitally. Each drum, cymbal, and hi-hat has a trigger wire. The bigger the setup, the more wires connect to the brain.

The brain has many sounds. In the old style of Music Minus One, some brains even play songs, with the drummer filling in the drum part . . . or even trading off with another "drummer." This is great practice for the beginning drummer. But if you're planning to play with a band, wood drums work a lot better. In the 1980s, when e-kits were just coming out, some bands used them in the studio and on stage and in their videos because they were so new and cool. But as every good drummer knows, nothing can approach the warm, rich, "true" sound of good old-fashioned wood drums.

Here are the components of an e-kit: snare drum, two toms, a floor tom, bass drum and pedal, two cymbals, and a brain module.

E-kit Setups

- The best e-kit for the beginner is the four pad—bass drum, two cymbals and a hi-hat. This gives you enough to work with without limiting your playing.

- E-drums have plastic heads like acoustic drums, to give you something of the feel, but when it comes to the art of drumming, they'll never replace the real thing.

- Because you're creating sound via earphones, the electronic drum set is perfect for an apartment setup. Even though you can get mufflers for wood drums, the e-kits are a far better practice kit. They can simulate the different drums and cymbals, and you can play along with song tracks and experiment with all sorts of sounds.

WOOD DRUMS: THE BEST

Wooden drums are more than just drum shells, metal hardware, and lacquer finish

Wood drums have to be the best drums on the market. They have warmth and dynamics. They have volume when needed. And they have the best sound around, because of the way they're made.

These drums start off as a piece of very thin wood—no thicker than a few sheets of printing paper. That's thin! Four to five layers of these paper-thin "plys" make up one drum shell. The layers are applied one by one with layers of glue in between. Then they're heated and squeezed together again. The result is a flat piece of wood similar to plywood. The wood is then put into a shell-bending machine. These shell-bending machines heat the wood so that it can be shaped. When

Making Drum Shells

- The painstaking craft involved in making drum shells hasn't changed through time, and is the same in every country.

- I love wood drums with thin shells.

Putting on Drum Hardware

- Machines may drill the holes with amazing accuracy, but the lugs, the drumheads, and the tuning screws have to be affixed by hand.

- Even the air-hole hardware is put on by hand. Correct placement is vitally important.

- Other drum hardware includes a system that holds the toms on the stand by hanging from the rims and mufflers for drums— always a welcome feature.

the shell comes out, it is a perfect circle shaped to the exact size needed by the operator of the machine. And then presto . . . you've got your drum shell. All drum shells are made like this. You can get shells of varying thickness, but the thinner the shell, the better the sound and the easier the playing.

After the shells are made, they must go through a building process in which the lugs, tuning rods, and other hardware is installed. The lugs are usually machine drilled. The bearing edge is also cut by machine, at an angle that enables the head to be positioned on the drum for the best sound.

After the hardware is installed, the finish is applied. A lacquer finish always looks great, but some drummers prefer a wrap finish—a specially formulated plastic. It's a matter of taste.

Cheaper drum sets use woods like eucalyptus and tuplipwood, because they're easy to procure and to work with. However they don't finish well. Beware of sets sold as "all birch" or "all maple," but that are really cheap wood with an outer layer of higher quality wood used for staining.

Wood Snare Drum

- The process for making wood snare drums involves a thicker ply of wood.

- Snare drums come in a wide variety of sizes.

- I have different snares for different kinds of songs. A 6- to 8-inch snare is good for a slow ballad, while the smaller 3- to 5-inch drum is better suited to a perky up-tempo number.

- The best way to find out which drums feel right to you is to try different ones out at a music store.

Cool Drum Finishes

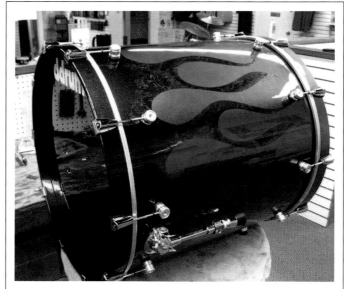

- I love lacquer finishes because they're so versatile. You can do anything with them—draw cartoons and murals on them or simulate sparkle. This satisfies my inner artist!

- Today, wrap finishes are crazier than ever. I like the flame effect. Really wild!

- Go to DDRUM.com to see some of the coolest finishes in the industry and check out what's happening.

- The finish is a statement. If you're artistic, you can even finish the kit yourself.

DIFFERENT WOODS FOR DRUMS

Many kinds of woods are used in drum making: Which one would you choose?

For years maple has been the most popular wood for drums because of its full, round sound. A drum made of maple has lots of bottom, mid-range frequency, and top-end treble, all of which combine for a great sound. In the 1920s and 1930s, Slingerland made a maple Radio King drum with a mahogany cover layer on the inside whose sound was truly amazing. But

today drums like these are very expensive. Fortunately other woods have also been found to be excellent for drums.

The rule of thumb is: Softer woods produce lower tones with less projection and harder woods produce higher tones with more projection. The "3 big" woods are mahogany, maple, and birch. Mahogany is the softest of these, and gives

Maple Drums

- In 1968 Ludwig built the first set of maple drums. They were a beautiful blond in color and had an amazing sound.

- Until very recently, most drummers used maple drums.

- Go to the music store, play some different wood drums, and see if you can hear the difference.

- Today drums are made from many different woods, even particle board! Yeah, those are cheap!

Birch Drums

- Birch drums started getting a name in the 1990s. I owned a few of them. My birch bass drums had an incredible sound, especially during recording sessions.

- The birch toms, on the other hand, needed more bottom.

- Try out some birch drums in the music store to get a feel for the sound.

- Try out the combo of maple bass drums and birch toms, or birch bass and maple toms. It's a really interesting experience.

the lowest tone. You'll want the best, though, like African mahogany. Maple has a higher pitch than mahogany, but a warmer tone than birch. Some drummers like a combination of birch bass drums and maple toms—the bass drums have loads of punch and are easy to mic and while the toms have the big, warm maple sound.

Walnut is a newer addition to the drum woods. Walnut drums aren't my favorites because they tend to have a very flat sound. Another new wood, babinga, delivers a really punchy sound and has the warm bottom sound of maple.

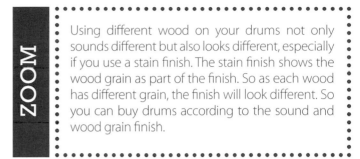

ZOOM

Using different wood on your drums not only sounds different but also looks different, especially if you use a stain finish. The stain finish shows the wood grain as part of the finish. So as each wood has different grain, the finish will look different. So you can buy drums according to the sound and wood grain finish.

Babinga Drums

- I became a babinga convert when I discovered that this wood had the full, rich sound of maple and the punch of birch.

- The babinga sound is warm and dynamic and delivers plenty of volume. I now play babinga toms.

- The size of my toms also helps get some punch. I use 12 x 8, 13 x 9, 16 x 16, and 16 x 18-inch babinga toms.

- Maple bass drums and babinga toms make a great combo.

Exotic Wood Finishes

- Some drum companies go the extra mile with exotic wood veneer finishes that are glued to the shell. The result can be quite impressive. A birdseye maple, for instance, becomes a beautiful piece of art.

- Other wood veneers include burl, oak cluster, and rainbow. Each has its own natural design. See which one appeals to you.

TYPES OF DRUM SETS

DRUM SET CONFIGURATIONS

There are many ways to build a drum set, whether beginner or pro

There are so many configurations of drum sets that an entire book could be written on that topic alone. So I'll keep it simple. Let's start with a good beginner setup, which should include one 22 x 16-inch bass drum, two rack toms—12 x 8 and 13 x 9 inches, one 16 x 16 or 14 x 14-inch floor tom, either a 5 x 14 or 3 x 14-inch snare (called a piccolo snare), a set of 14-inch hi-hats, one 18-inch ride cymbal, and one 16-inch

crash cymbal. You don't need an expensive wood kit to start with. Compressed particle board is fine. On a particle board kit, the snare drums are generally 5 x 14 inches and are made of steel. They're cheap, but they sound good enough.

You can also add to a $700 kit and customize it just for you. For instance there are literally thousands of cymbals out there, all with different sounds that will give you some nice

Basic Beginner Kit

- Beginner kits start at $299. Those new, not used, kits you see for $150 are much smaller and more appropriate for children.

- A full-size basic kit made of particle board is a price buster.

- While a cheap basic kit will get you started, if you're at all sure about playing drums, a better kit is a better investment.

Adding to Your Set

- You can add cheaper drums to your setup. They sound pretty good for the money. All you have to do is put some decent drumheads on them. When I put my Aquarian heads on a cheap set, it sounded great.

- And you can add more toms. A big 16 x 18-inch floor tom will give you a nice, deep tone. Add a 10 x 16-inch rack tom and you've got a five-tom kit. That's some good melody!

variation. Choose your own drumheads as well. A cheaper drum with good drumheads sound really good and saves you money. I put my signature heads on a cheap drum set and it sounded great!

Of course, if you know you're going to commit to the drums, a more expensive kit is definitely the way to go. Not only will it be higher quality, but you can add on to it. Some additions might include an 18-inch crash cymbal and a 16-inch "Carmine China" cymbal, some boom cymbal stands, and a 16 x 18-inch floor tom. Try out some different kits and configurations at your nearest drum store. And remember: Have fun!

Don't go out and spend a pile of money on your first drum kit. You can get a good kit for $299–$399.

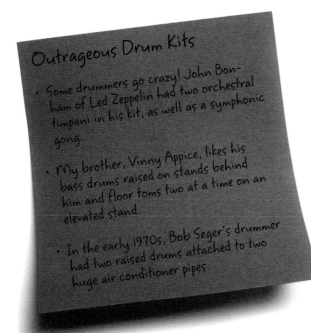

Outrageous Drum Kits

• Some drummers go crazy! John Bonham of Led Zeppelin had two orchestral timpani in his kit, as well as a symphonic gong.

• My brother, Vinny Appice, likes his bass drums raised on stands behind him and floor toms two at a time on an elevated stand.

• In the early 1970s, Bob Seger's drummer had two raised drums attached to two huge air conditioner pipes.

Wild Drum Kit Additions

• Latin touches are cool. Like some timbales. Or what about congas? Played with a stick?

• For a turbo-charged tone, I've even added some metal trash cans to the side of my drum kit! And I use a guitar wah-wah pedal on my snare drum!

• When designing your drum kit, anything is possible. Just open your mind and let some crazy ideas come out.

31

DOUBLE BASS DRUM KITS

The best way to set up different configurations of double bass drum kits

Double bass drum kits were made popular by the great Louie Bellson, drummer with, among other legendary names, Benny Goodman, Tommy Dorsey, Harry James, and Duke Ellington. Louie was the first drummer to play with two feet on the bass drums. His unique approach to the bass drum inspired many drummers to make their kits more creative.

Louie Bellson was one of the greats. He was not only a mind-boggling drummer but an amazing songwriter and lyricist as well. I knew Louie and loved him. When he died in February 2009, at the age of eighty-five, the drum world lost an awesome and beloved figure.

In the mid-1960s, many pop drummers played double

Two Bass Drum Setup

- Many drummers use the stock two bass drum set, which basically adds a bass drum to a five-piece kit.

- You should be able to hear five distinct tones from the highest toms to the left bass drum.

- The stock cymbal setup is one hat, one ride, and two crash cymbals. Note: A left-handed drummer's setup is the opposite of his right-handed counterpart.

Carmine Appice Bass Drum Setup—1968

- At the time this drum set was considered unique because of the drum sizes and clear finish.

- The bass drums were 26 x 14 inches—very big. I had to fill them with ripped up newspaper to muffle some of the overtones.

- Two of the three cymbals were mounted on the bass drums. The 22-inch ride and the 20-inch crash were also mounted on two L-shaped adjustable stands, while the third cymbal was on a cymbal floor stand.

bass drums. Cream's Ginger Baker, The Who's Keith Moon, and Vanilla Fudge's yours truly were all inspired by Louie's innovations.

With the double bass set up, each drum is tuned to a different note, like the toms.

The easiest double bass configuration consists of two 22 x 16-inch bass drums, one 14 x 5-inch snare, one 12 x 8-inch and one 13 x 9-inch rack tom (both of these on a floor tom stand), and one 16 x 16-inch floor tom.

Keith Moon Kit

- Keith's kit didn't have a hi-hat, because Keith played mostly on his ride or crash cymbals.

- The toms were spread three across over the two bass drums and mounted off the bass drums at a straight angle. There were also two floor toms on the side.

- Keith used different sets of drums. One set even had a see-through clear finish that doubled as an aquarium, with live goldfish swimming inside the drum!

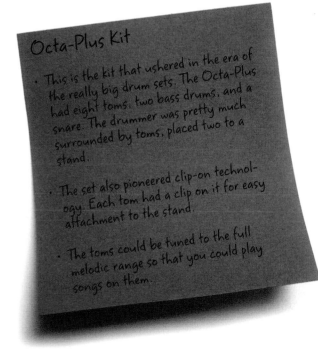

Octa-Plus Kit

- This is the kit that ushered in the era of the really big drum sets. The Octa-Plus had eight toms, two bass drums, and a snare. The drummer was pretty much surrounded by toms, placed two to a stand.

- The set also pioneered clip-on technology. Each tom had a clip on it for easy attachment to the stand.

- The toms could be tuned to the full melodic range so that you could play songs on them.

GETTING YOUR FIRST KIT

Be creative in finding that first kit—used drums can sound better than new

I don't know how many times I've been asked, "Does my first drum kit have to be new?" And I don't know how many times I've answered, "No!" In fact sometimes older drums sound better than new ones. My first drum set was a small, single-tension bass drum and a snare, with a 10-inch cymbal on a clip-on stand. Pretty minimal, but to me it was amazing.

All you need right now is something to give you the experience of playing the drums. Well, what about the drum pad? Most drummers practice on this because otherwise the tedious noise of practicing can be really annoying. But while it's a great portable tool, it can't approximate the feel of real drums. So you need to find a good, inexpensive beginner's

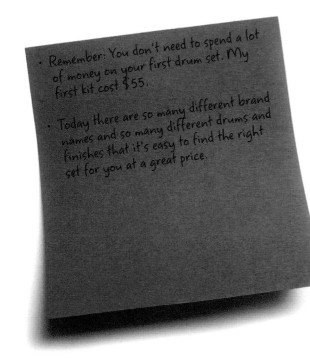

- Remember: You don't need to spend a lot of money on your first drum set. My first kit cost $55.

- Today there are so many different brand names and so many different drums and finishes that it's easy to find the right set for you at a great price.

First Drum Kit

- This is the kind of drum set I started on. The advantages were that it was cheap and gave me the feel of playing a real set.

- Today, if you get a small kit consisting of a bass drum and snare, both drums will probably have individual double-tension tuning rods.

- Today's cymbals are on a cymbal floor stand.

kit. I'd start with the want ads in the paper, or eBay, Craig's List, and other online sites, where you can find a used set for as little as $100 to $150.

Today you can get many brands of drums that are made in China and Korea. The best of cheapest drums are made in China. Every big music store, like Sam Ash or Guitar Center, has its own brand of Chinese-made drums. If they don't, they buy their brand from a drum company. DDRUM has a model called the d2 drum sets. These kits sell for under $225 new. I've played these kits and they sound really good.

These kits were designed and made for the beginner, and kits like these are great for a first kit.

Drum stores and music stores also sell used equipment and sometimes have quality used sets for under $200.

Your Second Kit

- Your next level of kit should include some tom-toms. My second kit had one tom and a hi-hat.

- This kit should include a bass drum, snare, tom, cymbal, and hi-hat. You can add a floor tom to the family too.

- The whole kit as pictured would include the full four-piece kit with two cymbals and a hi-hat. This is a great combo that will keep you busy for quite a while.

Transfer Kit

- Once you have a good quality four-piece kit, you can upgrade it to a professional kit by adding another rack tom and some more cymbals, like china cymbals, which make a shorter sound, and a different size crash cymbal.

- There are clip-on cowbell holders available. Or you can put a tambourine on a stand. This is how a pro kit is put together—bit by bit.

TUNING THE DRUMS

Learn to tune your kit and change drumheads, both as essential as keeping the beat

Playing the drums is fun; tuning the drums is work. Still there's an art to tuning, and you can't be a drummer, good or bad, unless you learn it.

Let's take the tom-tom. The first step is to remove the drumhead. With the drum key turn the tuning screw to the left until it loosens up. Then turn the screw near the lug to the left with your fingers until it is free. Do this to all the lugs.

Next, lift off the whole rim, keeping the tuning screws in place. Place the new head on the drum and push down on the top of the head around the drum. Then put the rim back on the drum and tighten the tuning rods manually until they're screwed in. Now you can do the actual tuning.

KNACK DRUMS FOR EVERYONE

Changing the Drumhead

- This photo shows the direction in which to turn the drum key in order to loosen the tuning screws.

- It's a good Idea to line up the lugs in the same position they came out of the drum.

- I recommend lubricating your tuning rods with 3 in One Oil for easy screwing and unscrewing.

- While the rim is off, take the opportunity to clean the surface of the rim that touches the head.

Putting the Head Back On

- For a good, rounded drumhead, place the head on the drum and push it down all over to make sure that it's sitting flat on the rim.

- Put the rim back on the drum as indicated in the photo. The tuning screws go back in, with the drum key template at the top of the rim. Twist the rods to the right to tune.

- Tighten the tuning rods by hand and then fine tune with the drum key. Tighten and fine tune until the pitch is the same all around the drum near the rim.

Start by turning the drum key to the right to get a medium tightness to the head. Begin with one lug and go across the drum. Skip a lug and go across again. Repeat until all lugs have been tuned. Once you've tuned all the drums, go around and hit the heads lightly in front the tuning rod with the drum key. The pitches should all be the same. If they aren't, tighten or loosen until all the pitches are even. This is how you get rid of overring.

Do the same thing to the bottom head until both bottom and top heads have the same pitch and tension.

For rapid head removal, you can buy a drum key drill bit that goes onto an electric drill and has the drum key template on it. I highly recommend this tool—it makes putting the heads on and taking them off super easy.

Turning Screw Sizes

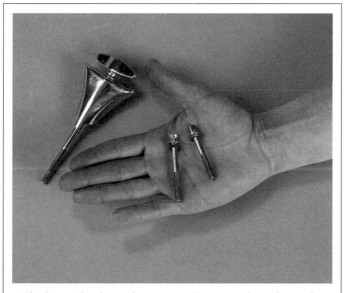

- The larger the drum, the longer the tuning screw. That's your drum set physics lesson for today.

- The bass drum has a T tuning rod that makes it much easier to tune without a key.

- Some new bass drums do not have the T tuning rod. If you have one of those, you'll have to use a drum key instead.

Changing the Bass Drumhead

- When changing the bass drumhead, loosen all the tuning screws all the way until they come off the lug.

- Pull off the wood rim and the old head. Put the new head on and replace the rim in the same position.

- Tighten the tuning screws to a medium tightness. Then go around to the back head and get the tone. Hit the front head near the tuning rod and tighten or loosen the tuning screw to match the tone. Repeat in front of each lug.

CHANGING SNARE BOTTOM HEADS

Here are some tips on changing the snare bottom head, the most difficult to change

The snare bottom head is by far most difficult head in the drum kit to change. That's because the actual snare wires and the snare wire plastic belts live under the snare.

Begin by loosening the tuning screws as you would the top head. Then remove one side of the plastic belt. Caution: Don't take off both sides of the belt. Only remove the side that is

not connected to the snare throw-off switch. You also must remember to mark the belt so that it goes back in the same position. Tighten and loosen the belt screws with either a regular Phillips head screwdriver or a drum key.

Once the belt is off, take the tuning screws off the drum. Next remove the rim, which will only come partially off the

KNACK DRUMS FOR EVERYONE

Snare Bottom Head

- Changing the snare bottom head is a challenge. Lay the snare upside down so the bottom is facing up. To loosen the screws, follow the arrows on the photo.

- Make sure you remember where all the screws go. Lay them out in position or mark the areas accordingly.

Removing the Snare Belt

- The snare plastic belt holds the tension of the snares. To change the bottom drumhead, you only need to remove one end of the belt.

- Remove the side opposite the throw-off switch. It acts as a connector and is held in with two screws. Loosen

the screws with a screwdriver or drum key.

- It's very important to mark where the screws go on the belt so that you'll get the correct tension and you won't change the snare's sound.

drum because it will still be connected by one side of the belt. Pull the rim off just enough to be able to remove the snare bottom head.

Put the new snare head on. Put the rim back on and put back all the tuning screws. Tighten to a medium tightness. Then go around to all the lugs and tune them to the same pitch. Hook the belt back up to the connector at the spot you marked. This is easier to do with the snare throw-off in the tom loose position.

····· GREEN ● LIGHT ·····
When changing the snare bottom head for the first time, go to a music store for help!

Putting On a New Head

- With the drum still lying on the top head, pull the rim as far as you can off the snare bottom and pull off the old head.

- Put the new head with the rim back onto the head. Insert and tighten all the tuning rods. Go to all the lugs and make sure the

pitch is the same.

- Reconnect the belt to the connector using the guide marks. Turn the snare throw-off switch back to the "on" position. Hit the top and bottom heads until the pitch is the same between them.

Fine Tuning the Snare

- Fine tune the drum by tightening or loosening the snares on the throw-off switch. You may have to adjust the two screws on the connector.

- The snares need to be straight across and the ends need to be tight and even.

- After completing the fine tuning, you can make the heads tighter.

TUNING & HEADS

39

USING DIFFERENT DRUMHEADS

The type of drumheads you use depends on the music you're playing: rock, jazz, rhythm and blues

When I started playing drums in the early 1960s, calfskin heads were all that were available. Today all drums come with plastic heads.

The most widely used heads in the industry are Remo drumheads. Remo was the first company to make plastic heads. Of these, the "Ambassador" was the most popular. This was a fairly thin head that had a white coating that was great for wire brushes, which were used in ballads and particularly in jazz music in the 1930s and 1940s.

Rock drummers liked playing the Ambassador in the studio because of its awesome sound and versatility. Soon it became the state of the art drumhead for the industry and practically

Coated Heads

- The first head to be made of plastic was the Remo Ambassador, and it was an instant success.

- When you play with wire brushes, you want a coated drumhead.

- Coated heads were traditionally used for swing, jazz, Latin, and other "softer" beats. They aren't great for hard rock, however, because they can't withstand really rough action.

Carmine Drumheads

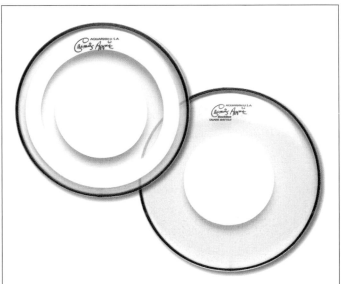

- I worked with the Aquarian Company to create my own set of drumheads, which are very strong and lasted for months at a time.

- Before the Carmine head came out, I'd have to change heads every day or two. Now, I might change them every couple of months.

- You really don't want to use brushes on these heads, because they don't have the same kind of dynamics as the Ambassador heads. But they're great for rock.

- The Carmine heads come in all sizes.

every drum that was manufactured came with an Ambassador head. As rock playing got more intense, however, stronger heads became necessary. Although the Ambassador was still used in the studio, it wasn't tough enough to withstand a lot of bashing. So newer heads came out that were double thickness, with an extra piece of plastic in the center. Remo had the Black Dots and Aquarian had a head called the Rock Dot. The Dot heads lasted longer and were custom made for rock music.

So, different heads are used for different types of music. As far as choosing the heads for you, it's really trial and error, depending in part on the type of music you want to play, but here are some recommendations

If you want a drumhead that lasts long and gives you good sound, I recommend Aquarian drumheads. I've used them for many years and they never break

Other than Remo and Aquarian, there are Evans heads. With many models to choose from Evans is one of the top selling head companies in the United States.

Pinstripe Heads

- Pinstripes have a good all around rich tone. They can be identified by the penlike circle going around the head.

- Many famous drummers use pinstripe heads because they're strong and have a good rock sound.

- Sometimes I'd use pinstripes in the studio, because of their open sound.

- The Remo pinstripe drumhead is a classic.

Black Dots and Other Heads

- Black Dot heads were the first to feature a second layer of plastic in a circle in the middle of the head.

- Ludwig has the Silver Dot, which, like the Black Dot, is also a great head for playing rock.

- DW made some interesting—and handy—drumheads that featured numbers on them to indicate where and in what order to tune the drums.

41

NOTES TO TUNE TO

Using the basic whole note scale to tune your drums and play melodies on them

We've already established that you need to know how to tune your drums well. But how do you know what notes to tune to?

Some drummers don't know about notes. They just tune by ear, to whatever sounds good to them. I actually do a little of both. I get a starting note with either my highest or lowest tom. Once I reach the note that I like, I then hear the next note in my head.

It all goes back to the basic whole note scale: Do, Re, Mi, Fa, So, La, Ti, Do. If you sing those notes, you've got the full octave. Number them 1 to 8. The tones that I tune to are the numbers 1, 3, 5, and 7. In music this is called a seventh chord.

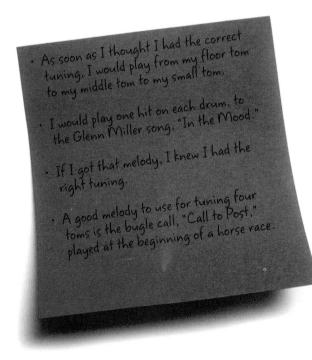

- As soon as I thought I had the correct tuning, I would play from my floor tom to my middle tom to my small tom.

- I would play one hit on each drum, to the Glenn Miller song, "In the Mood."

- If I got that melody, I knew I had the right tuning.

- A good melody to use for tuning four toms is the bugle call, "Call to Post," played at the beginning of a horse race.

Tuning Sequence

- Here you see the tuning sequence in order.

- If you become a real drummer, you'll need to memorize the turning sequence because you'll be doing it every day for the rest of your life.

- Use the drill bit key, ratchet key, or drum key to tune these to get them medium tight. Then fine tune with the drum key.

- Remember to hit the head right at the lug point to make certain the pitches are all the same.

Starting with the "Do" as number 1 on my floor tom, I tune the other two toms to 3 and 5. If you have four or more toms, you can keep going up the scale until you start all over again. Tuning is a personal thing. My system might not work for you, but by experimenting, you'll find the one that does.

I do not include the bass drum in this equation. The bass drum should have its own tone. Sometimes you need to tune the bass drum higher to actually achieve the low note. Many of Motown Records' bass drums were tuned high to get the bottom they wanted on the record.

Tuning to 1-3-5 Notes

- The 1-3-5 tuning sequence is great sequence for tuning your toms.

- Drums go out of tune all the time. After playing them a while, the tuning usually loosens up and you'll have to go through the process of tuning all over again.

- Use 1-3-5 tuning to play little melodies on the toms.

Tuning Out of Tune

- Tuning out of tune lets you get a different tuning on the kit without changing the tuning by moving the drums to different positions.

- Let's say you're using the 1-3-5-7 tuning sequence. You can take the "5" note on the rack tom and move it to where the "7" note drum is, and vice versa.

- This creates some interesting patterns without changing the tuning. Notes jump out at you differently, challenging you to hear things in a new way.

43

THE DRUM TOOL KIT

Every drum set needs a tool kit, including screwdrivers, pliers, scissors, and various drum keys

As a drummer you also double as a handyman. Every drummer must have a tool kit that includes screwdrivers, pliers, and other indispensable implements. Even though drum companies are becoming more and more determined to create kits that are "operated" by the drum key, I advise having an extended tool kit on hand.

Your drum tool kit should include a couple of screwdrivers, straight and Phillips; a pair of pliers; a small scissors; a small flashlight; a small hacksaw; and your various drum keys. A tackle box from Walmart or some other discount store makes an excellent toolbox.

You should also have some spares on hand. Spare whats?

Your Tool Kit

- Tool kit layout: pliers, straight screwdriver, phillips screwdriver, drum keys, small hack saw, flashlight, spare snare wires, snare wire belt spares, felt washers, metal washers for cymbals, duct tape, 3 in One Oil.

- You can buy survival kits that contain the things you'll need for regular maintenance and emergencies.

- Always carry extras of little things like wing nuts, tuning screws, an extra spring for your pedal—anything that, if lost or broken, could derail your gig.

Things That Break

- When things break, you've got to be ready to fix them. Snare wires, for instance, will come off, and you'll have to know how to change them.

- Flipping the snare throw-off switch to the tom position, loosen the two screws with a screwdriver and pull out the belt. Repeat on the other side. Get new snare wires from your tool kit and put them on, reversing the procedure.

- Carry a drum key on your key chain. This way, you'll never be without a drum key when you need it. And believe me, this happens when you least expect it.

Well, spare plastic belts for the snare, spare snare wires, extra wing nuts for the cymbal stands, extra felt washers of different sizes for the cymbals and hi-hat, duct tape, and 3 in One Oil. Sabian puts out what they call a "Survival Kit" that contains many of these items. The name is right on; I can't imagine life without my Survival Kit.

Think of your drum tools as part of your drum kit. You should have them with you at all times. When you're setting up for a gig and you drop your drum key on a dark stage, you've got your flashlight. If your cymbal stand wing nut comes loose,

out come the pliers. If your snare wire belt snaps, you've got a new one on hand, and the tools with which to put it on. Take a tip from a veteran rocker: You've got to be ready for any and every emergency!

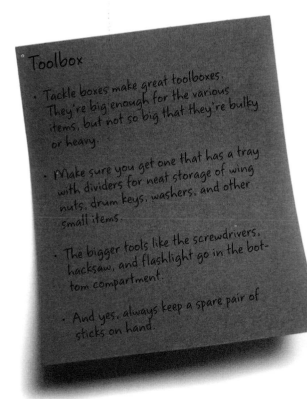

Toolbox

- Tackle boxes make great toolboxes. They're big enough for the various items, but not so big that they're bulky or heavy.

- Make sure you get one that has a tray with dividers for neat storage of wing nuts, drum keys, washers, and other small items.

- The bigger tools like the screwdrivers, hacksaw, and flashlight go in the bottom compartment.

- And yes, always keep a spare pair of sticks on hand.

Ultra Toolbox

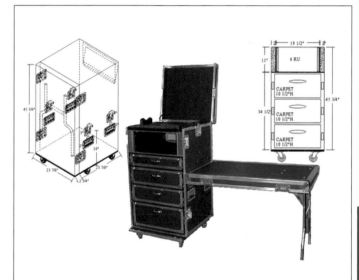

- When you turn pro, you get to have the ultra toolbox.

- There is the road case made by Anvil or Calzone that sits on the side of the stage with a drum tech hanging around it and has the ultimate in tools.

- The ultra toolbox should include an electric drill with drum related bits, electric screwdrivers, extra drum pedals and parts, and anything else you'll need to make life on the road easier.

MUFFLING DRUMS

If it's time to turn the volume down, here are some ways to muffle your drums

Drums are notorious for causing family and neighborhood upheavals. As long as you have to live around others, you can be sure that at some point they'll want to kill you when you get the urge to practice at midnight or blow the roof off while drumming away to music turned on at full blast. This is where muffling comes in.

Muffling is essential for two reasons: creating a better sound and making playing possible in an apartment or other living situations.

Let's start with the bass drum. There are different bass drum muffling systems to choose from. The pillow bass muffler goes inside the drum and dampens the sound, taking out all

Bass Drum Pillows

- DW, Evan, and HQ all make drum pillows, which dampen the bass drum sound.

- To eliminate the dead bass drumhead feel, you can move the pillow so that it does not hit the back head of the drum.

- I prefer the DW pillow because it's a little smaller than the others.

Silencers

- Unlike the pillows, the silencers really do silence the drums. They're made of rubber and sit on the drum.

- The bass drum silencers really soften the sound. Like the electronic drum kits, they're great for practicing in an apartment.

- There are also silencers for the cymbals and hi-hats— round or odd shaped pieces of rubber that go onto each cymbal, killing the sound.

of the ring and giving you a dull thud instead. There are drum silencers made for the entire set that range in size from 6 to 24 inches. These are circular rubber pads that actually sit on the drums. There are different ways of keeping them upright against the drum so the pedal can hit them.

These apparatuses come under the classification of silencers. There's another kind of muffling system, however, that's designed to enhance the sound of the drum. Products like Moon Gel and the original Richie Ring take out drumhead overtones without silencing the drums.

• • • • • • • • • • • • RED ● LIGHT • • • • • • • • • • • •

Don't get a muffling system until you know exactly what you want from it. Do you want to muffle the sound? Silence it entirely? Or enhance it? You can search for mufflers or silencers online. Just make sure to put "drum" in the keywords or you'll end up getting ten million hits for car mufflers!

Moon Gel

- Recording studios have used Moon Gel and tape for years. Moon Gel is a muffling system that eliminates unwanted overtones. It's mainly used on snare drums and toms.

- You can also use tape on the toms and the snare. If the drum has too much ring, start with a small piece of tape or some Moon Gel until you get a good sound and no ringing.

Richie Rings

- Richie Rings are made of plastic drumhead material cut into "O" rings.

- The Richie Ring was a great innovation. No gels or tape to mess with. They just fit right on the drums.

- The down side of the Richie Ring was that it tended to kill the ring on the bass drum. The solution? Newspaper fill.

TUNING & HEADS

47

STICKS

Like drumheads, drumsticks—wood, metal, or other materials—have changed over time

Are your sticks the most important part of the drum kit? Well, just try playing without them!

Like everything else in the world of drums, sticks have come a long way since cave dwellers and tribesmen used tree branches to beat on log drums.

At one time sticks were only made of wood. Today they are made of wood, metal, and other materials. I myself love the old-fashioned hickory wood sticks.

The replacement of the wood tip by the nylon tip ushered in a big craze that's still going on. It also led to the creation of one of the biggest brand names in the stick business, Regal Tip. Regal began making these tips in the early 1960s. Nylon

Stick Size

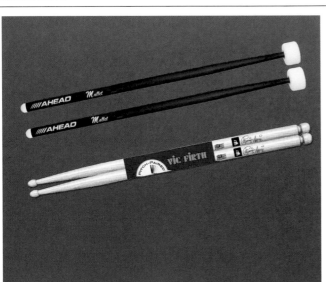

- Sticks come in various lengths and widths. If you play a lot with a particular stick, your hands will get used to it.

- Most sticks are made of hickory. Metal sticks, which are much heavier, were made for practice.

- Back in the day you'd pick out your sticks in a music store, rolling them on a table to get the best matched set. Today sticks come matched by size, weight, and width and are rolled to get only straight sticks in a pair.

Plastic Tips

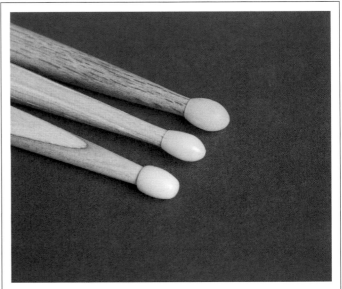

- All sticks today have either a wood or plastic tip. Plastic tips are really great for playing jazz grooves on the cymbals.

- When the plastic tip first came out in the 1960s, it would fly off the stick if you played hard. Today's tips will never come off.

- My first signature stick was a Regal plastic tip. I loved it, but when I was asked to endorse the Vic Firth sticks, I changed to a wood tip.

tips gave a new clarity to the sticks when playing the ride cymbal and were especially good for jazz and ballads.

Everyone seemed to be playing Regal Tip sticks in the Sixties. Then the Pro-Mark stick came along. Pro-Marks were made of different woods and definitely "made their mark." Then, in the 1980s a timpanist for the Boston Philharmonic started making sticks in his garage for his drummer friends. He sold so many of them that he opened up a thriving business: Vic Firth Drum Sticks.

In addition to the regular drumsticks, there are mallets.

These have felt ball ends and are primarily used in timpani playing. They make a "swwisshhing" kind of cymbal roll. And wire brushes have been part of the jazz/swing world for years.

Picking a Stick

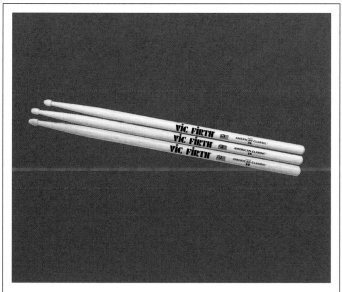

- You can't play the drums well if you're not comfortable with your sticks.

- Start with an average stick size like a 7A. If that seems too small, try a 5A. The solid and powerful 5B will probably be too big.

- Picking out your drumsticks is like picking out your clothes. You want sticks that fit you—and look cool, too!

Latest Stick Technology

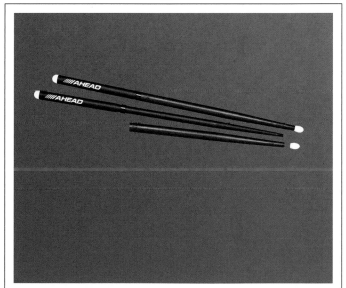

- AHEAD manufactures drumsticks that are truly ahead of their time.

- They feature tuned handle diameters, superhard replacement polyurethane covers that protect both sticks and gear, and a vibration reduction system that reduces hand fatigue and is

always perfectly balanced and matched with cushioned grips.

- Unlike wood sticks, which will wear out in one spot and eventually break, AHEAD sticks are supposed to be break proof.

PRACTICE STICKS

What are practice sticks, why do you need them, and which is better for practicing?

What are practice sticks, and why do you need them? Well practice sticks are sticks that are oversized in length and are used for practicing on a drum pad. The idea is that if you practice with bigger, fatter sticks, your hands will move that much faster and more easily when you get on the drums with normal sticks. I'm not sure if this is true, but maybe it is because I did the practice stick routine when I started out and it was a lot easier to play with the regular sticks.

The best practice sticks are the ones made by Vic Firth, Pro-Mark and Regal Tip.

I recommend the 2B stick, which is less expensive but big enough to make a difference. Vic Firth and Pro-Mark also

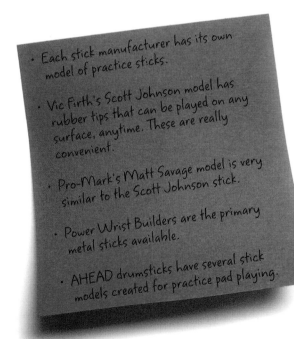

- Each stick manufacturer has its own model of practice sticks.

- Vic Firth's Scott Johnson model has rubber tips that can be played on any surface, anytime. These are really convenient.

- Pro-Mark's Matt Savage model is very similar to the Scott Johnson stick.

- Power Wrist Builders are the primary metal sticks available.

- AHEAD drumsticks have several stick models created for practice pad playing.

Wood Sticks

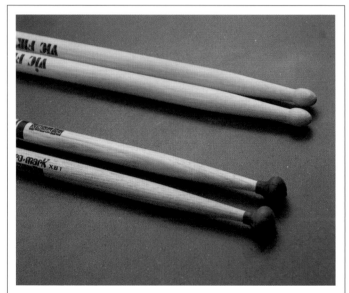

- The rubber-tipped 2B sticks can be played on any surface, anywhere.

- Wood practice sticks can be made of hickory or maple, depending on the manufacturer.

- Go to a music store and try out different sticks. I would recommend getting a pair of 2Bs and a pair of rubber-tipped sticks.

make rubber-tipped practice sticks that give you the bounce of a practice pad. You can also get actual metal sticks called Power Wrist Builders that are made of aluminum and brass and will really last a lifetime. These sticks come in different weights so that you can start light and gradually go to the heavier models to build up your wrists.

•••••••••••••••• RED ● LIGHT ••••••••••••••

Because it's like doing a workout for your wrists, use metal sticks with caution. Make sure you start off with light-weight sticks. Sticks that are too heavy will lead to wrist pain. If this happens, stop using them immediately and switch to lighter sticks.

Metal Sticks

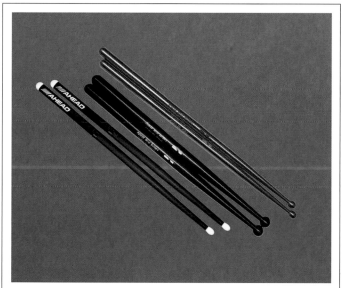

- PWB sticks are solid metal and are much more expensive than wood sticks. But they'll last a lifetime.

- Start out with the aluminum sticks, and when you're ready to increase the weight, go to the brass models.

- Cheaper metal sticks are available; you can find them online, for instance, at sites like DRUMBUM.com.

- Metal sticks can hurt your wrists. Begin with short interval practice and alternate with a pair of wood practice sticks.

Practice Sticks

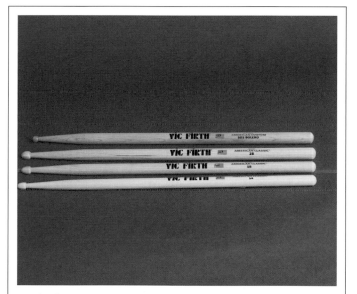

- Whether or not to use practice sticks is a matter of opinion. Some teachers recommend them, while others believe it's fine to practice with your regular sticks.

- If you want to give practice sticks a try, start out with the 2B stick, which is a lot

cheaper than the metal alternative and won't harm your wrists.

- There's also the bigger 5B stick, which should help you develop your wrists with the correct exercises.

DRUMSTICKS

THE CARMINE STICKS
How the double-tipped sticks came about, what they do, and why they're different

They say that necessity is the mother of invention, and that was certainly true for the Carmine Stick. When I was playing live in the 1960s, there weren't any big sound systems. So I had to use the butt end of my sticks to give me more power—and more sound. However, because the butt end wasn't the part of the stick that was meant to be hitting the drum, the stick action was not as good.

I played like this for many years. Then, in the late 1970s, I thought to myself, "What if I put a tip on the butt end? Wouldn't that give me better stick action?" I tried it out and sure enough, it worked. In 1982 I partnered with Regal Tip to develop the double-tipped Carmine Appice Stick. The regular

Carmine Stick versus the Standard Stick

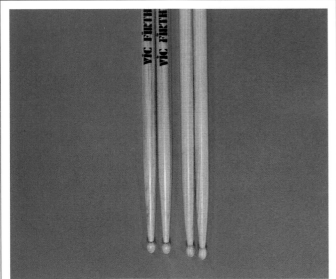

- The stick I've been playing for years is basically a 5A in weight, length, and thickness.

- You can see the similarities between my stick and a standard 5A. The tapered parts are pretty much the same.

- Originally I used a plastic-tipped stick. But because a plastic tip is better suited to jazz or light cymbal work, I found that I really didn't use it very much.

Butt End Tip

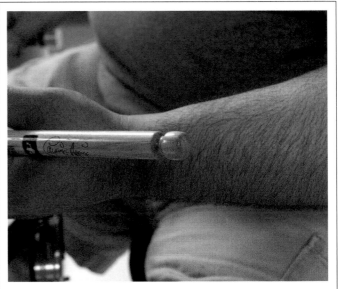

- This is the butt end tip of the Carmine Stick. It's sort of carved into the butt end like a bead.

- Playing with the butt end makes the stick last longer and also gives the sound a boost, making it thicker and more powerful. You can really hear the difference.

tip was plastic, with a wood tip on the butt end. I remained with Regal until 1989, when I moved to the Vic Firth Stick Company. With Vic, I kept the same design; the only difference was that both ends had a wood tip.

With the Carmine Stick, you get a real two-in-one deal: power and action from the butt end and sensitivity from the regular stick tip.

ZOOM

If you play with the butt end of the Carmine Appice Stick, you'll notice that your hands will be wrapped around the part of the stick that is tapered. This will feel a little strange and will take some getting used to.

Regular Tip

- The regular end of the Carmine Stick acts like a regular wood-tipped stick. When you use it on the cymbal, you get a "ping" sound that's not quite as clear as it would be with a plastic tip but is nice for less-intense playing.

- Because the tapered end of the stick is weaker than the butt end, I usually play softer songs with the normal tip end of the stick.

- This is a stick made of hickory.

Balance

- Because the tip on the butt end actually acts as a weight, your get better balance when you play with the small tip, and the stick moves faster.

- No matter which grip you use, the weight on the butt end works for you.

- I've had many people tell me that they love the way the stick feels when playing this way.

- You can get the Carmine Stick at most music stores, or you can order it from www.vicfirth.com.

DRUMSTICKS

CHOOSING STICKS
The A,B,S's of sticks—how to get it right when choosing your sticks

Which sticks you choose depends on what music you want to play. Here are some questions to ask yourself: What type of band will you be playing with? Do you want wood or nylon tips? (For instance, what kind of sound do you want on the cymbals?) What volume will you be playing at—hard, soft, or medium? How do they feel in your hands? If they're not comfortable, they're not right for you. Do you tend to get sweaty hands? If so, you'll want to think twice about getting varnished or laquered sticks, which will be difficult for you to grip.

If you're planning to play rock drums, you'll need a stick like a 5B. B sticks are for rock and pop playing, while the A sticks are best for orchestra and jazz playing. And the S sticks are made for marching band and are much larger.

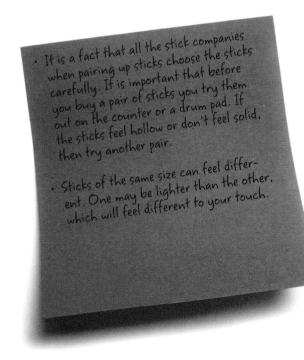

- It is a fact that all the stick companies when pairing up sticks choose the sticks carefully. It is important that before you buy a pair of sticks you try them out on the counter or a drum pad. If the sticks feel hollow or don't feel solid, then try another pair.

- Sticks of the same size can feel different. One may be lighter than the other, which will feel different to your touch.

5A and 5B Sticks

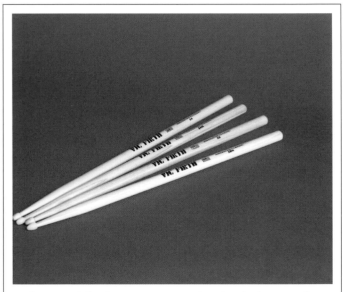

- The 5A stick has become another milestone in the rock world. It is a light/heavy stick that can give you great action.

- The 5A hickory stick is the stick to use for playing rock and pop. When you hit the drum, it's very solid.

- The 5B is the heavier of these two sticks. It delivers more power if you need it. It feels bigger in your hands as the diameter is bigger.

- Both these sticks come in wood and nylon tips.

Don't just go and order your sticks online without trying them out at a music store first. There's no other way to know which size stick will feel most comfortable in your hand. Try out a 5A, 5B, 7A, and 8A and see which stick feels right when you hold it.

When pairing your sticks, choose carefully. Because they can vary slightly in weight, sticks of the same size can feel totally different when you're actually holding them.

········· GREEN●LIGHT ·············

It is important to experiment with sticks of various sizes. Don't settle for the first stick you try. Be patient and discriminating, and like the right wand that came to Harry Potter, the right stick will come to you.

7A and 8A Sticks

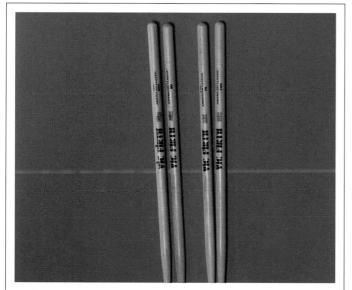

- These A sticks are lighter and are really great for playing jazz, which requires more sensitivity and dynamics.

- The 8A is a little thinner and is for the ultralight player.

- You can get the 7A's and 8A's with either the wood or nylon tip. I think the nylon tip works better for the ride cymbal that is so important to jazz.

Stick Sizes Differ by Company

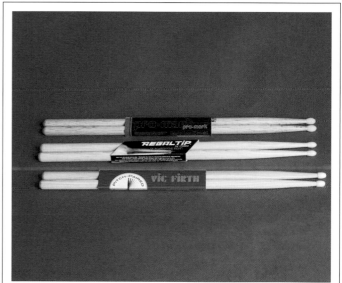

- A Regal Tip 5A is not the same as a Vic Firth 5A. If you like the Vic Firth, don't assume you'll be just as happy with the Regal Tip.

- Signature models like the Carmine Appice Stick will have their own unique properties. You won't know

if they'll fit your needs until you try them out.

- If you like Buddy Rich or Steve Gadd, it doesn't mean you'll like the sticks they like.

DRUMSTICKS

MALLETS & BRUSHES

Mallets can be used on a drum set or on a timpani, but what can brushes do?

Sticks aren't the only way to play drums. Mallets and brushes are a lot of fun too. Think of your striking instruments as the different paintbrushes an artist uses to create different effects.

Mallets are very thin drumsticks with a piece of felt wrapped around something that looks like a ball attached to the end of each stick. These ball ends are used on drums or timpani to create a softer, rounder sound than standard sticks.

The ball ends of mallets vary in size, and even the felt material can vary depending on the sound it's intended to create. Tight felt has a harder sound, while the "furry" felt creates a much softer tone. Brushes are made out of very long pieces

Tight Mallet

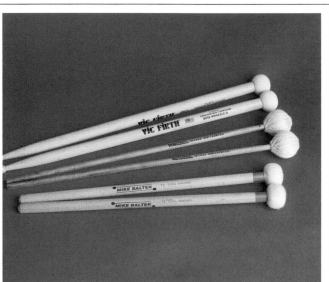

- The tight mallet produces a much softer sound than the drumstick.

- A good way to play with mallets is to turn off the snares on your snare drum, which basically turns the snare into a tom-tom and allows you to really hear the soft mallet sound.

- Mallets were made for cymbals, transforming crashes into soft, mellow tones.

Furry Mallet

- The furry mallet is the softer of the two mallet types. It creates beautiful washes of sound and long, flowing-water-like tones on the cymbals.

- Hitting the big floor toms with the furry mallet can simulate an orchestral timpani.

- Snare solos with furry mallets are really interesting. When the snares are turned off, the result is a very melodic tone.

of wire that form a sort of V shape that extends from a small round metal casing. Brushes are a standard item in jazz groups and commercial society bands. Sometimes they're used in rock for bluesy shuffle numbers.

Brush playing is an art form all its own and takes time and patience to perfect. The left hand turns in a circle on the snare while the right hand plays rhythms on the snare and other parts of the drums. The result is a very soft, whispery sound.

ZOOM

The legendary Buddy Rich was a phenomenal drummer and brush artist. I got to know Buddy very well, and he and Gene Krupa were my two main idols. Buddy was probably one of the most animalistic, vicious drummers who ever lived. He was so fast he took your breath away. I don't think there was anything he couldn't do on the drums.

Brush Construction

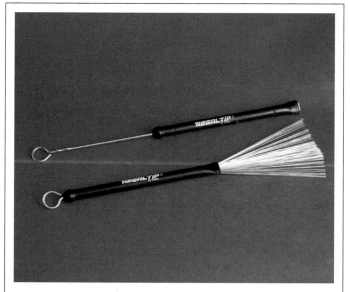

- Because it was difficult to store brushes conveniently, somebody came up with the great idea of storing them in their own casing.

- A rubber or plastic covering over the metal casing makes it easier for the drummer to hold the brush.

- The brush wires are very strong. They have to be in order to withstand heavy playing without getting bent.

How to Play Using Brushes

- Playing with brushes differs from playing with sticks in just about every way, from feel to sound to technique.

- The tempo of the song will determine how fast or slow you brush. Follow the direction of the left-hand movement in the photo.

- Meanwhile the right hand is playing the actual rhythm of the song, with the accents.

- Together, both hands develop a unique kind of rhythm.

DRUMSTICKS

STICK BAGS

What's the big deal about a stick bag, and which is the right bag for you?

Your stick bag is more than just a stick transporter. It holds an array of sticks, mallets, brushes, and other items. It can even hold tools, drum keys, felts, wing nuts, and other necessities.

Different companies make different stick bags. There's pretty much no limit to stick bag creativity; DDRUM makes a stick bag attached to a cymbal case as a backpack, for example.

What should you look for in a stick bag? A good starter stick bag should hold about twelve pairs of sticks on the inside and have at least two pockets on the outside for tools and small accessories. It should be water resistant and should open and close with a zipper, a must for traveling because it prevents things from falling out.

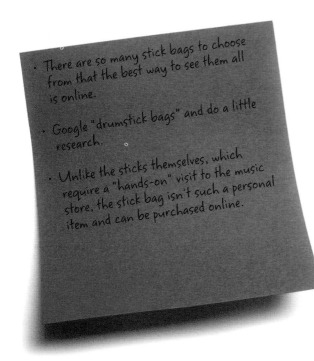

- There are so many stick bags to choose from that the best way to see them all is online.

- Google "drumstick bags" and do a little research.

- Unlike the sticks themselves, which require a "hands-on" visit to the music store, the stick bag isn't such a personal item and can be purchased online.

Best Buy

- I think the Vic Firth 1twelve-pair bag is the best buy. It's made of water-resistant nylon and has plenty of room for everything you need.

- This bag has strong string on the ends, so that you can hang the bag from the tension rods of the floor tom.

- The standard Pro-Mark bag has three pockets and a soft protective lining.

- You can check out these two bags, along with other bags in their price range, online.

You might also consider getting a small spare bag, one that holds no more than pairs of sticks and is perfect when you're going to play a few songs on someone else's kit.

As far as price goes, I recommend the canvas bags. The leather bags are more expensive and don't really give you any more bang for your buck.

Once you find a bag you like, you'll have it for a long time. I've had mine for at least ten years.

················· RED ● LIGHT ··············

Some of the larger stick bags hold too many sticks and accessories and are hard to carry. As a beginner you don't need anything this complicated. Smaller and cheaper is the way to go.

Deluxe Bag

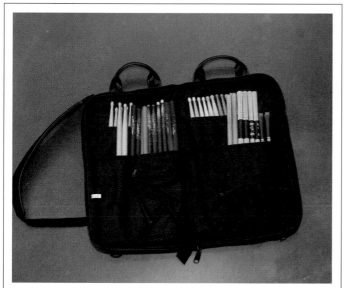

- The more expensive Vic Firth models are made of leather and hold twenty-four pairs of sticks and mallets.

- It's water resistant and comes in a leatherlike vinyl with double stitching throughout.

- This is the deluxe bag made for the professional drummer.

- The Zildjian Session Stick Bag includes a front pouch. It's large enough to accommodate and organize sticks, brushes, mallets, and other implements.

A Wild Bag

- The Meinl Zebra Bag: This durable item is made from heavy-duty, padded nylon and features four spacious sections for drumsticks.

- It includes an external pocket for drum accessories, a shoulder strap, and extension straps.

- Features include pleated heavy canvas material, double stitching, retractable hanger cords, two large zippered compartments, eight roomy stick or mallet compartments, and flame design inside and out.

DRUMSTICKS

DRUM PEDALS

From the classic Speed King to today's DW line, drum pedals are what make your set go

Without the invention of the bass drum pedal, there wouldn't be a drum set. The bass drum pedal started out with just one kind of beater (the part of the pedal that beats on the drum). The original beaters were made of a furry felt and delivered a soft hit. They were replaced by the hard felt beaters, which produced a much harder sound.

Ludwig set the standard with the Speed King, one of the all-time classic pedals. The Speed King was fast and simple to operate and had great adjustments. The concept behind the Speed King was simple: You pushed on the pedal and the beater hit the drum. A spring action brought the foot plate back into position for rapid repeat action. These springs

Speed King Pedal

- The Speed King design produced a pedal that was easy to operate and had plenty of power.

- If you wanted a tighter pedal with more spring, you just tightened down the screw. For a looser pedal you loosened the screw.

- The Speed King also featured a beater height adjustment.

- Some of the greatest drummers in history used Speed King pedals.

DW 5000 Chain Pedal

- In the 1980s the DW 5000 took over the Speed King's throne. This pedal featured the revolutionary chain drive.

- The DW 5000 was the first pedal to offer the plastic/felt combination beater,

which allowed for two different sounds. One side delivered a hard felt sound. When you flipped it over, you got the harder plastic sound, which actually imitated the wood beater that was a popular alternative to the felt beater.

could be adjusted to whatever tension you desired. The adjustments were what made the Speed King so easy to use. All you did was turn the pedal over and adjust two screws. That's it.

Today pedals are much more complicated. A basic pedal has a chain drive for strength. There are adjustments for the springs, camshafts, beater height, and angles. Some pedals have so many adjustments that they're really confusing to operate.

So I recommend starting out with the good old Speed King pedal. It's inexpensive, easy to operate, and comes with a great sounding hard felt beater that I prefer to the more modern beaters that are half plastic for a hard sound and half felt for a softer sound.

Yamaha, Pacific Drums, Pearl and other companies make cheaper pedals, but they don't have the classic old school pedal technology that really makes the Speed King *King!*

Today's DW Pedals

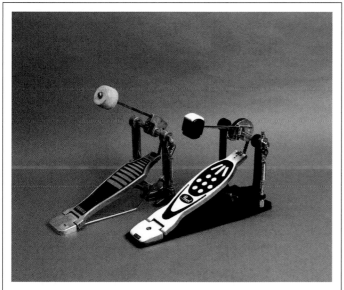

- If you want a really great pedal, the DW brand is the one to get.

- The newer pedals like the DW 9000 are more compli-cated and expensive. They have many adjustments and are really top of the line—a good way to go for the experienced drummer.

- A DW has adjustments for springs, cam, beater height, beat distance from the head, spring tension—you name it.

Beater Adjustments

- Most of today's pedals have adjustments for the beaters. This means you can control not only the height of the beater, but also the angle at which it sits on the pedal.

- These adjustments control the power of the hit. If the beater sits up higher on the bass drum, it delivers a longer hit. If it sits lower, the hit is shorter. You can adjust the beater distance from the head to give you more power.

BEATERS

How many beaters are there to choose from, and what do they do?

Once upon a time, there was only one kind of beater available for a drum set. The first beaters consisted of a big fuzzy-furry ball on the end of metal rod. With the Sixties and the evolution of hard rock, beaters also evolved, with a different shape and harder felt balls. Then came the wood beater, which delivered an even harder, more powerful hit that led to the development of stronger drumheads with a thicker center

to withstand beater damage. Round pieces of Mylar plastic called "kick pads" attached to the head for extra protection.

Today you have choice of felt, wood, fiberglass, and combination beaters. Combination beaters have a solid plastic side that, when turned 180 degrees, becomes a felt beater. Easy!

Beaters with felt ends are best for rock or jazz "kick" drums. If, however, you need a beater with more "slap" to it, the

KNACK DRUMS FOR EVERYONE

Felt Beaters

- Of the two felt beaters shown here, the one on the bottom is hard felt for the harder hit, the other—the fuzzy round one—for the softer hit.

- Recently Vator reintroduced the vintage fuzzy beater. It looks just like the old one— your basic ball on a metal rod—and has the same kind of sound.

Wooden Beaters

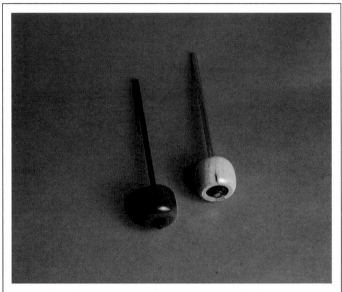

- Wooden beaters are head killers. They've got awesome power and so much attack that they can dent the drumhead.

- While wood beaters come in different shapes and sizes, they all have pretty much the same sound.

- It is a good idea to have both a felt beater and a wood beater in your kit. If you're playing in a rock band, use the wood beater. If you've got a jazz gig, the felt beater is the one you want.

beaters made of harder materials are preferable.

Why does the type of beater you choose make such a difference? Because you want the best sound you can get out of your bass drum. Like the various woods that are used for drums, the different beaters will give you a different sound. I personally love the uniquely warm sound of the felt beaters on a bass drum pedal.

When you go to a music store, try putting a felt beater on the pedal and listen to the difference in sound.

• • • • • • • • • • • • • RED ● LIGHT • • • • • • • • • • • • •

If you are planning to play the bass drum with a wood or plastic beater, you *must* put a kick pad on the drum, even if you have a dot on the head.

Two-sided Beaters

- These two-sided plastic-felt beaters were invented by DW in the late 1980s and were considered a great innovation.

- All you did was turn the beater 180 degrees to change the sound from hard to soft.

- The plastic had a similar sound to a wood beater and the felt part closely approximated the sound of a traditional felt beater. Each side hit the drum from a slightly different angle.

- The original felt and wood beaters have a better sound.

T Beaters

- "T's" are the newest design in beaters. They have a smaller area range, resulting in a sound with more attack and less warmth.

- T beaters come in either plastic or combinations of wood and plastic and felt and plastic. All three types produce different tones.

- Many younger drummers who play fast bass drums prefer the quick, hard attack of the T beaters. But others don't like their sound. If you're interested in them, try them out first.

PEDAL ADJUSTMENTS

Attaching your pedal, adjusting the spring and beater, and maintaining them for smooth operation

The first thing you should know is your pedal brand. The one we'll be talking about here is the DW 5000. Next you need to know how to attach the pedal to the bass drum. Put the pedal near the bass drum; you'll see a metal clamp with a T screw on it. The bass drum shell goes in between the base of the pedal and the screw clamp. Now tighten the screw until the pedal is secure.

Try out the pedal. If it feels too loose, tighten the spring by turning the nut above it counterclockwise, pulling down on the long nut on the bottom and tightening up the top nut. To loosen the pedal, do the opposite. Aside from the Speed King, most pedals operate on this principle.

DW 5000 Pedal

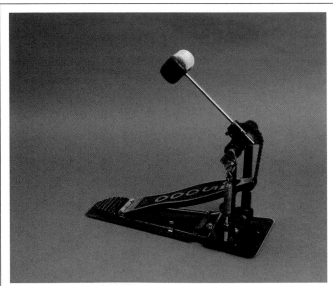

- These are the parts of the DW 5000 pedal: pedal board, cam, beater, oil holes, beater holder, spring, spring tension screw and nuts, clamp to bass drum, screw anchors, chain drive, chain drive adjust screw (underneath pedal board), spindle.

- It's always a good idea to keep extra parts on hand. The chain drive is a signature feature of the DW 5000 pedals. Pushing down on the pedal pulls the chain down and causes the beater to hit the drum cam.

Oiling Your Pedal

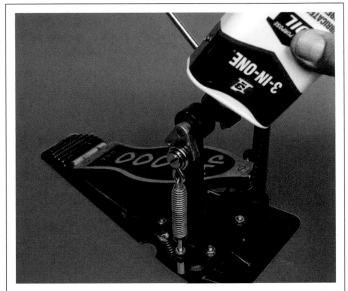

- All brands of pedals require regular oiling to keep them running correctly. If they're not oiled, they'll get noisy and sluggish.

- 3 in One Oil comes in a can with a top that fits into the oiling holes.

- When a Speed King pedal needs oiling, it squeaks. There are little oiling holes on each pedal that look like Allen screw holes. Put the 3 in One can up to the holes and squirt in two or three drops.

Now check the beater height. On the cam that goes across the pedal is the shaft where the beater goes. Loosening the screw with a drum key, slide the beater in, adjust the height, and select the side of the beater you want to use—plastic or felt. These are the two main adjustments for this kind of pedal.

There is also a chain adjustment. You can find this on top of the chain, to the right of the cam. Using a drum key, move the metal (which has a slit in it) back and forth to find the best position for the action you want. This adjustment becomes a fine-tuning mechanism for the chain, changing the angle and, consequently, the feel of the pedal.

Other Pedal Features

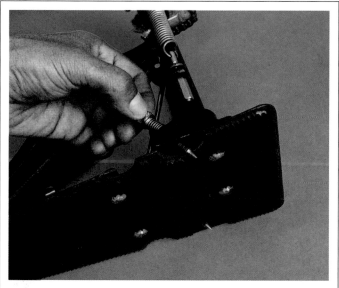

- You can also adjust the anchor screws on the base of the pedal to prevent the pedal and bass drum from moving. Note: Anchor screws can ruin a floor, so always set up your drums on a rug.

- A footplate on the DW pedal keeps the pedal really sturdy.

Using Velcro

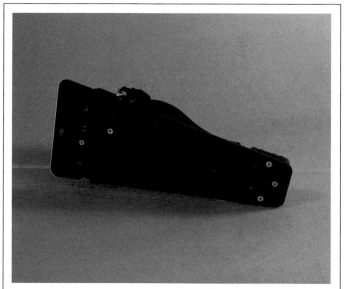

- You can attach the footplate to a rug with Velcro. Together with the pedal anchors, Velcro helps keep the bass drum in place so that you can play it as hard as you want.

- Sometimes the Velcro will make it difficult to move the bass drum when the pedal is hooked up to it. If you find this happening, take the pedal off, move the drum, and put the pedal back on.

BASS DRUM DOUBLE PEDALS

Let's look at double pedals, how they work, and whether you need them

Double pedals came on the market in the 1980s. They were introduced by DW, the number one company in pedal technology. Up until then, if you wanted to play double bass drums, you had two bass drums. With the double pedal setup, you could play a single bass drum with two different pedals. This isn't the same as playing two bass drums. When you play two bass drums, you hear two distinct notes. With the double pedal there's only one note, but the double pedals enable you to go faster and get a more even sounding tone.

So do you need a double pedal? Not really—when you're just starting out. As you get better, however, you may want to start experimenting with them.

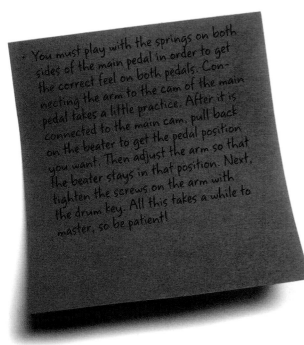

- You must play with the springs on both sides of the main pedal in order to get the correct feel on both pedals. Connecting the arm to the cam of the main pedal takes a little practice. After it is connected to the main cam, pull back on the beater to get the pedal position you want. Then adjust the arm so that the beater stays in that position. Next, tighten the screws on the arm with the drum key. All this takes a while to master, so be patient!

DW 5000 Double Pedal

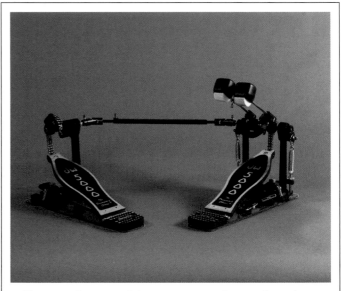

- These are the parts of the DW 5000 double pedal: two pedal boards, two cams, two beaters, oil holes in both pedals, two beater holders, two springs, two spring tension screws and nuts, clamp to bass drum, screw anchors, two chain drives, double-chain-drive adjust screw (underneath pedal board), two-chain spindle.

Double pedals operate the same way as single pedals. The main pedal hooks up to the bass drum and has two springs, plus an adjustable bar or arm. The arm connects to the cam on the main pedal that connects to the satellite pedal. This satellite pedal has no spring, so when you hook it up, you must connect the arm to the cam, turn the satellite pedal to the desired pedal board height, and tighten the arm. All the adjustments are the same as on the stock DW pedal. The only addition is the arm and the second spring and pedal board.

Other Double Pedals

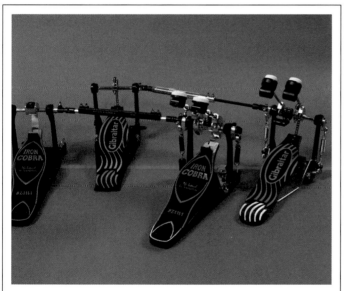

- Every major drum and accessory company in the United States and China now makes and markets double pedals, ranging in price from $99 to over $400.

- To see all the available pedals, Google "double pedals for bass drums." Some of the best pedal brands are DW, Pearl, and Pacific Pedals. Pacific is a DW product and is a very well made pedal.

- I would suggest playing your drum set for a while with a single bass drum before going on to the double pedal.

Those Crazy Sleishman Pedals

- For a really different double pedal, try the Sleishman. The footboards sit on the right and left of the main part of the pedal, which hooks up to the bass drum. The positioning of these pedals definitely takes some getting used to.

- Sleishmans are totally sci-fi. They look like they've come out of a futuristic movie and are guaranteed to get people's attention.

PEDAL FOOT POSITIONS
Different ways to use your foot on the pedals to play effectively and avoid injury

The bass drums and hi-hat pedals can be a challenge. You need good coordination, and without proper positioning and technique, you can strain muscles and tendons.

The first good pedal method is the "heel-down" approach. Let's start with how to sit on the drum stool. Sit with your legs at a right angle to the floor. This gives you maximum power and strength. The weight is then distributed to your butt, where it belongs. Your snare drum should be sitting between your legs, and your pedals should feel comfortable when you hit them. If your legs are too far apart, you risk getting injured, so position the pedals so that you're not straining your legs or ankles.

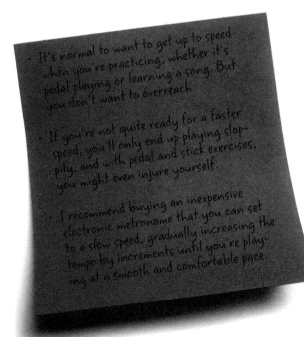

- It's normal to want to get up to speed when you're practicing, whether it's pedal playing or learning a song. But you don't want to overreach.

- If you're not quite ready for a faster speed, you'll only end up playing sloppily, and with pedal and stick exercises, you might even injure yourself.

- I recommend buying an inexpensive electronic metronome that you can set to a slow speed, gradually increasing the tempo by increments until you're playing at a smooth and comfortable pace.

Sitting Properly

- Foot exercises may cause muscle aches, but don't stop practicing unless you experience sharp or severe pain. By building up the reps gradually, your muscles will become stronger and the discomfort will disappear.

- Pay close attention to your seat height. Too high or too low, and you'll experience discomfort not associated with the exercises themselves. If you feel twinges or straining in your legs, feet, shoulders, and/or back as soon as you start to play, adjust the seat until you can hit the pedals comfortably.

With your heel down on the back of the pedal board, raise the front part of your foot and push down on the pedal to hit the drum. Do a count of 1-2-3-4, repeating this exercise. Repeat with your left foot on the hi-hat pedal. This will get your feet going.

Keep this up for five minutes on each foot, building strength and stamina. If you can't do five minutes, start with two or three and work up to five.

Now let's get comfortable with the back-and-forth foot motion used for the hi-hat. To the count of 1-2-3-4, bring

your heel down on the end of the footboard on the 1 and 3 counts. On the 2 and the 4 counts, hit the pedal with the ball of your foot, pushing the hi-hat closed. On the 2 and 4 counts, you're putting the accent on the second and fourth beats of the bar. One, *TWO,* three, *FOUR.*

Practice every day for at least five minutes in order for your brain and body to absorb the new information. Eventually, the process will become automatic—like riding a bike.

Heel-Up Method

- When you're playing rock music, use the heel-up method of pedal playing.

- Here, the heel does not touch the back of the pedal board. Instead, you bring your whole leg up and down again, but at the last minute, just before your foot actually hits the pedal,

  you snap your ankle to hit the drum.

- Practice to the 1-2-3-4 count.

- Remember: It's important to start slowly and build speed. Use the metronome.

Music Terms

- *Tempo*—Speed at which a piece is played.

- *Metronome*—Practice device that allows you to set and control the tempo, keeping the beat with a series of clocklike ticks; a metronome can either be hand wound or electronic.

- *Rocking pedal method*— When you rock you foot back and forth from heel to toe on the hi-hat.

- *Heel-up method*—A way to play the pedal in order to get more power on the bass drums; generally used in rock drumming.

THE METRONOME

Use an old-style metronome or a new electronic version to improve your practice

The metronome is a device that produces a regulated pulse that sets a steady tempo. The word *metronome* comes from the Greek *metron,* meaning "measure," and *nomos,* meaning "regulating." Although the earliest metronome dates from the ninth century, the modern mechanical metronome was invented in 1812. While the mechanical, or hand-wound, metronome is still in use, the electronic metronome has become very popular.

The metronome sets the speed of any musical piece by counting the beats per minute (BPM). It can go from 40 to 208 BPM. The nonelectronic metronomes operate on a pendulum principle, with a weight that you can set on notches. The pendulum then clicks back and forth at the set tempo.

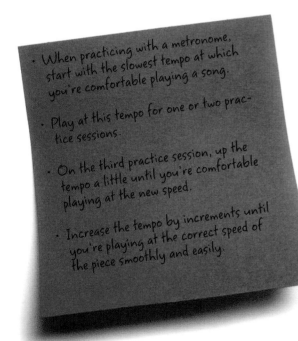

- When practicing with a metronome, start with the slowest tempo at which you're comfortable playing a song.

- Play at this tempo for one or two practice sessions.

- On the third practice session, up the tempo a little until you're comfortable playing at the new speed.

- Increase the tempo by increments until you're playing at the correct speed of the piece smoothly and easily.

Pendulum Metronome

- A metronome is like having a conductor standing next to you, pounding out the tempo and pushing you to stay in time.

- Many musicians, especially drummers, have metronomes as part of their daily workout. It's like the Stairmaster, or treadmill, or Lifecycle.

- You set the machine at a lower speed and work up to the faster speeds as you increase your endurance. In the case of music, it's not so much endurance as facility that you want to achieve.

Some of today's more ingenious metronomes can also perform as a click track to use in the recording studio and are capable of programming a whole song with different tempo and time signature changes. They can be used onstage with earphones to enable you to have a click track while playing a show. These electronic metronomes can also be used to start songs. The Tama Rhythm Watch/Song Starter, for instance, does everything I mentioned above. It also programs up to maybe twenty songs or more with the correct starting tempo for the song. This is a great performance aid.

ZOOM

The old-style metronome is accurate and easy to use. To set the tempo move the weight up or down the pendulum and give the pendulum a slight push. It will tick back and forth to a steady rhythm. These metronomes are small and portable, and they run the old-fashioned way—wound by hand.

Tama Rhythm Watch

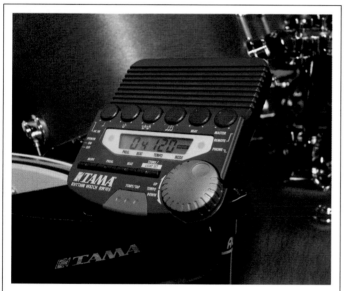

- The Tama has many different uses. You can change the sounds of the click track; for instance, from a wood block to a cowbell.

- There are memory settings and a knob that quickly turns up the tempo. There are also separate knobs for volume for each kind of note value.

- One of the best things about the Tama is being able to start each song on stage at the correct tempo.

Pricing Metronomes

- As a beginner you don't need to spend any more than $20 on an electronic metronome that will give you everything you need.

- The $40 Boss DB-30 has a tap tempo feature on it—you tap a beat on your pad and it figures out the tempo.

- If you've got money to burn, there's the $150 model, which is more than just a metronome. It's virtually an entire practice station.

- Google "electronic metronomes" and check out the different possibilities.

CHOOSING CYMBALS

Choose your cymbals from a number of companies: Zildjian, Sabian, Paiste, and others

Boy, have cymbals changed. They come in colors now—black, red, woo-hoo! Makes me feel old, to think that in my heyday, all we had was boring old brass. And once upon a time, there was only one cymbal manufacturer—Zildjian. Then along came Paiste cymbals, which were very popular with the drummers of the late 1960s. Today there are a whole

host of cymbal companies to choose from—Zildjian, Paiste, Sabian, Wuhan, Istambul, and Meinl are the biggest names, but the list goes on. This book will only look at a few types of cymbals; the rest is up to you. You'll need to figure out which ones are right for you. Are you playing rock or jazz? If so, check out a hand-hammered cymbal. These are the

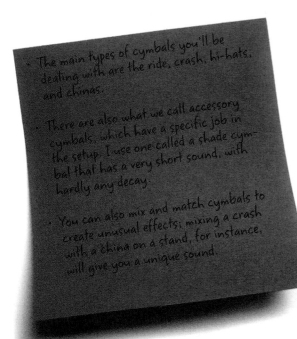

- The main types of cymbals you'll be dealing with are the ride, crash, hi-hats, and chinas.

- There are also what we call accessory cymbals, which have a specific job in the setup. I use one called a shade cymbal that has a very short sound, with hardly any decay.

- You can also mix and match cymbals to create unusual effects; mixing a crash with a china on a stand, for instance, will give you a unique sound.

Zildjian K

- The Zildjian K was the first successful hand-hammered cymbal, noted for its beautiful warm tone.

- The K has a short decay and a great sound on the bell. The A, another famous and widely used Zildjian cymbal, has a big sound with much more decay.

- Both range in size from 6-inch to at least 24-inch rides. Go to the cymbal sound room of a music store and try out as many cymbals as you can take.

traditional cymbals. The Sabian hand-hammered cymbal has the same construction and sound as a Zildjian K, and both are equally fine models.

I use 18-inch and 20-inch HH Sabian crashes. They sound great. They have a short decay (the length of time the cymbal rings), which works for me when I'm playing rock. I also use a Signature ride cymbal called the Definition Ride 21. This is a great hand-hammered quality cymbal made with a B8 material known to cut through with a fierce bell sound. (The bell is the center area of the cymbal that looks like a flying saucer.)

ZOOM

Splash cymbals are very small cymbals, 6, 7, and 8 inches in size, that have a quick, "splashy" kind of sound and add good tone variation to the drum set. All the cymbal companies make these kinds of cymbals in different weights.

Traditional Sabian Cymbals

- Sabian cymbals are actually made and the company is owned by Robert Zildjian.

- The Sabian's hand-hammered HH is expensive but well worth the price.

- The Sabian AA's have a longer ring and a big, open sound.

- New Sabian models include the HHX, which is labeled a dark-sounding cymbal, and the BB, a bronze cymbal with a brighter sound.

Paiste Cymbals

- The best Paiste cymbals are the old 602 models, which have a dark sound with great bell response.

- The 2002's had a brighter sound than the 602's. You can still get 2002 rides, crashes, and hi-hats, and

some of the best china cymbals are still the 18-inch Paiste 2002's.

- In the realm of accessories, the greatest one—which every rock drummer had— was a big Paiste gong on a big stand.

HI-HAT CYMBALS

Mixing and matching your hi-hat cymbals from among different brands, sizes, and weights

Hi-hats are a matched pair of cymbals that clash when you use the hi-hat pedal.

Hi-hat technology has been developing for many years. Like most drums equipment, there are an incredible number of hi-hat models now on the market. The cost of hi-hats can range from $60 all the way up to hundreds of dollars.

I like the 14-inch Sabian HH cymbals. These are excellent all-round cymbals for rock, jazz, Latin, and basically whatever you want to play. The one drawback for the beginner is that they're not cheap, running around $400. The B8 Pro, however, is a good hi-hat to start with. You can get this model for around $125.

Starter Hi-Hats

- The Sabian B8 hi-hat cymbals are a great deal. Priced at under $110, they've got a good pro sound you'll love.

- The Zildjian ZBT hi-hat is a nice pro-sounding cymbal. If money's really tight, there's the 13-inch pair in the $60 range.

- The Paiste PST series is also inexpensive, $68 to $77, with a medium weight top and a heavy bottom.

Pro Hi-Hats

- All the cymbal companies make high end pro hi-hats. The Zildjian K has been around for years and prices out at around $400.

- The Sabian AA series will give you a very high quality hi-hat for around $260—a great buy. This model is an excellent choice in terms of both quality and budget.

- In the end, though, go back to the music store to check out hi-hats for yourself.

What kind of sound are you looking for in a hi-hat? Some hi-hats create sounds that are crisp and clean; others are dark and "dirty" sounding. It is difficult to single these out just by name. With time you'll get to know the characteristics of a particular cymbal model.

You can mix and match some of the hit-hats by using a heavyweight bottom and a lightweight top cymbal, say a 15-inch top and a 14-inch bottom. Cymbals are a very personal thing, so you must research and then try out each set of hi-hat cymbals you think you might want. The only way to meet your hi-hat soul mates is to date as many hi-hats as you can.

Some companies made hi-hats especially designed to push the air out when the cymbals close. This gives some cool dynamics to your playing. Hi-hats can also come with improved pedal action.

Experimenting with Sound

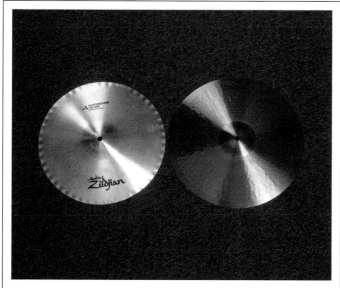

- One of the best ways to create new sounds is by experimenting with your cymbals.

- For some interesting variations, try a 16-inch top and a 14-inch bottom hi-hat. Or a 15-inch top and 14-inch bottom.

- If you can still find them, I believe Sabian made cymbals with holes in the bottom to let the air out. These "air hole" cymbals can add considerable dynamics to your set when mixed and matched.

Paiste Sound Edge

- The Paiste Sound Edge hi-hat is based on the concept that if you make spaces in the cymbals to let the air escape, you'll cut down on air pressure and the pedal action will be easier and faster.

- With the Sound Edge hi-hats, the bottom cymbal has a beveled edge. When the top cymbal comes down on the bottom one, the air is pushed out through the beveled edge. You can really feel the difference in the cymbal action.

CYMBAL PACKS

If you are new to the drums, cymbal packs are a good way to get started

By now you're probably experiencing cymbal overload—and I haven't even begun to talk about the other hundreds of models out there! So, you might want to take a smart shortcut with a ready-made cymbal pack.

The cymbal pack comes with three or four cymbals that usually include a hi-hat set, a crash, and a ride. They're specially designed and priced for beginning drummers.

Zildjian offers a pack, the Zildjian ZBT cymbals, at a good price. With the ZBT, price can't stand between you and a sensational sounding set of cymbals. The ZBT's use revolutionary new manufacturing techniques developed by the Zildjian Sound Lab that release fast, bright, high-volume sound from

KNACK DRUMS FOR EVERYONE

Sabian Packs

- The Sabian Super B8 pro set is a superdeal, with four cymbals, including a 14-inch set of hi-hats, 14- and 16-inch crashes, and a 20-inch ride.

- My signature line with Sabian is also B8 material. So, you are getting a true pro sound here for much less in the dollar department.

- Sometimes companies throw in free items to the pack. Check online before you buy to see if any of these deals are available.

Zildjian Packs

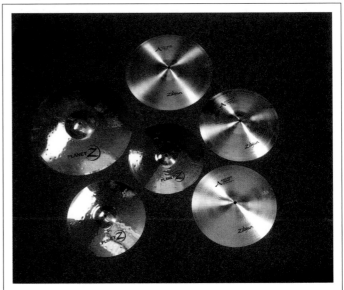

- Zildjian's Planet 23 cymbal pack only has an 18-inch ride/crash and a set of 14-inch hi-hats, but it's also only around $100.

- Another Planet 23 pack includes two 14-inch hi-hats, a 16-inch crash, and a 20-inch ride.

- The more expensive Zildjian A series includes two 14-inch hi-hats, a 16-inch crash, and 20-inch ride. They may throw in a small crash for free.

the power-packed ZBT alloy. Sizes include the 14-inch hi-hats, 16-inch crash, and a 20-inch ride. Throw in a cymbal bag, and what a deal. The Meinl MCS Cymbal Pack with Free Filter China contains 14-inch medium hi-hats, a 16-inch medium crash, and a 20-inch medium ride, plus a free filter china. These Meinl cymbals are all harmonically matched for the most musical sound. The Sabian B8 Cymbal Pack was designed according to Sabian's high standards—without the high price. Outfitting any drum set with these cymbals will provide a pro sound at a fraction of the price of pro cymbals.

Meinl Packs

- The German cymbal company Meinl makes some nice cymbal packs, among which is the award-winning Generation X, an add-on setup that includes a 16-inch crash, 18-inch crash/ride, and free 14-inch filter china.

ZOOM

You must go into music stores and look at all the various cymbal packs. It is very hard to do this online—for one thing you can't hear the cymbals. And you can look at the differences in the equipment, from the cheap cymbals to the expensive cymbal packs. Also not every music store carries everything, so you'll have to shop around to hear what you are buying.

CYMBALS & HI-HATS

- Cymbal packs are pretty new. They were created to give the drummer a preselected set of cymbals so he doesn't need to go to a store and play each cymbal. Once the idea caught on, most of the companies started creating packs. Packs range from cheap to expensive models.

CYMBAL SHORT SOUNDS

Combining different cymbals can help you create new sounds and give "bite" to your playing

Different cymbals have different ring lengths. Up until now we've been talking about cymbals that have a decay, or long sound. A Sabian A rings more than a hand-hammered cymbal. The difference in the length of ring is called decay. Other cymbals have short rings. When you hit your two hi-hats together, they make a short sound. China cymbals are a type

of short sound cymbal. Wuhan Cymbal Company makes chinas with really short sounds. And the smaller the cymbal, the shorter the sound. If you hit a 14-inch Wuhan china, the sound will dissipate faster than an 18-inch china.

Another type of short sound can be produced by putting two cymbals together. When you push the hi-hat pedal

Short-Sound Cymbal Combos

- To make the china/splash short sound, take a felt washer from your cymbals stand or your survival kit. Cut a one-eighth-inch slit in the washer with a razor knife. Then tear it with your fingers to produce a very thin felt washer.

- Lay your china cymbal on the stand with the bell face down. Put the thin washer on the china cymbal. Lay a 7 or 8-inch splash cymbal over the washer. Then, put the rest of the washers back on the stand, securing them with a metal washer and screwing it down firmly.

Dual-Cymbal Short Sounds

- This is a simple, effective way to get a short sound. You'll need two cymbals. The cymbals can be any size, but smaller cymbals—those under 16 inches—work better.

- Put one cymbal on a stand and another smaller-sized cymbal on top of it. Put as many felt washers on it to make it a tight fit. Top it off with a metal washer.

down and push the cymbals together, and then hit the cymbals, you get a short sound.

Similarly, you can create different short sounds by putting different cymbals together on one stand. I like to do this with one of my Carmine Chinas and a 7-inch splash cymbal. I put the splash inside my upside down china with a one-eighth-inch felt washer between the cymbals. The rest of the felt washers go on top of the cymbal, with a metal washer on top of everything. I tighten the nut until it's very tight. When I hit the china and the splash at the same time, I get a new short sound.

Chinas Together

- This china short sound is a lot of fun to create and play.

- Put two 14-inch chinas together on a cymbal stand like a set of hi-hats. Put the felt washers on top and make the nut really tight. When you hit the cymbals, you'll get a very short sound with "bite" to it. This is because a china cymbal has more attack, so two of them together produce a really sharp sound.

- The cheap chinas sound great!

·········· GREEN ● LIGHT ··········

Listen to your favorite drum tracks. See if you can pick out differences in how long cymbals ring and how the difference between a short sound and a long sound (decay) changes the way the song feels.

CYMBALS & HI-HATS

- Experimenting with short sounds can be exciting and fun. Even if you have some really cheap, trashy cymbals, you can combine them to produce unique effects.

- The sizes don't really matter as long as they're not too big. A 20-inch ride won't sound that great, but 12, 14, 15, or 16-inch cymbals will be very effective, as they have a smaller sound with more attack.

- Remember: Short sounds are as much about attack as they are about sound.

79

WILD CYMBALS

If you want to produce "thunder" or the sound of clanging trash can lids, there's a cymbal for you

Today there are more wild accessory cymbals than you can shake a drumstick at. All the cymbal companies feature some sort of special effects cymbals, each of which has a unique sound and purpose. I worked with Sabian to create the Carmine Appice Shade Cymbal, which is so special you have to direct-order it from the company. I'm proud of this model,

because it sounds like no other cymbal.

Some cymbals sound like trash can lids, while others have a bell sound that's tuned to a specific note. Some really out-there cymbals are shaped like big crosses and sport a silver finish. Factory Metal even makes a ride cymbal without the bell that sounds like a piece of scrap metal!

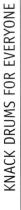

Sabian Effects Cymbals

Factory Metal

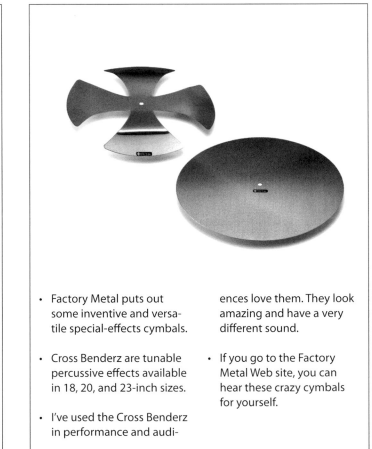

- The Sabian ALU Bell Effects looks like an oversized cymbal bell and sounds, as you might expect, like a bell.

- The Sabian Chopper's innovative three-layer design fits on a cymbal stand and delivers superfast white-

noise responses. The chopper can also add a distinctly different flavor when used in place of a hi-hat.

- The Sabian Thunder Sheet is a sheet of treated bronze that produces a thunderlike special effect when hit.

- Factory Metal puts out some inventive and versatile special-effects cymbals.

- Cross Benderz are tunable percussive effects available in 18, 20, and 23-inch sizes.

- I've used the Cross Benderz in performance and audi-

ences love them. They look amazing and have a very different sound.

- If you go to the Factory Metal Web site, you can hear these crazy cymbals for yourself.

Wuhan and Sabian make a small cymbal with a gong sound. UFIP has a cymbal that sounds like a tambourine, but looks like someone cut a triangle out of a regular cymbal. Sabian makes cymbal effects called Thunder Sheets that really do sound like thunder.

And how about some colored cymbals to really let 'em know you're there? Most companies make black cymbals; the drawback is that the paint cuts down on the ring. But it is a great look. Whether or not you're willing to sacrifice a little sound for a lot of cool is up to you.

ZOOM

As with anything else, it's very important for you to do your online research before buying any special-effects cymbals. Google all the big names in cymbals and then search "special effects." You won't believe what's out there! And don't forget to give these cymbals a listen before you buy.

Carmine Appice Shade

- This cymbal is called a "shade" because it's shaped like a lampshade. Hit it hard and you get a loud and trashy short sound that's great for accents and quick, clear, loud patterns. Hit it softly and it sounds like a breath of air.

- You can buy the shade in a music store new from DDRUM.

- I've been playing the Shade since 1992, and these cymbals continue to mesmerize me with their dynamic range and awesome sound.

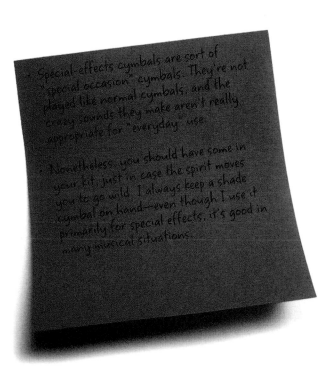

- Special-effects cymbals are sort of "special occasion" cymbals. They're not played like normal cymbals, and the crazy sounds they make aren't really appropriate for "everyday" use.

- Nonetheless, you should have some in your kit, just in case the spirit moves you to go wild. I always keep a shade cymbal on hand—even though I use it primarily for special effects, it's good in many musical situations.

CHOOSING A CYMBAL SETUP

A few ideas for beginners or players who want to rethink their drum setup

Every basic cymbal setup should include a set of hi-hats, a ride, and at least one crash. The average drum set would have all the above and an extra crash. So, how do choose your setup? You might want to start by thinking about the cymbal setups some of your drum idols use. If you've got a favorite drummer whose cymbal sound you really like, find

out what cymbals he uses. Then try them out at a store.

If you're not into idols, go to the music store and check out some medium-sized cymbals like the 20-inch medium ride Sabian AA cymbal, the 16-inch Paiste PST 5 medium crash, the 18-inch Zildjian ZHT medium crash, and a set of Sabian B8 pro 14-inch medium cymbals. Notice how the same size

Drum Setup

- Your cymbals should be positioned in a tight, close-knit setup that has a ride, two crashes, hi-hats, and a china. The china sits up over the ride on a boom stand for easy access.

- The ride is on the right between the rack and floor toms. The 16-inch crash is

on the left side of the kit, and the 18-inch crash is on the right side, near the floor tom. You can also reverse these.

- You can keep the cymbals low for quick and easy access. This setup looks very relaxed.

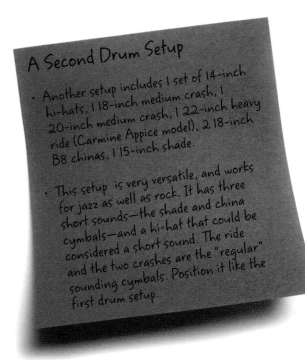

A Second Drum Setup

- Another setup includes 1 set of 14-inch hi-hats, 1 18-inch medium crash, 1 20-inch medium crash, 1 22-inch heavy ride (Carmine Appice model), 2 18-inch B8 chinas, 1 15-inch shade.

- This setup is very versatile, and works for jazz as well as rock. It has three short sounds—the shade and china cymbals—and a hi-hat that could be considered a short sound. The ride and the two crashes are the "regular" sounding cymbals. Position it like the first drum setup.

cymbals from the various companies each have their own sound.

Once you've decided on your cymbals, you need to set them up. You should place your ride cymbal to the right of your rack tom, between the rack and the floor tom. The crashes should be left of the rack toms and to the right of the floor tom. Since everyone's arm length is different, make sure the cymbals are positioned within easy reach. The hi-hat pedal should be to the left of the snare drum; keep it as close to the snare as possible without crowding the drum.

For a short sound you can add a china cymbal to your setup. Place the china where you feel you can reach it easily. Chinas can go high up on a boom stand or in between other cymbals on the set.

Choosing Your Cymbals

- When picking out your cymbals, choose them in this order: hi-hat, ride, primary crash, and secondary crash.

- At the music store, when you find the cymbals you like, go across the room and listen as someone else hits them. This way you'll hear

them as an audience would be hearing them.

- Cymbals loose brightness with age. So when it comes to new cymbals, look on the bright side! It's better to have a little too much brightness at the outset.

Cleaning Up

- You only have to clean your cymbals once or twice a year. And since some cymbals have a more brilliant finish than others, too much cleaning can actually dull them.

- You can get cymbal cleaner through any cymbal manufacturer or at music stores.

- Always make sure to dry the cymbals really well in order to avoid water damage. If the cymbal isn't completely dry, it can sometimes turn green.

MUSIC THEORY FOR DRUMS

The beginning of drum music: fundamentals of rhythm, key signatures, and note values

It's time to learn how to read music. First, let's learn the fundamentals of rhythm, key signatures, and note values—the basics of music theory.

When you listen to a rock song and tap to the beat with your foot or fingers, you're actually counting 1-2-3-4 along with the music. Every 1-2-3-4 makes up a bar or a measure. In this type of music, the count is always 1 to 4—the next count after "four" is always "one." Count 1-2-3-4, and you've completed a measure.

Every piece of music has what we call a time signature right

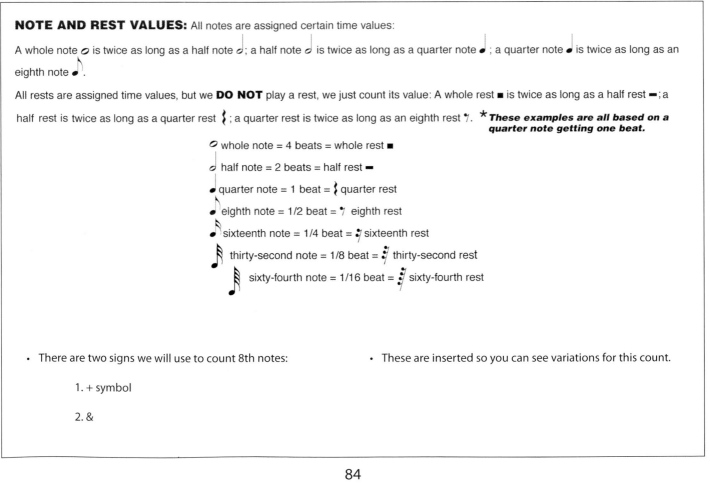

NOTE AND REST VALUES: All notes are assigned certain time values:

A whole note 𝅝 is twice as long as a half note 𝅗𝅥; a half note 𝅗𝅥 is twice as long as a quarter note ♩; a quarter note ♩ is twice as long as an eighth note ♪.

All rests are assigned time values, but we **DO NOT** play a rest, we just count its value: A whole rest 𝄻 is twice as long as a half rest 𝄼; a half rest is twice as long as a quarter rest 𝄽; a quarter rest is twice as long as an eighth rest 𝄾. ****These examples are all based on a quarter note getting one beat.***

𝅝 whole note = 4 beats = whole rest 𝄻

𝅗𝅥 half note = 2 beats = half rest 𝄼

♩ quarter note = 1 beat = 𝄽 quarter rest

♪ eighth note = 1/2 beat = 𝄾 eighth rest

𝅘𝅥𝅯 sixteenth note = 1/4 beat = 𝄿 sixteenth rest

𝅘𝅥𝅰 thirty-second note = 1/8 beat = 𝅀 thirty-second rest

𝅘𝅥𝅱 sixty-fourth note = 1/16 beat = 𝅁 sixty-fourth rest

- There are two signs we will use to count 8th notes:

  1. + symbol

  2. &

- These are inserted so you can see variations for this count.

at the beginning. It looks like two numbers separated by a division sign. The 1-2-3-4 rhythm is known as 4/4 time. The 4/4 is telling you that there are four beats to a measure, with a quarter note equaling one beat.

The quarter note is an example of a note value. The basic notes you'll be dealing with are the following: Whole Note: The longest note, equal to four quarter notes or an entire measure in 4/4 time. Half Note: Equals two quarter notes and receives two counts in a 4/4 measure. Held twice as long as the quarter note, and half as long as the whole note. Quarter

Note: In 4/4 time the quarter note gets one count and there are four quarter notes to a measure. It's twice as fast as the half note, and four times as fast as the whole note. Eighth Note: Eighth notes are twice as fast as quarter notes. A 4/4 measure would contain eight such notes, counted like this: "1+2+3+4+." Sixteenth Note: An eighth note equals two sixteenth notes, and a quarter note equals four sixteenth notes, so a sixteenth note is four times as fast as a quarter note, with sixteen of them equaling one measure in 4/4 time.

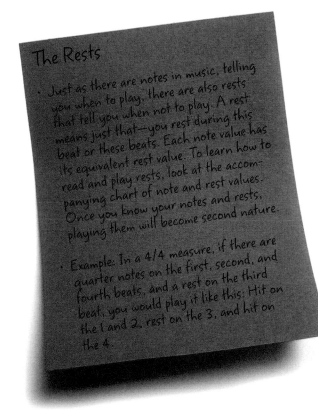

Counting/Playing 4/4 Time

- Whole notes: One to a measure. Hit on "1" and count "2-3-4."

- Half notes: Two to a measure. Hit on "1," count "2," hit on "3," count "4."

- Quarter notes: Four to a measure. Play on every beat: 1-2-3-4.

- Eighth notes: Eight to a measure. Play eight beats, counting them "1+2+3+4+," with the numbers indicating the quarter notes.

- Sixteenth notes: Sixteen to a measure. Play sixteen beats, counting them "1e&A, 2e&A, 3e&A, 4e&A."

The Rests

- Just as there are notes in music, telling you when to play, there are also rests that tell you when not to play. A rest means just that—you rest during this beat or these beats. Each note value has its equivalent rest value. To learn how to read and play rests, look at the accompanying chart of note and rest values. Once you know your notes and rests, playing them will become second nature.

- Example: In a 4/4 measure, if there are quarter notes on the first, second, and fourth beats, and a rest on the third beat, you would play it like this: Hit on the 1 and 2, rest on the 3, and hit on the 4.

DRUM THEORY

MUSIC "SIGN LANGUAGE"

Learning the signs that guide your playing: bass and treble clefs and time signatures

The first thing you'll see on the five-line music staff is a clef. It may be a bass clef, a treble clef, or a neutral clef and it's always found at the beginning of a piece. (See below.) The clef tells you where you'll be playing on your instrument—in the bass range, or up higher in the treble, or in the middle.

The next thing you see is the time signature. This tells you how many beats there are to a measure, and what kind of note equals one beat. At the end of the measure, there is a line called the bar line. The bar lines separate the measures in a piece.

Some Common Music Signs

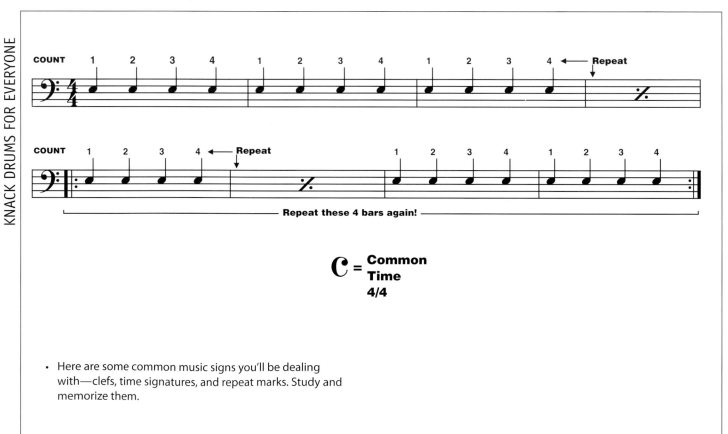

- Here are some common music signs you'll be dealing with—clefs, time signatures, and repeat marks. Study and memorize them.

Sometimes there will be a sign to repeat a section of a piece. You'll find this sign—a pair of dots that looks like a colon, with a bar line and a darker bar line—at the end of the section. This means repeat the bar or bars you are playing. There is another repeat mark that tells you to repeat the bar(s) right in front of the mark. This looks like one measure with a forty-five degree angle line going through the bar with a dot on each side. If it has a "2" above it means repeat the last two bars, a "4" equals 4 bars, and so on.

Now let's look more closely at time signatures. Say you're in 4/4 time. The top number 4 means, "How many beats in a measure?" The bottom 4 means, "What kind of note equals one beat?" In 4/4 time, there are four beats per measure, and the quarter note receives one beat.

So, in 3/4 time, how many beats are there to a measure? If you said "3," give yourself a brownie point. And what kind of note equals a beat? Did I hear quarter note? Right!

Counting a Measure

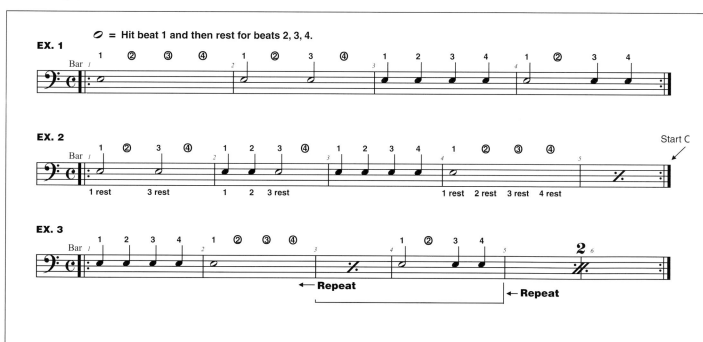

- Look at these measures and count them. You don't have to play them; just read and beat out the notes, making sure to take into account the repeat marks.

COUNTING NOTES
Learn how to properly play the notes

All notes except the whole note consist of a black ball (the head) and a stem rising from the head. The numerical equivalent of the note is indicated by a flag at the stem's top. A quarter note has no flag. A single flag indicates an eighth note, two flags a sixteenth note, three flags a thirty-second note, and so on. The whole note is just a large white ball with no stem.

In the 4/4 time exercises that follow, count aloud and obey any repeat marks, going back to the beginning of the piece and repeating it.

Exercise 1 is a 4-bar phrase, or series of bars that make up a section. Bar 1 has a single whole note. Just hit on the "1" and rest on "2-3-4." Count it like this: 1, rest, rest, rest. Bar 2: half notes. Remember that two half notes equal a whole note.

Reading and Counting Notes

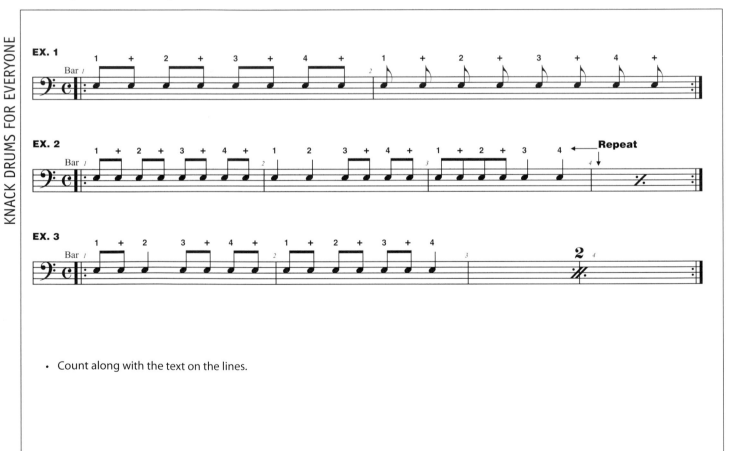

- Count along with the text on the lines.

Play on the "1," rest on "2," play on the "3" and rest on "4." Bar 3: four quarter notes. Play each one to the 1-2-3-4 count. Bar 4 has a half note and two quarter notes. So, you'll play on 1, rest on 2, and play on 3 and 4.

Exercise 2 is a five-bar exercise. It has the same elements as the first exercise, except it has a last bar with a repeat mark that indicates repetition of the bar right in front of it. Then there's a sign for repeating the whole line.

Exercise 3 is a six-bar phrase. Bar 1 has four quarter notes. Bar

2 just has a whole note. Bar 3 repeats bar two. Bar 4 has a half note (play on 1, rest on 2) and two quarter notes (play on 3 and 4). Now you come to a repeat sign, indicating that you're to repeat the preceding two bars. So repeat bars 3 and 4.

Continue Reading and Counting

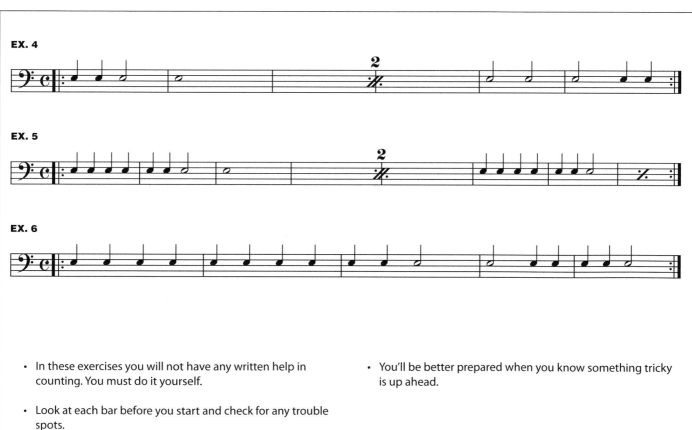

- In these exercises you will not have any written help in counting. You must do it yourself.

- Look at each bar before you start and check for any trouble spots.

- You'll be better prepared when you know something tricky is up ahead.

EIGHTH NOTES

Getting to know eighth notes—they make up the foundation of rock music

Jazz was based on the "shuffle" and has a triplet feel to it; the notes are played in groups of three.

Rock is based on an eighth note feel, meaning that the music is essentially in 4/4 time.

So let's look at the eighth note. An eighth note has a single flag. Two eighth notes equal one quarter note. With eighths, instead of 1-2-3-4, which would be four beats or quarter notes to the measure, you count "1+2+3+4+." That's twice as fast as quarter notes.

Exercise 1: Two bars of eighth notes: 1+2+3+4+. But the bars

Counting Eighth Notes

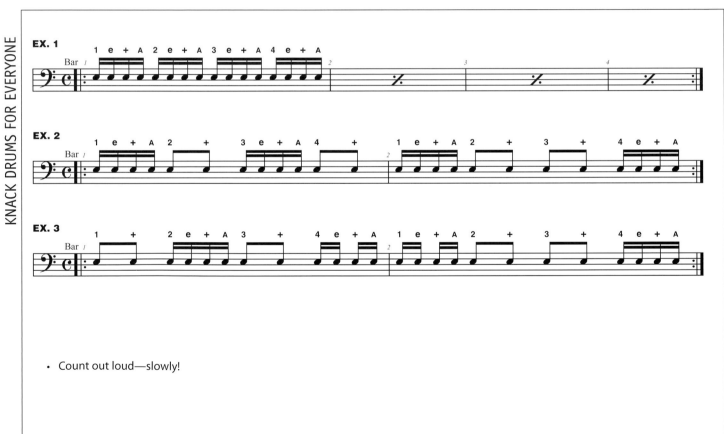

- Count out loud—slowly!

look different. That's because we put a line over the eighths in bar 1 to make it easier to see how many notes you're looking at. Eighth notes are usually written as you see them in bar 1. Use bar 2 to train your eyes to see it in a different way. The repeat marks in bar 2 tell you to repeat the line.

Exercise 2: Again, two bars that look different but the eighth note count is the same. In bar 2 the quarter notes come in on the 1-2, with the eighth notes coming in on the 3-and-4-and. Pay attention to the tempo. Count "1-2-3-4" to establish the tempo, and then play the exercise. In bar 3 the eighth notes are counted on "1+2+," while the 3-4 counts are quarter notes. Finally, bar 4 tells you to repeat bar 3. Then repeat the entire line.

Exercise 3: Bar 1 has a lot of eighth notes. "1+" are eighths, "2" is quarter note, and "3+4+" are eighths. Bar 2 has the eighths on "1+2+3+" and the quarter on "4." The last two bars are a repeat of the previous two bars. Then repeat the line.

Writing in the Counts

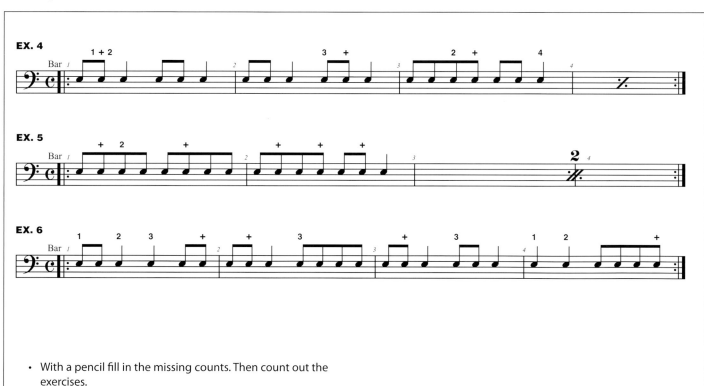

- With a pencil fill in the missing counts. Then count out the exercises.

SIXTEENTH NOTES
Sixteenths are harder to count, but that makes them all the more fun to play!

Sixteenth notes can be great fun, but they take some building up to. Because there are more of them—sixteen to a measure in 4/4 time—they're more difficult to read. And because they go twice as fast as eighth notes, and four times as fast as quarters, they require more technique and facility.

With sixteen beats to a measure, the count goes like this: "1-e&-a-2-e&-a-3-e&-a-4-e&-a." (See Exercise 1.) That's a bit of a tongue twister, so work up to it. Start with a slow tempo of 1-2-3-4, adding the eighth note count of 1+2+3+4-and, and then adding the sixteenth note count, "1-e&-a-2-e&-a," and so on.

Counting Sixteenth Notes

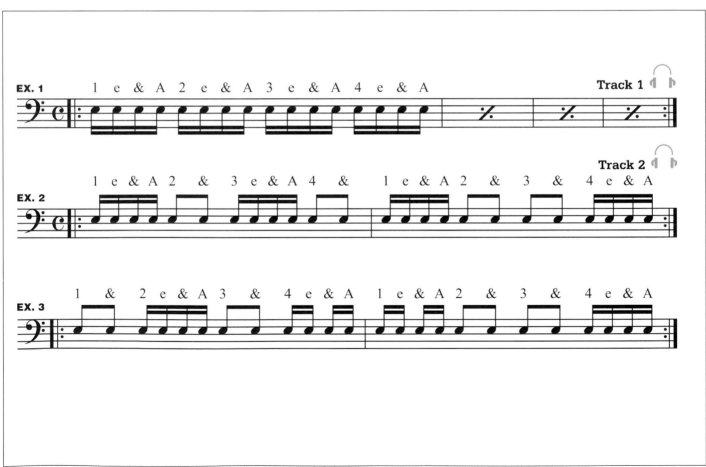

Sixteenth notes look like eighth notes except that they have two flags instead of one. What follows are some sixteenth note patterns that you should familiarize yourself with.

Exercise 1: Bar 1 has your typical 16 counts to the measure: "1-e&-a-2-e&-a-3-e&-a-4-e&-a." Bars 2, 3, and 4 repeat this pattern. This equals a four-bar line. Study this line and count it out.

Exercise 2: In bar 1, the 1 beat is in sixteenths—"1-&a." The 2 beat is an eighth note—"2+." Beat 3 is another sixteenth, and beat 4 is another eighth. Bar 2 has the first beat as a sixteenth, the second and third beats as eighth notes, and the fourth beat as a sixteenth. The line then repeats, so you count these two bars twice.

Exercise 3: Try this one yourself without my help.

Exercises 4, 5, and 6: Fill in the count yourself with a pencil. Remember to count slowly—if you go too fast, you just end up wasting time and having to do it over.

Fill in the Sixteenth Note Count

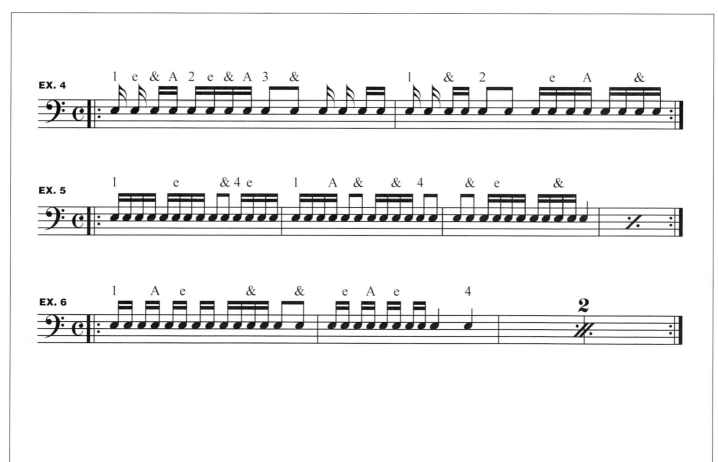

DRUM THEORY

NOTE COMBINATIONS

Let's review all the notes we've learned so far, and count them in different patterns

By now you know what whole, half, quarter, eighth, and sixteenth notes look like, and how to count them. So it's time to move on to counting these notes in a series of patterns. Are you ready? Let's do it!

Exercise 1. This is an eight-bar pattern that combines

everything you've learned so far. Bar 1 consists of a single whole note. The first two beats of bar 2 are sixteenths, with a half note on 3 and a rest on 4. Bar 3 has quarter notes on 1, 2, and 3, and sixteenths on 4. In bar 4 there are eighth notes on the first beat, sixteenths on the second, and quarter notes

Counting

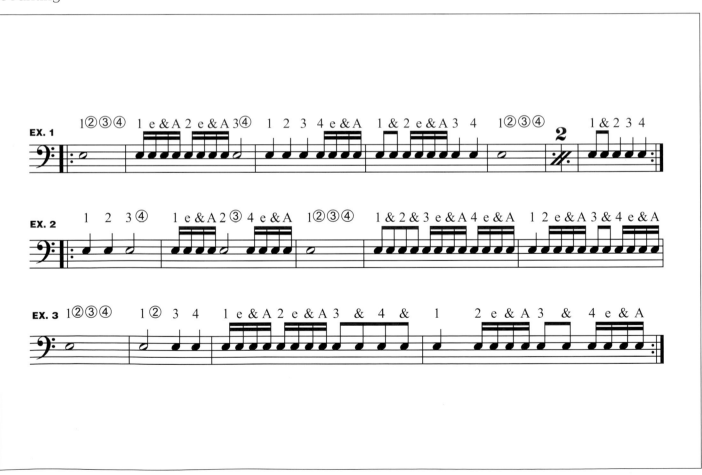

KNACK DRUMS FOR EVERYONE

on 3 and 4. Bar 5 is a whole note, followed by a repeat sign telling you to repeat bars 4 and 5. And bar 8 has eighth notes on 1 and 2, and quarter notes on 3 and 4. Finally, repeat the whole line.

Exercise 2. Bar 1: Quarter notes on 1 and 2, a half note on 3, and a rest on 4. Bar 2: Sixteenth notes on 1, half note on 2, rest on 3, sixteenths on 4. Bar 3: Whole note. Bar 4: Eighth notes on 1 and 2, sixteenths on 3 and 4. Bar 5: Quarter note on 1, sixteenths on 2, eighth notes on 3, sixteenths on 4. Bar 6:

Whole note. Bar 7: Half note on 1, rest on 2, quarter notes on 3 and 4. Bar 8: Sixteenths on 1 and 2, eighths on 3 and 4. Bar 9: Quarter note on 1, sixteenths on 2, eighths on 3, sixteenths on 4. The repeat marks tell you to repeat all nine bars.

Now count out the exercises that follow.

Filling in the Blanks

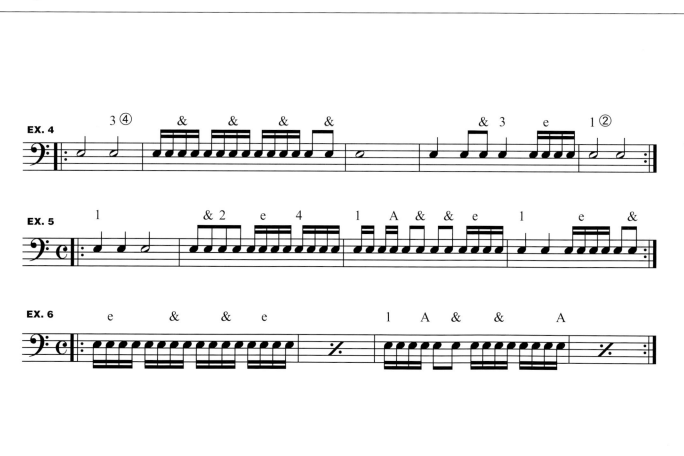

THE DRUM PRACTICE PAD
What is a drum practice pad and why do you need one?

Earlier in the book I mentioned practice pads. A practice pad is a piece of wood, plastic, or metal with a layer of rubber on top that you practice on instead of your drums. Of course you're not going to get the full effect of the drum set, but it's a lot better than nothing and is totally transportable, adding a lot of extra practice possibilities to your day.

There are quite a few types of drum pads on the market. The angled wood drum pad is the kind I learned on. It consists of two pieces of wood put together at a right angle, simulating the feeling of the snare drum on an angled stand. The rubber striking surface is in the middle of the top piece. Because there is space under the striking surface, you get a louder, warmer sound—a welcome inspiration when practicing.

Then there are the flat surface drum pads. Vic Firth, Aquarian,

Angled Practice Pads

- The only angled drum pad I could find on the Internet is this one at earfloss.com. You may find others at your music store.

- I like the way this pad sounds. It's louder than the newer flat pads, because of the space under the striking surface.

- The angled pads are very comfortable for a drummer who uses traditional grip.

- At 5 inches or so square, these pads are a lot easier to carry around than your drum set!

Flat Practice Pads

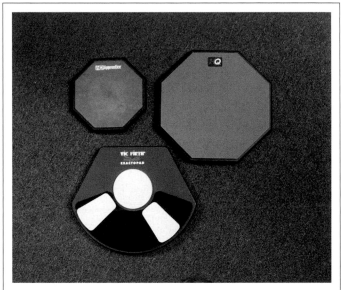

- There are many types of flat practice pads. The most popular practice pads are the flat ones made by Vic Firth, Evans, Pro-Mark, and HQ.

- The two-sided Vic Firth Heavy Hitter 12D offers two playing surfaces, each with a different color, feel, and sound.

- Then there are the simple flat pads like the Evans Apprentice and HQ 6.

Evans, HQ, and Pro-Mark are just a few of the companies that make the flat surface pads, all of which are similar in concept but vary in price. There are also pads that go onto the actual drum set to give you a kind of drum feel. This type of pad sometimes sounds louder than a regular drum pad.

A variation on the drum pad is the Nee Pad, which goes on your knee. It's attached with an elastic belt, and you can sit there and practice on yourself! It's totally silent and convenient and whoever invented it deserves the Nobel Prize for Peace and Quiet! Practice pads go from $8.99 on up.

Other Pad Designs

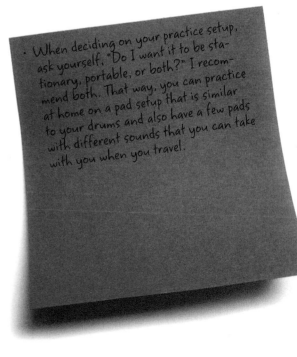

- When deciding on your practice setup, ask yourself, "Do I want it to be stationary, portable, or both?" I recommend both. That way, you can practice at home on a pad setup that is similar to your drums and also have a few pads with different sounds that you can take with you when you travel.

- The Gladstone is a rubberized pad that fits on your snare drum. Because it goes on your snare, you feel like you're playing the drum, not the pad.

- You can also get a Gladstone for your bass drum, enabling you to practice your foot as well as your stick action.

- There's also a foot practice pedal called the Hansenfutz practice pedal that's portable and great for travel.

DRUMHEAD & FOOT PADS

Some alternatives to the standard wood pads and creative foot practice pad solutions

In addition to the standard wood practice pads, the drumhead companies make a pad that actually looks like a drumhead and is padded, making it extra quiet.

Remo Drumhead Company makes the very portable Ambassador drumhead practice pad that gives you the feel of playing on a real drumhead and sells for just $8. They also carry the Remo practice pad, an 8-inch head on a pad with a rim, for $18. There's even a tunable version for $22.

Another good drumhead pad is the HB 14-inch snare practice pad—cheap and effective.

Now we come to the foot practice pads. Gibraltar and Pearl make bass drum pads with adjustments to set the pads at

Head Pads

- Remo pads are very quiet and lightweight, and deliver a lot of bang (or is that thud?) for the buck.

- The Remo pads have no rim, but they do have a nice feel. For a little more money, however, you can find drumhead pads with rims.

- These two drumhead pads have rims and are tunable. You can actually change the feel by tuning them, simulating a real drum.

Foot Practice Pads

- Bass drum pads are a fairly recent addition to the market. They're more expensive—$50 and up.

- You adjust the action on these pads from the pedal itself.

- Gibraltar, Pearl, and Sound Effects Percussion make the most popular bass drum pads. You can find the Sound Effects Percussion and Gibraltar pads online at Musician's Friend for around $50. The Pearl pads will cost you at least $20 more, So shop around for a deal.

approximately the same place as the pedal would be. You then attach the pad to the pedal to get the feel you want. Both Gibraltar and Pearl bass pads have a metal frame that sits on the floor, with a rubber pad where the pedal hits.

I've already mentioned the Hansenfutz practice pads. The Hansenfutz is actually a self-contained pedal that goes onto a rug, with Velcro, to hold it in place. You can adjust it like a real pedal, so that it feels like the real thing. Another plus: The Hansenfutz is at least $20 cheaper than the Pearl or Gibraltar models.

•••••••••••••• GREEN●LIGHT ••••••••••••••

Live in an apartment building with thin walls? Live in a quiet suburb with overly sensitive neighbors who complain about the noise of a pin dropping? Invest in practice pads. It might be the only way you can practice without having your neighbors on your case all the time.

Hansenfutz Pedal

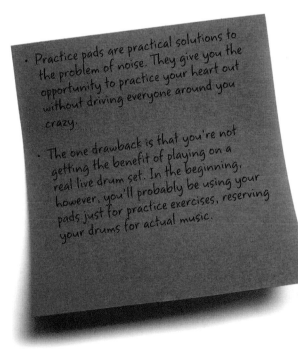

- Practice pads are practical solutions to the problem of noise. They give you the opportunity to practice your heart out without driving everyone around you crazy.

- The one drawback is that you're not getting the benefit of playing on a real live drum set. In the beginning, however, you'll probably be using your pads just for practice exercises, reserving your drums for actual music.

- This unique new bass drum practice device is not a pad. It's a pedal that gives you the feel of a bass drum pedal. You can also get one for the hi-hat.

- The Hansenfutz is very portable and has adjustments that loosen or tighten the pedal. This practice pedal is much more lightweight than the other alternatives. You can also turn it into a bass drum trigger pedal for electronics.

PRACTICE

99

PRACTICE PAD DRUM SETS

There are tom, hi-hat, and cymbal practice pads that set up like drum sets

In addition to individual hand and foot practice pads, there are pads that can be set up like an actual drum set. These setups include the tom, hi-hat, and cymbal pads. As far as practice pads go, these are definitely the most fun to work with.

For a good pad setup in an affordable price range, I recommend the DW Go Anywhere Practice Pad Pack. The Go Anywhere includes four adjustable pads and a bass drum pedal attachment. They're really easy to set up, and you can find them online for $139. An even cheaper setup is the TKO, which also comes with four pads and a pedal setup. The TKO is not as compact as the DW, but it's also a lot cheaper—$94 online. At the higher end, there's the Remo five-piece set up,

Drum Set Pads

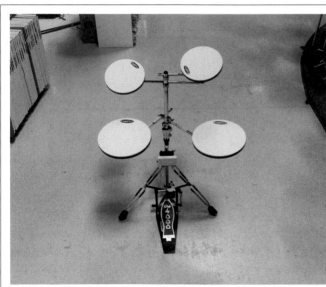

- Drum set pads are lots of fun to practice on because you can configure them to simulate your own drum set.

- The DW Go Anywhere kit has four pads and a bass drum pedal pad. It's the easiest of the practice setups to assemble and take down.

- The TKO five-piece setup is also a good, solid package.

- The Cecilio drum pad set comes with five tunable pads and an easy setup on one stand, similar to the DW.

Remo 5 Setup

- The Remo 5 has a unique design. The tubular setup is very sturdy and fully adjustable, allowing for just about any configuration of the parts. It comes with pads ranging in size from 6 to 10 inches, all of which are tunable.

- Because of its size the Remo 5 is one of the most difficult practice pad kits to set up and take down, so if you go with this one, consider it a permanent fixture.

which sells for over $200. Because the Remo is much larger than the cheaper models, once you set it up, you pretty much leave it up.

There are also cymbal practice setups. Some are plastic and resemble cymbals, but without the ring. Another way to go is the cymbal muffler route. These devices are made of cloth or rubber and hang on the cymbal, deadening the sound.

Zildjian mutes are attached to the cymbals with adhesive. They kill the sound completely and are very affordable at just $22.

Cymbal Mutes

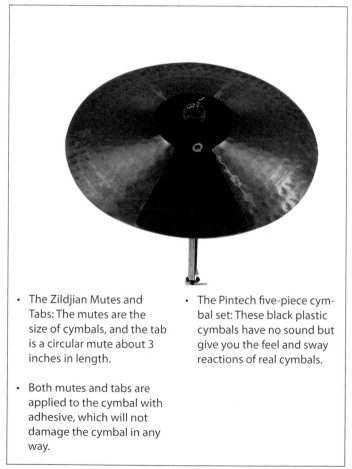

- The Zildjian Mutes and Tabs: The mutes are the size of cymbals, and the tab is a circular mute about 3 inches in length.

- Both mutes and tabs are applied to the cymbal with adhesive, which will not damage the cymbal in any way.

- The Pintech five-piece cymbal set: These black plastic cymbals have no sound but give you the feel and sway reactions of real cymbals.

············ YELLOW ● LIGHT ···············

When you use a practice drum setup, always put a rug underneath it to protect your floors. If you live in an apartment, make sure the pads are not touching any walls you share with your neighbors, because the sound really travels.

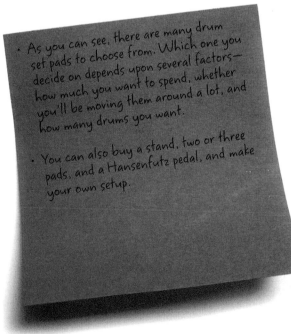

- As you can see, there are many drum set pads to choose from. Which one you decide on depends upon several factors—how much you want to spend, whether you'll be moving them around a lot, and how many drums you want.

- You can also buy a stand, two or three pads, and a Hansenfutz pedal, and make your own setup.

PRACTICE

101

MUFFLING DRUMS FOR PRACTICE

There are many ways to muffle a drum set for practice—here are a few

If you have a drum set in your home or apartment and you want to muffle it, there are many ways to do so. If you just want minimal muffling, you can stuff a pillow into the bass drum and tape some rolled up rags to the snare and tom. You'll still get plenty of sound; it just won't be as big. If you really want to deaden the bass drum, keep packing it with

pillows until the sound disappears.

Rubber pads shaped like drumheads cut the sound even more. These pads come in the various drum sizes and fit right on the heads. When you hit them, there's hardly any sound. For the bass drum, you'd use a mute. HQ, for instance, has a good one for $35. And we've talked about cymbal mutes.

Drum Silencers

- You can purchase drum silencers in a pack for around $32, depending on the sizes. You can also buy individual tom and snare silencers for around $7.

- If you have more than a four-piece drum set, you'll need to buy some individual tom silencers.

- These silencers work really well. You just put them on the drum and presto—no sound.

- HQ Sound Percussion and Vic Firth both make silencer packs and drum mutes.

Bass Drum Mutes

- Vic Firth and HQ Sound Off both have a pre pack that includes a 22-inch bass drum mute as well as the snare and tom silencers.

- HQ makes a neoprene pad that covers bass drumheads and reduces the kick sound without unduly altering the feel of the pedal.

- The Sound Off mute hooks up onto the bass drum rim. It's specially designed for excellent bass drum pedal response. This was the only mute of its kind I could find online. It's available for under $35.

Caution: It's quite a job to remove pillows from the bass drum, a big drawback when you're playing a gig. You generally have to take the front head off—a pain—and then retune the drum. If you're doing more than just practicing at home, I recommend getting a bass drum silencer like the HQ Percussion Sound Effects bass drum mute, which goes on the outside of the batter head and is very easy to put on and take off.

Easy Way Out

- If you don't want to spend your hard-earned money on fancy silencers and mutes, take the easy way out and visit the old ragbag.

- In order to stuff your bass drum with pillows, you have to first remove the head. You can also fill the drum with strips of old newspaper.

- For the other drums towels work great. Cut them in a circle, double them up, and put them on the heads.

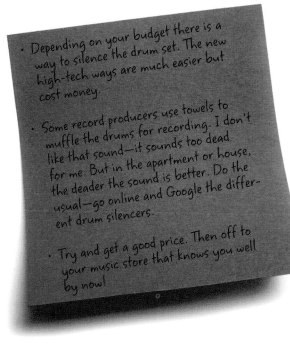

- Depending on your budget there is a way to silence the drum set. The new high-tech ways are much easier but cost money.

- Some record producers use towels to muffle the drums for recording. I don't like that sound—it sounds too dead for me. But in the apartment or house, the deader the sound is better. Do the usual—go online and Google the different drum silencers.

- Try and get a good price. Then off to your music store that knows you well by now!

PRACTICE

MOUNTABLE DRUM PADS

Mountable drum pads are a cheap, smart, and durable solution to practice problems

We've talked about different kinds of drum pad setups and muffling devices. But if you're practicing with larger sticks or metal sticks, which will damage silencers, I suggest buying the rubberized drum pads that are mounted on their own adjustable stands and can take a lot of punishment.

Both the HQ 6-inch mountable drum pad and the Vic Firth

12-inch mountable pad are octagon-shaped rubber pads that can be mounted on a cymbal stand. These pads sell for $25. Remo has a drum pad stand that's sold separately and would be cheaper than buying an expensive cymbal stand. There are all sorts of variations on this stand, starting at $30. Some even come with stick holders.

More about Remo Pads

- The Remo drum pads are my favorites. With the rims and the tunable heads, you get the feel and response of a real drum.

- Remo pads come in many different sizes. When mounted on a stand, they can be adjusted to the

exact height and position that's comfortable for you.

- The HQ, Vic Firth and other mountable pads are pretty much all the same and sell for $19 and up. The Vic Firth Heavy Hitter is $31 online.

Cymbal Stands for Pads

- Virtually all the screw-on pads should fit on the cymbal stands.

- You can find a wide variety of cymbal stands online for around $28. Choose one that's strong enough for the pad.

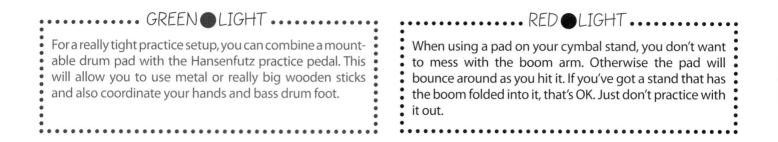

······· GREEN ● LIGHT ·············

For a really tight practice setup, you can combine a mountable drum pad with the Hansenfutz practice pedal. This will allow you to use metal or really big wooden sticks and also coordinate your hands and bass drum foot.

·············· RED ● LIGHT ·············

When using a pad on your cymbal stand, you don't want to mess with the boom arm. Otherwise the pad will bounce around as you hit it. If you've got a stand that has the boom folded into it, that's OK. Just don't practice with it out.

Drum Pad Stands

- The Remo pad stand (RST100000-P) is specifically designed for use with single practice pads.

- Remo stands are similar to a single cymbal stand, but sturdier. You can also add stick holders to them.

- The Cannon Percussion Practice Pad Stand will take Remo, Drum Buddy, and many other pads.

- The Cannon is fully adjustable and a little cheaper than the Remo stand. Cannon is known for good quality at a good price.

Setting Up the Pads

- It's important to read the instructions that come with drum pads and pad sets. The drum set pads setups, in particular, can get complicated.

- These single pad setups may all be a little different. Some screw into the cymbal stand. Some supply the screws. Others don't.

- Add the Hansenfutz pedal to the right of the pad. This would be your main bass drum pedal.

- You could add a hi-hat pedal on your left.

PRACTICE

PRACTICE, PRACTICE, PRACTICE

What's the best way to practice and how much time should you spend practicing?

In chapter 8, we learned how to count notes. From Chapter 9 on, we'll be learning how to hold the sticks, how to read music—how to play drums.

Environment is very important. If at all possible, you should have a separate space in your home or apartment that can be devoted to practicing your drums. If you live alone, this won't be difficult, but if you've got family or roommates around, you definitely don't want to be setting up in the living room or other communal areas. When I was learning, I practiced in an enclosed porch, and at another point I had a setup in my basement.

You'll probably have to carve out a space for yourself in the

Practice Equipment

- Here's the practice equipment you'll need:

1. A CD or an iPod with self-powered headphones or a power board; enough volume to hear the music over the drum set.

2. A sturdy music stand for drum books.

3. Adequate lighting; consider a small light that attaches to your music stand.

4. A mirror so you can correct stroke and technique mistakes.

5. A metronome with a headset jack.

When and How to Practice

- The more time you devote to your practicing, the more you'll get out of it.

- A good way to divide your practice session is to spend 50 percent of it on the drums without silencers, and 50 percent on the pads.

- You'll want to practice with either your metal sticks or your big wood practice sticks, especially when you're learning the rudiments and working on increasing your speed.

- Remember: The key to effective practice is to start slowly and build up speed.

basement, or the garage, or anywhere else where you won't be distracted. It's essential to be able to focus, because you'll not only be learning to read and play music—you'll also be concentrating on a click track at the same time.

You must practice for at least one hour a day. That's the minimum. If you're working or in school, you'll have to fit it in to your schedule and absolutely commit to it.

Take heart, though—it's been my experience that most students love the drums so much that they can't tear themselves away from them.

•••••••••••••• GREEN ● LIGHT ••••••••••••••

An ideal practice setup would include a music stand with a light, a metronome with a headset jack, a DVD player with TV monitor, a rug to protect the floor, a drum pad setup or a set of mufflers/silencers, an iPod or CD player, and a set of headphones.

Building the Foundation

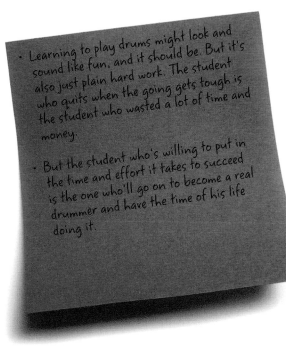

- Learning to play drums might look and sound like fun, and it should be. But it's also just plain hard work. The student who quits when the going gets tough is the student who wasted a lot of time and money.

- But the student who's willing to put in the time and effort it takes to succeed is the one who'll go on to become a real drummer and have the time of his life doing it.

- Learning anything new takes time, and drums are no exception. It's easy to get discouraged when you're a beginner, but you must have patience.

- Expect good and bad days—sometimes things will seem just flow, and other times you might prac- tice one thing for days with no improvement.

- When this happens, know that it's only a temporary situation.

- Just when you feel you're at a standstill, you'll suddenly take a great leap forward.

PRACTICE

HOLDING THE STICKS

Different ways of holding the sticks and how your grip affects the music

There are three ways to hold your drumsticks: 1) the traditional grip, 2) the match grip, and 3) the Carmine grip.

The traditional grip dates back to the old marching drummers. It was a "leftie" operation in which the drummer reached around the drum with his left hand and gripped the stick so he could drum and march at the same time.

In the traditional grip the right hand grips the stick like a hammer; the left hand like a pencil.

In the 1960s Ringo Starr shocked the drum world by using the "match grip." You hold both sticks the same way—as if you're gripping a hammer—so that they "match." I've been playing match grip ever since 1967, but I have done my own

Holding Your Sticks

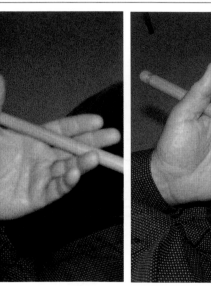

- When you wrap your fingers around the stick, it should be positioned between your thumb and the first joint of your index finger.

- Grab the stick about one-third of the way from the butt end. This will give you good balance.

- When holding the stick between your fingers, hold it tightly enough to control it and loosely enough to let it bounce.

- Do these exercises with your practice sticks.

The Stroke

- Hold the stick about three inches from the drum and strike the drum with a snap of the wrist. Feel the rebound and bring the stick up.

- The stroke is not finished until you've completed the down-and-up motion. The wrist controls it all.

- Do the stroke on the snare drum and on a drum pad. Try to achieve an even sound.

- Draw a 4-inch circle in the middle of your drum or pad. Try to hit every stroke inside the circle.

variation on it, which I'll discuss a little later.

Let's try the match grip. Grab the right-hand stick between your index finger and your thumb. Holding it firmly but not too tightly, wrap the rest of your hand around the stick. Give it some breathing room. Now hold the stick with the palm of your hand face down toward the ground until it's facing left at a forty-five degree angle. Now lift the stick in midair by bringing your wrist up almost to a ninety-degree angle. Then bring your wrist down until it's straight and even with your arm.

After you get the feel of the up-and-down motion, begin hitting your drum pad, making sure not to hold the stick too tightly. You should be able to pull it out of your hand easily. As you hit the pad, you'll feel the stick wanting to bounce back. This is called the rebound. With enough practice you'll be able to control the rebound. Repeat this exercise in 4/4 time with quarter notes, counting "1-2-3-4."

Thumbs-Up Grip

- This grip is similar to the match grip, except that your thumbs are face up instead of face down.

- You can do thumbs up while using your wrist as well. This approach makes it easier to get around the drum set.

- Once you get the wrist working, you can add the arm for power. I do this all the time, and you can't believe how much more power you get.

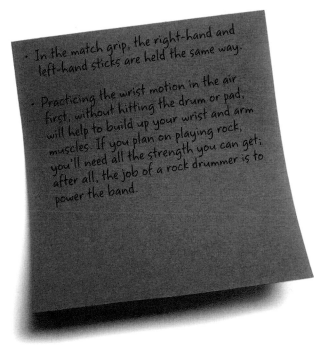

- In the match grip, the right-hand and left-hand sticks are held the same way.

- Practicing the wrist motion in the air first, without hitting the drum or pad, will help to build up your wrist and arm muscles. If you plan on playing rock, you'll need all the strength you can get; after all, the job of a rock drummer is to power the band.

LEFT-HAND TRADITIONAL GRIP
Traditional grip versus match grip: Is one grip better than the other?

When we refer to the traditional grip, we're really talking about the way you hold your left hand. The right hand assumes the same position as it does in the match grip, but the stick rests in the fleshy part between your thumb and first finger in the left hand.

Start by opening your left hand and turning it upside down. Now put your stick straight across your hand so that it fits into the base of your thumb between the thumb and the index finger and extends between your middle and fourth fingers. Once the stick is secure in that position, fold your index and middle fingers over so that they rest lightly on the stick.

Next twist your wrist to the right. This enables the stick to move down to the pad or drum. Bring your stick up again to the original position. This completes the stroke. You must

Traditional Grip—Left Hand

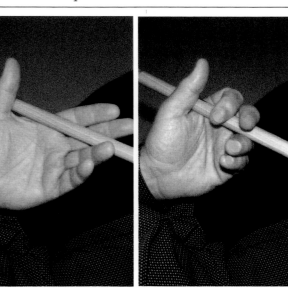

- Practice the left-hand exercise over and over until you feel it getting easier and smoother. The twist of the wrist is the key.

- Don't grip the stick too tightly with your index and third fingers. Remember, just like you, your stick needs room to breathe.

- Practice hitting the drum or pad using the traditional grip to the 1-2-3-4 count over and over, to familiarize yourself with the grip and build up your left hand.

Match Grip—Left Hand

- The left-hand match grip is exactly the same as the right-hand match grip, but as I said, you'll have to devote more practice time to your weaker hand.

- Practice to a steady 1-2-3-4 rhythm with the match grip, trying to get an even sound from both hands.

- Remember to keep a mirror on hand when practicing your grips, to monitor your stroke. The stick needs to go straight up and down.

practice this stick exercise in midair over and over to build up your wrist.

After air drumming for a while, try hitting your drum pad or drum with the traditional grip. As we did with the match grip, practice to the count of 1-2-3-4. Repeat this exercise for a few minutes at each practice session, trying to keep a steady rhythm.

········· YELLOW ● LIGHT ·············

Unless you're a southpaw, your left hand will most likely be weaker than your right. So you'll want to do more left-hand practice in the beginning, to build up left-hand strength.

Thumbs Up—Left Hand

- The same advice applies to the thumbs-up grip. Even though it's the same for both hands, one hand will be weaker than the other.

- Check in the mirror to make sure your thumbs remain up as you play the different exercises.

- Once you become more comfortable with the thumbs-up approach, you'll be surprised at how much more speed it will give you. The thumbs-up grip is especially good for speed and playing sticking patterns.

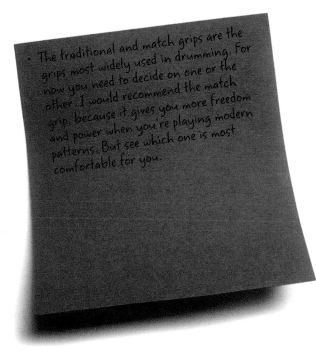

The traditional and match grips are the grips most widely used in drumming. For now you need to decide on one or the other. I would recommend the match grip, because it gives you more freedom and power when you're playing modern patterns. But see which one is most comfortable for you.

STICK HANDLING

THE CARMINE GRIP

My own personalized grip: how it came about and how it differs from the other grips

The Carmine grip came about completely by accident. In 1967 I was playing in Arizona in some really blistering heat. I was sweating so much that the stick kept flying out of my right hand. I moved one finger to keep a tighter grip on the stick, and thus was the Carmine grip born. I also do a stick twirl while using this grip.

The Carmine grip has some good, strong speed to it. Let's try it. Pick up the stick with your right hand and assume the match grip. Now move the index finger of your right over the stick, to the left. Your index finger and thumb should now be in an upside down U shape while the stick protrudes between the index and middle fingers.

Carmine Grip

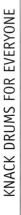

Left-Hand Carmine Grip

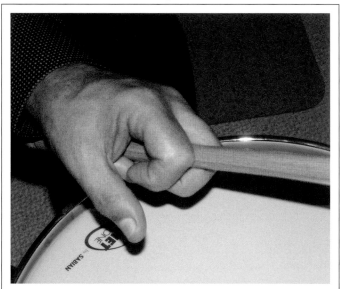

- Practice this grip with the left and right hand. Repeat the wrist action in the air until you can do it easily.

- As you get more proficient with this grip, your fingers will open a little to get speed to control the rebound.

- Do the repetition count and keep a steady rhythm while slowly increasing speed. Hold the rhythm for two to three minutes at a time.

- Practice this grip slowly with each hand, bringing the stick up high in the up-down stroke.

- Use the mirror to check the height of the sticks, with correct up-down strokes.

- When you practice with this grip at a slow tempo, your fingers will naturally curl into a fist, with the stick coming out of it. As you get faster, open your fingers up and push them fast against the stick to gain speed.

Now do the wrist movement in the air, as you did with the match grip. It will feel different because of the new position of the stick between your index and middle fingers. After you've practiced air drumming, try it on the pad or the drum as we've done with the other grips, to the 1-2-3-4 count, repeating the exercise until you're comfortable with the new grip.

·················· RED ● LIGHT ··············
Practicing the different grips will cause a blister to form on your index finger. This blister will then turn into a callus, a drummer's mark of distinction. When you get a blister, wrap at least two fabric Band-Aids completely around it and keep your finger bandaged until the callus forms.

Single-Roll Carmine Grip

- The Carmine grip gives you a fast single roll—one hit of each stick R=right, L=Left.

- Do RL-RL-RL-RL-RL over and over until you get the sticks going fast and it turns into a fast roll. This can take a while.

- Use the mirror to check your stick height. You may have to adjust it to get it to sound even.

- You can also try one hand like this and one hand match grip. Do the previous exercise that way.

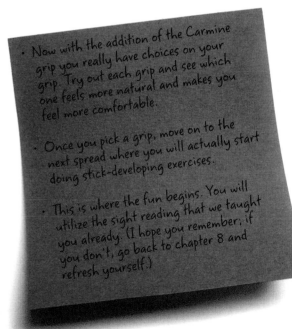

- Now with the addition of the Carmine grip you really have choices on your grip. Try out each grip and see which one feels more natural and makes you feel more comfortable.

- Once you pick a grip, move on to the next spread where you will actually start doing stick-developing exercises.

- This is where the fun begins. You will utilize the sight reading that we taught you already. (I hope you remember; if you don't, go back to chapter 8 and refresh yourself.)

STICK HANDLING

EXERCISES FOR THE HANDS
The following exercises will help you develop your hand—practice them over and over!

Now it's time to pick your grip and start developing your hands and wrists. First thing you need to do is get in front of the mirror and put the sticks in your hands with your desired grip.

Got your grip picked out? *OK—here we go!*

In front of the mirror, do the following exercises. Remember:

We're aiming for evenness and control, and eventually, speed. So start out really slowly.

Exercise 1: Right-hand. This is a constant pattern with just the right hand. It goes like this:

RRRR RRRR RRRR.

Hand Exercises

- Here are some more hand-development exercises.
- Do them two times, five minutes each time, with each hand, in every practice session.

Repeat this for five minutes, using the up-down wrist motion technique we learned. Start out slowly, gradually increasing your speed until you're going as fast as you can. Then slow down a little and stay at that tempo for five minutes. By the way that's a long time for these exercises. After five minutes stop, take a two-minute break, and try the exercise again for another five minutes.

Now, repeat the entire process for the left hand:
LLLL LLLL LLLL.

··········· GREEN ● LIGHT ·············

With both of these exercises, you need to make sure they are even strokes throughout, and use the mirror for the height and stroke check. Height should be the same thoughout.

And More Hand Exercises

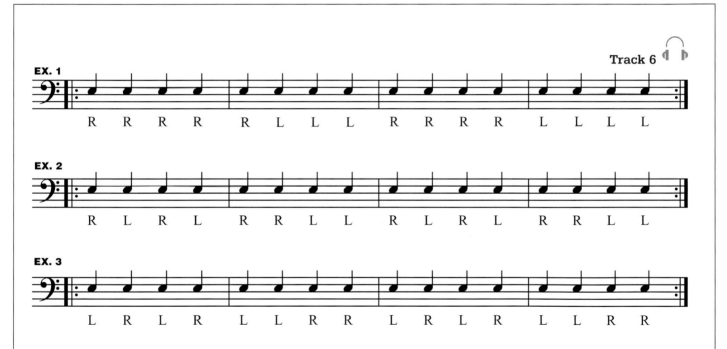

- Remember to use the mirror to check your stick height and stroke. It should be the same for both hands.

- You'll need to do these exercises every day for at least a week before you begin noticing their effect. It's a slow, tedious process, but this is the way you develop hand strength and dexterity.

STICK HANDLING

A NEW TIME SIGNATURE

Here we look at a stick exercise in 3/4 time, adding the right foot to the equation

Up until now, we've stayed solely in 4/4 time. Now it's time to acquaint you with 3/4 time. The principle is exactly the same as 4/4 time, except that instead of four beats to a measure, with the quarter note receiving one beat, there are only three. So, you would count "1-2-3" to a measure.

Three-four time is also known as "waltz time." The waltz is danced in three-beat measures, with the accent on the first beat, like this: *1-2-3, 1-2-3, 1-2-3*. You know, like the old "Blue Danube" waltz. Not that you'll be playing any waltzes, but this gives you the feel of standard 3/4 time.

Hand-foot Exercise in 3/4 Time

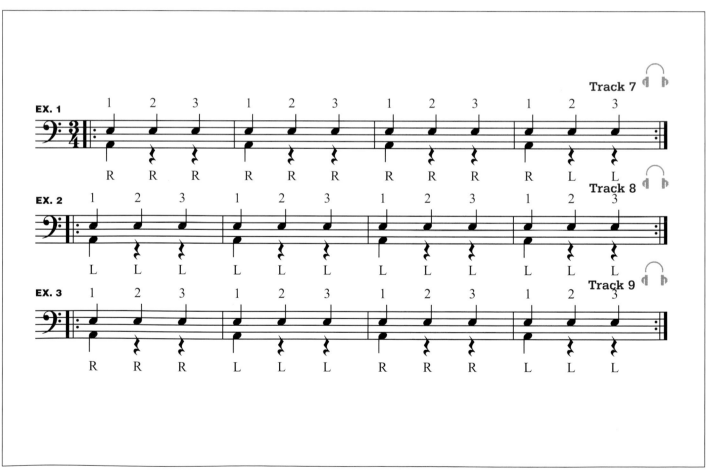

KNACK DRUMS FOR EVERYONE

Exercise 1: Right-hand roll in 3/4 time: With your right hand, and counting 1-2-3, 1-2-3, 1-2-3, practice the following: RRR RRR RRR. Do this over and over, starting slowly, picking up speed until you're going as fast as you comfortably can, and then slowing down and holding the tempo for five minutes. Then rest for two minutes and repeat the exercise.

Exercise 2: Left-hand roll in 3/4 time: Do the same thing with your left hand: LLL LLL LLL, and so on.

Exercise 3: Adding the bass drum foot: The sooner you begin coordinating your hands with your bass drum foot, the better. When you add the bass drum to these exercises, your right foot hits the drum on the count of "ONE." This takes coordination and may take a little time to get used to, but just keep practicing. Examples 1-3 following illustrate where your foot comes in.

Now, let's go back to 4/4 time and practice some new hand exercises, adding your right foot on the count of "ONE." The exercises below go back and forth between bars of 3/4 and bars of 4/4. Practice daily to master hand coordination.

Hand-Foot Exercise in 4/4 and 3/4 Time

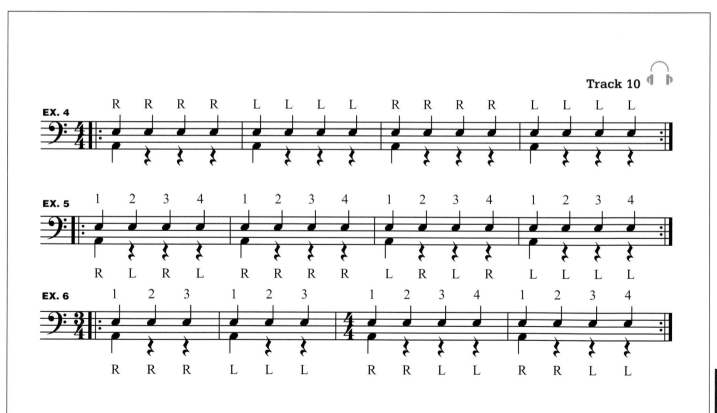

STICK HANDLING

MIXED HAND-FOOT PRACTICE

Different ways of developing hand coordination including mixing up the sticking for quick hand development

In this spread we will add more exercises in 3/4 and 4/4 time, throwing in some new sticking while keeping your right foot on the "ONE" count. The object here is to develop your hands, build speed, and build hand-hand and hand-foot coordination. As usual start slowly, build up speed, and stay at a tempo

that you can keep up for five minutes.

Exercise 1: Mixed sticking

In this exercise you'll be doing more alternating between hands and time signatures. It goes like this: RLR LLLL, counted 1-2-3, 1-2-3-4, 1-2-3, 1-2-3-4, and so on. Remember: Your foot

Mixed Sticking Exercises

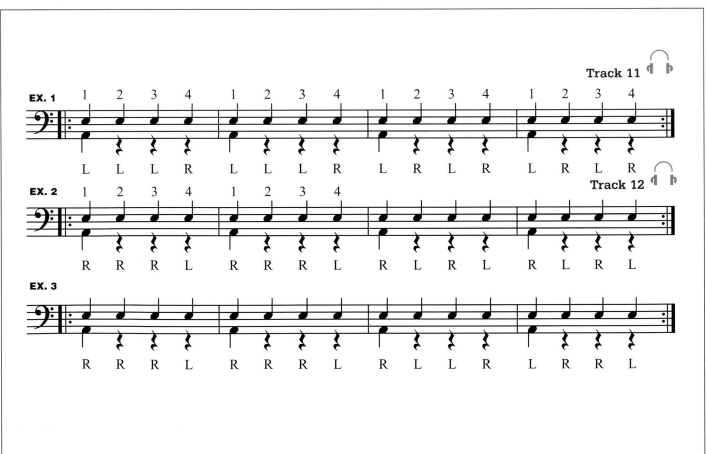

always hits on the count of "ONE."

Next try this pattern to the same count: LRL RRRR LRL RRRR. Remember: It takes time to build up strength and coordination. Patience is a must!

Play each of the exercises that follow for two minutes instead of five. They're great for both practice and later use as drum fills, so you'll want to learn them well. Play them on the drum pad in front of the mirror to make sure your up-down strokes are looking good.

More Mixed Sticking Exercises

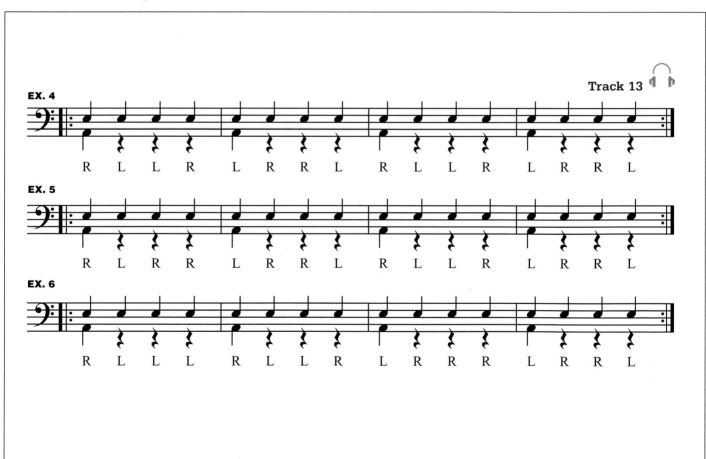

MORE HAND DEVELOPMENT EXERCISES
Here are some cool hand-foot exercises and a taste of reading simple music

By now you're able to hold your sticks, read and count notes, play in 3/4 and 4/4 time, and play on a pad or drum. In this chapter we'll go on with some more challenging exercises for developing your hands and your bass drum foot. From now on we'll be abbreviating "right hand," "left hand," and

"right foot" as RH, LH, and RF. Bass drum is BD. Practice the exercises slowly as usual, gradually building up speed.

Exercise 1 is for the RH and BD foot. You'll be reading the notes and rests and playing the BD on the counts of 1 and 3.

This is a four-bar phrase in 4/4 time.

More Hand Development and Reading

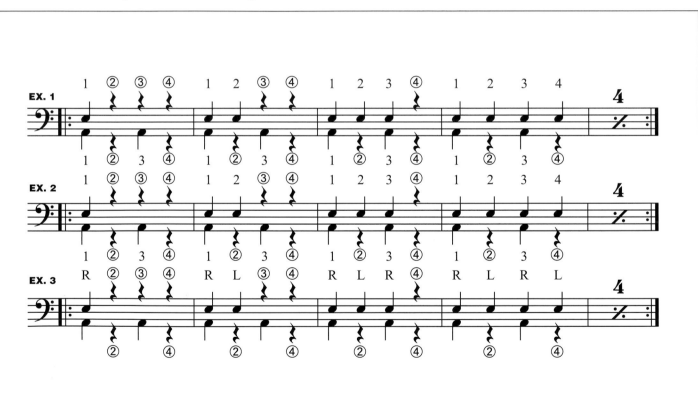

Bar 1: RH and RF play on 1. You count the three quarter-note rests (2-3-4), playing the BD again on 3.

Bar 2: RH plays on 1 and 2; 3 and 4 are rests. BD comes in on 1 and 3.

Bar 3: RH on 1-2-3; rest on 4. BD on 1 and 3.

Bar 4: RH plays on 1-2-3-4. No rests.

The repeat sign tells you to repeat the entire phrase, so that you'll actually be playing eight bars in all.

············· GREEN ● LIGHT ·············

Remember: There are two ways to play with your right foot: the heel-down method, in which your heel is on the pedal base, and the heel-up method, where the ball of your foot is on the pedal. Of the two heel up is the more powerful. Also remember to practice this and all the exercises for five minutes at a time for at least half an hour a day. Repetition is the only way to get a pattern down.

More Hand Reading Exercises

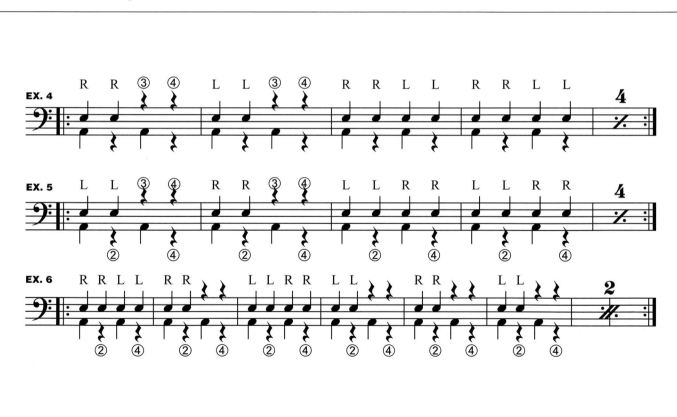

3/4 TIME EXERCISES

Let's try some more sticking exercises to make you more proficient in 3/4 time

Congratulations. You're coming along great. Now let's switch to 3/4 time. We'll be starting with RLL and LRR sticking.

Exercise 1: A really cool pattern

Bars 1-3: RH on 1; LH on 2 and 3 (RLL). BD on 1. Repeat.

Bar 4: RRR on 1-2-3. BD on 1.

Bars 5-7: Here the sticking changes. It's RL on 1-2 with BD on 1. Rest on 3.

Bar 8: Same as bar 4: RRR on 1-2-3; BD on 1. By now you know what that repeat sign means.

More Hand Exercises in 3/4

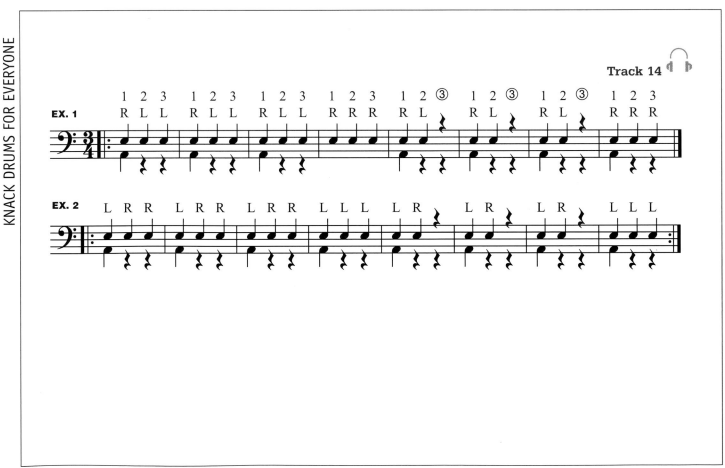

······ GREEN ● LIGHT ······

These sticking exercises should be practiced with a metronome. Start at a slow, comfortable speed and gradually
push it up by increments. And at this point you should be
playing along with the audio track, too.

And Still More. . .

SOME MORE MUSICAL TERMS

When getting ready to read music, it's important to first learn essential terms and definitions

Here's a more comprehensive list of definitions you'll want to memorize.

Accents. An indication in musical notation that tells you to give a certain note more emphasis or prominence.

Bar Line. The line that separates measures or bars.

Batter head. Also known as *top head*. The head on the drum that is struck with the sticks.

Bottom head. Also known as *resonant head*. The head that controls the drum's resonance.

Dot. Has half the value of the note in front of it.

Drum fill. A short, energetic musical passage or riff usually played in a break in the music to hold the listener's attention.

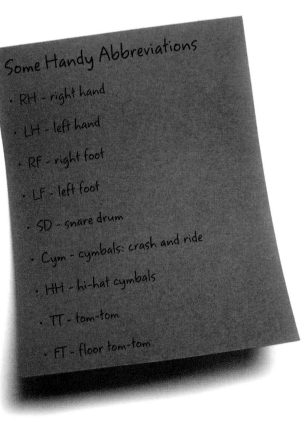

Some Handy Abbreviations

- RH - right hand
- LH - left hand
- RF - right foot
- LF - left foot
- SD - snare drum
- Cym - cymbals: crash and ride
- HH - hi-hat cymbals
- TT - tom-tom
- FT - floor tom-tom

More Musical Terms

The following are musical terms you should know with signs that go with them:

- Accelerando - speed up the musical piece
- Crescendo - gradually get louder
- Decrescendo Diminuendo - gradually make the music softer; usually shortened to Decrescendo
- Fermata - hold or pause like at the end of a song; a big ending
- Ritardando - gradually slow down

Flag. The curved line "flying" from the stem of the note at the end opposite the head, indicating the note value.

Gig. A job or performance that pays the bills!

Measure or Bar. The most basic unit of music. Contains a specific number of beats separated by a bar line.

Note head. The round end of the note. It's either a black ball or, in the case of a whole note, a black circle with white inside.

Paradiddle. A pattern of drumbeats characterized by four basic beats and alternating left-handed and right-handed strokes on the successive primary beats. Can be single,

double, or triple paradiddle.

Phrase. A series of measures that makes or expands a musical statement or idea. A four-bar phrase is four consecutive bars that may introduce or expand the theme or development of a piece or song.

Rebound. The "bounce back" effect you get when your stick/sticks hit the batter head.

Rim shot. The sound produced by hitting the rim and the head of the drum at the same time.

Stem. The thin line that extends from the head of the note.

Dynamics

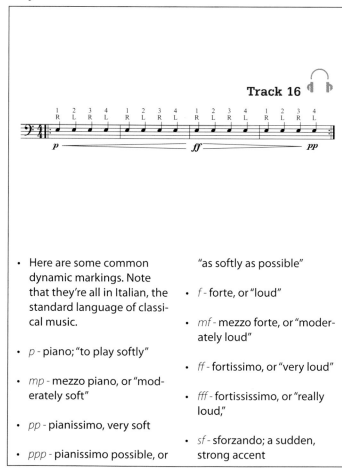

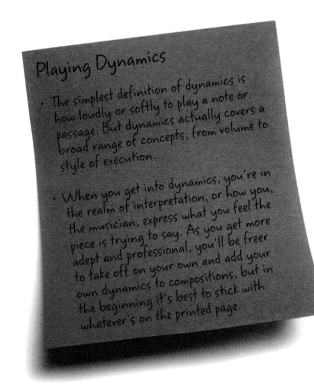

- Here are some common dynamic markings. Note that they're all in Italian, the standard language of classical music.

- *p* - piano; "to play softly"

- *mp* - mezzo piano, or "moderately soft"

- *pp* - pianissimo, very soft

- *ppp* - pianissimo possible, or

"as softly as possible"

- *f* - forte, or "loud"

- *mf* - mezzo forte, or "moderately loud"

- *ff* - fortissimo, or "very loud"

- *fff* - fortississimo, or "really loud,"

- *sf* - sforzando; a sudden, strong accent

SIMPLE QUARTER NOTE READING
Now start reading and playing the hand and right foot line with quarter notes

In this section you'll start reading notes while coordinating sticks and the bass drum on all the beats—something we haven't done yet.

First, let's look at some simple quarter note readings.

Exercise 1: Your hands and foot are both playing on the quarter notes. Be careful to follow the R and L sticking at the top of the exercise.

I have included some quarter note and half note rests in these exercises. All you have to do is count and watch what your hands and foot are doing. Remember the repeat marks.

Simple Quarter Note Reading

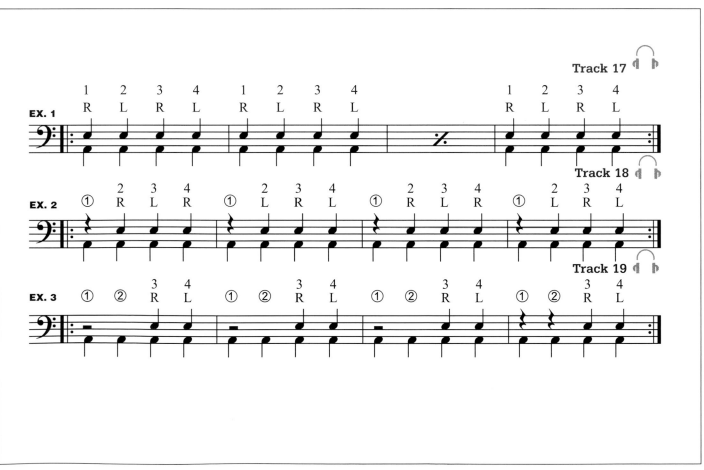

KNACK DRUMS FOR EVERYONE

Try Exercise 1 now. Exercise 2: Play the quarter notes with your foot. The hands have a quarter rest on the count of 1. Then alternate hands RLR on 2-3-4. Once you've mastered those, move on to these additional quarter note exercises. Exercise 3: Hold the half note rest for counts 1-2. Then play 3-4 with your sticks. The bass drum is still on the quarter notes. Exercise 4: Here the hands play a different pattern. The R and L hands play on the counts of 1 and 2; 3 is a rest. Then the R hand plays on 4. Repeat. The charts for these exercises follow.

· · · · · · · · · · RED ●LIGHT · · · · · · · · · · · ·

I can't emphasize this enough: Because it takes time to learn hand-foot-eye coordination, take your practice slowly. Start by reading all the lines. Then practice the sticking alone, and finally the steady foot pattern. When you've got each element down, you can put them all together.

Additional Quarter Note Reading

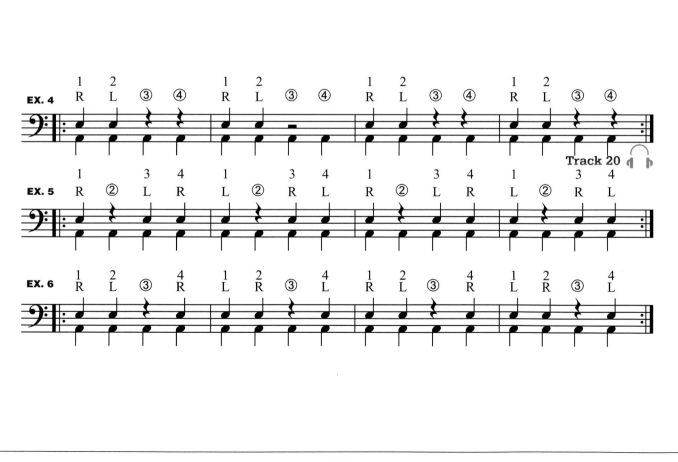

MORE QUARTER NOTE READING

Reverse sticking and the importance of strengthening both hands to become more than a one-handed drummer

It's a fact that when it comes to sticking, many drummers just aren't ambidextrous. Because they haven't taken the time to work with and develop each hand, they rely on their stronger hand, which limits them. These exercises are intended to prevent you from becoming a one-handed drummer.

A good way to practice these exercises is to reverse the sticking. In other words, if the exercise starts with the right hand, start with your left and alternate the sticking. I have put two stickings in each exercise. Sticking 1 starts with the right hand and Sticking 2 with the left. The more you

Quarter Notes with Two Stickings

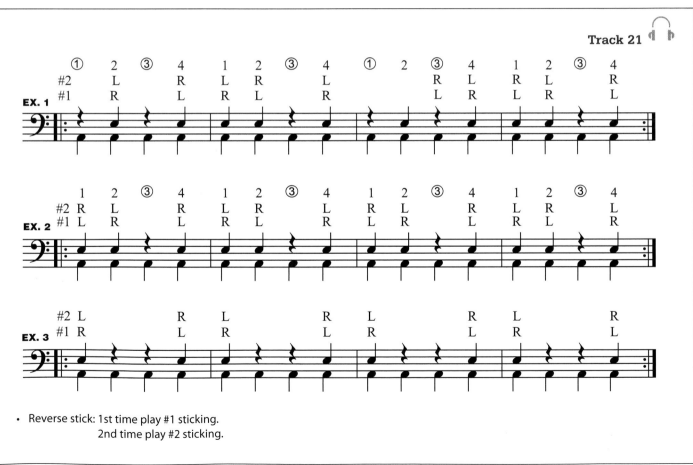

KNACK DRUMS FOR EVERYONE

Track 21

- Reverse stick: 1st time play #1 sticking.
  2nd time play #2 sticking.

practice alternate sticking, the stronger your weaker hand will become, and the more evenly you'll play.

Exercise 1: Sticking 1

Bar 1: R on 2 and 4 counts.

Bar 2: R-L on 1-2, rest on 3, R on 4. Repeat.

Then practice Sticking 2. Do each exercise twice. Go through exercises 1, 2, and 3, using the two stickings.

Now for the quarter note exercise. This is a two-sticking, 12-bar exercise. Here you'll be playing twelve bars of different patterns one after another, giving you a chance to practice all the patterns you've learned so far. When you do the entire exercise with the repeat, you'll actually be playing twenty-four bars.

Twelve-Bar Quarter Note Exercise with Two Stickings

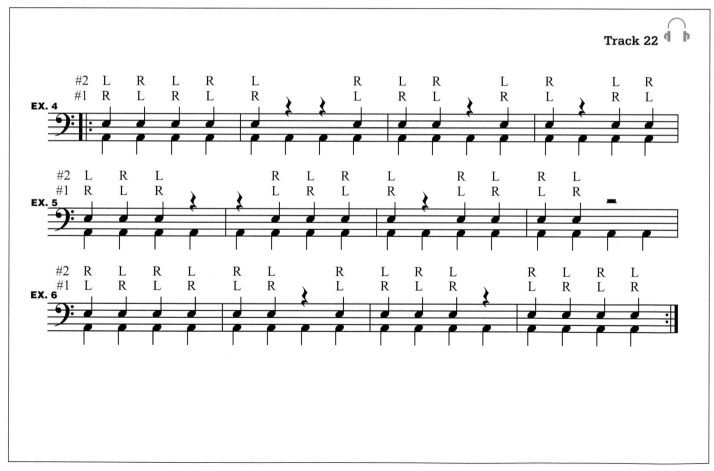

SIMPLE EIGHTH NOTE READING

Become familiar with the eighth note patterns that form the basis of rock music

Rock music is based on eighth notes. The exercises in this section incorporate both quarter and eighth notes, without rests, with two lines of sticking. Do the first sticking exercise starting with the RH for eight bars each. Then repeat it using Sticking 2, starting with the LH.

A reminder: A four beat measure of eighth notes is counted, "1+2+3+4+."

Exercise 1: Scan the exercise to familiarize yourself with it. As you can see, the BD foot plays quarter notes on 1-2-3-4 while the hands do a RLR sticking on 1-2-3, and a LR sticking on 4.

Simple Eighth Notes

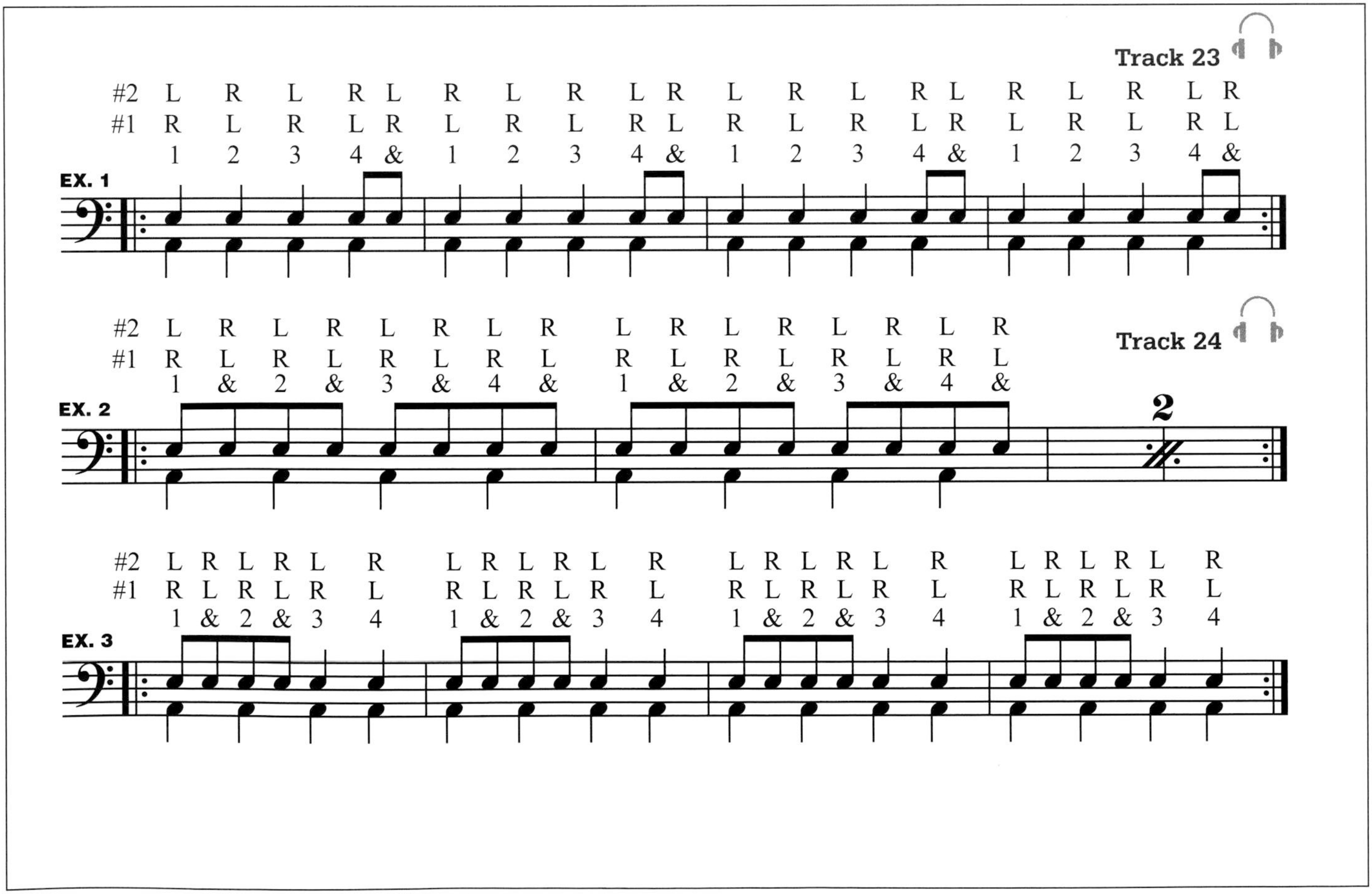

KNACK DRUMS FOR EVERYONE

This then repeats for eight bars. Pick a comfortable tempo and go for it!

Exercise 2: This is an entire bar of eighth notes, with the BD on the quarter note beat. Use the two stickings.

········· GREEN ● LIGHT ·············

Look at all the following exercises and play them through with the two stickings. You can even play them to a rock song, making sure to concentrate on the counting and sticking.

More Eighth Notes

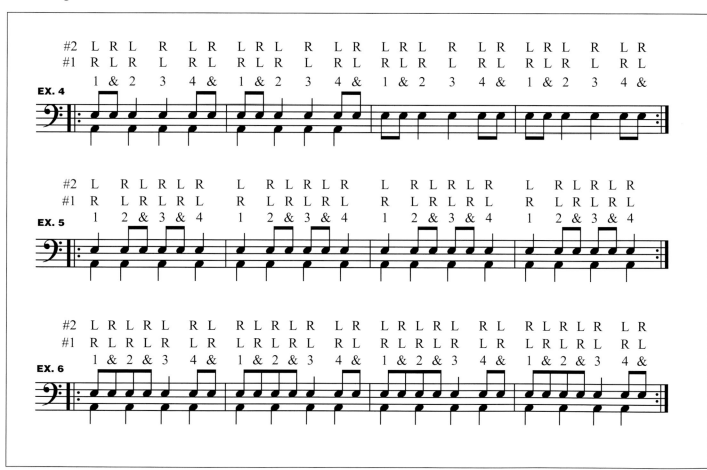

SOME TWELVE-BAR EXERCISES

A couple of fun and challenging 12-bar exercises to expand your drumming technique

I hope you rocked with the eighth notes in the last spread. Now it's time to expand to some 12-bar patterns that will give you a little more to work with.

Exercise 1 is a 12-bar exercise based on the previous spread. Each bar is a different pattern, with the exception of the BD

part, which you'll be very familiar with by now—it comes in on the 1-2-3-4 counts. Read through the exercise first. Then try it slowly with the RH and then repeat it with the LH sticking.

Exercise 2 is a little different. Notice that the BD has its own

Eighth Note 12-Bar Exercises

part now and is not just coming in on the steady quarter note beat. Let's go through a few bars together.

Bar 1: RLR on 1-2-3. BD rests on those counts and comes in on 4. Bar 2: LR on 1-2, BD on 3, L on 4. The BD rests on 1-2 and 4. Now, let's look at bar 7. Bar 7: This bar has eighth notes, quarter notes, and rests. The RH comes in on 1; the BD follows on 2-3, and you do a LR sticking on the 4-and. This exercise is great for practicing hands-and-foot combinations.

Advanced 12-Bar Exercises

EIGHTH NOTES & RESTS

Learning to play eighth note rests, creating different rhythms in your drum patterns

So far we've done exercises with eighth notes, quarter notes, and quarter rests. Now we're going to add eighth note rests, with strokes on the "and" part of the beat.

In this spread we have six lines of exercises with eighth note rests in various spots. As you do these patterns, you'll notice that the eighth note rests create some really fascinatin' rhythms.

Exercise 1: Here we have the BD playing quarter notes in every bar. It starts off with the RH on 1. Then there's the eighth note rest on 2, with the RH playing on the "+" part of the count. The bar concludes with a RL sticking on 3-4. Play each bar with

Eighth Notes and Rests

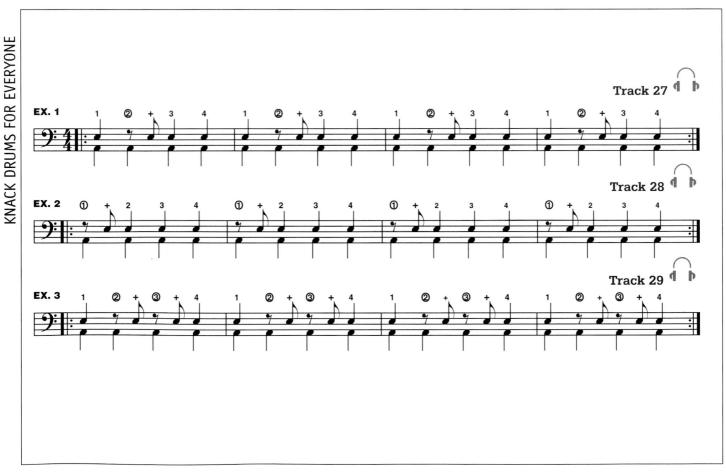

the repeat, for a total of eight bars. Exercise 2: All bars: Rest on 1, R on "+," L on 2-3-4. Repeat. Then repeat the entire exercise with reverse sticking. Exercise 3: Bar 1: R on 1-and; eighth rest on 2, L on "+"; eighth rest on 3, R on "+"; eighth rest on 4, L on "+." This is basic syncopation—the foundation of jazz and rock. *Syncopation* is when you rest on the strong or beginning beat and play on the weak or "off" beat. Always practice with a metronome, gradually increasing the speed until you can rip through them! And do them with both stickings.

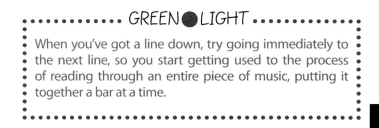

· · · · · · · · · · · · *GREEN ● LIGHT* · · · · · · · · · · · · ·

When you've got a line down, try going immediately to the next line, so you start getting used to the process of reading through an entire piece of music, putting it together a bar at a time.

Additional Eighth Notes and Rests

MORE EIGHTH NOTES & RESTS

Practice eighth notes and rests in a 12-bar exercise and continue to improve your playing

By now there should be a noticeable improvement in your playing. Your hands and bass drum foot should be getting stronger and more independent, your sticking should be more even, and hand-foot coordination should be getting easier to accomplish. See what I mean about the importance

of daily practice? It really pays off, doesn't it?

Let's continue with some more eighth note patterns.

Exercise 1: This one's cool. Rest on 1, R on "and"; rest on 2, L on "and"; rest on 3, R on "and;" LR on 4-and. Again the BD plays quarter notes throughout the exercises. Play this for

More Eighth Notes and Rests

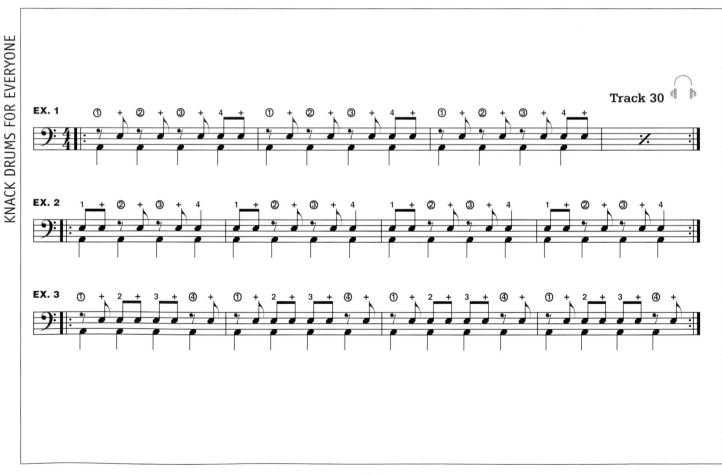

eight bars or more and it makes a great drum fill.

Exercise 2

Bar 1: RL on 1-and; rest on 2, R on "and"; rest on 3, L on "and"; R on 4. Repeat.

The first two bars of the 12-bar exercise are interesting because there are multiple notes on "and" counts. It begins with a RL sticking on the 1-and. The "and" counts of "2-and-3-and-4-and" are played with RLR sticking.

Bar 2: Starts with LRL sticking on the "and" counts of "1-and-2-and-3-and," ending with RL on 4. Even if you play only these two bars over and over, you'll establish a great rhythm.

Practice this 12-bar exercise with the repeat, using the metronome. Go really slowly at first because this exercise is a little more complicated than the previous ones; each bar is slightly different.

12-Bar Exercise with Eighth Notes and Rests

Track 31

SIXTEENTHS WITH QUARTER NOTES

How to play sixteenth notes quickly and evenly, adding speed to your playing

In Chapter 8 you learned how to count sixteenth notes. Now you get to play them. Just a refresher: two eighth notes to a quarter note, two sixteenth notes to an eighth note, four sixteenth notes to a quarter note. So sixteenths are counted "1-A-and-a."

Exercise 1: Bar 1: Starts off with RLRL sticking on " 1-e&-a" and RLR on 2-3-4. Bar 2: The same pattern with reverse sticking. Read it over first. Then play the entire exercise with the repeat.

Exercise 2: Bar 1: RLRL on "1-e&-a," R on 2, L on 3, LRLR on "4-e&-a." The next measure is a *time-out*, that is, a four-beat

Sixteenth Notes with Quarters

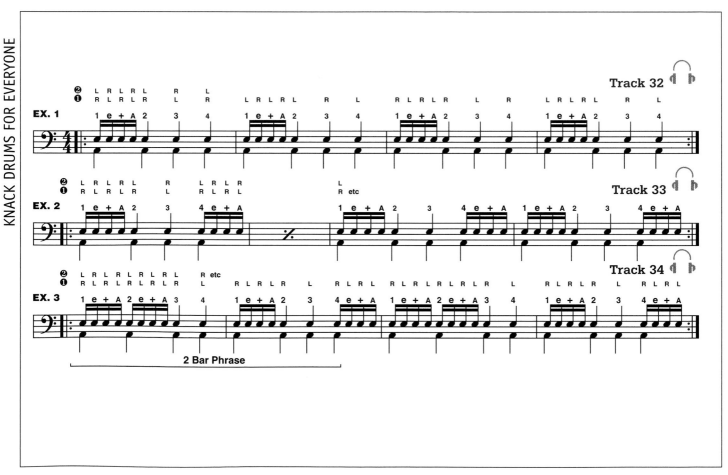

rest. Bar 3: Same as bar 1. Bar 4: Same as bars 1 and 3, without the BD. Repeat. Then do the exercise with Sticking 2.

Exercise 3: This looks a lot more complicated but don't let the extra notes intimidate you. Bar 1: Follow the sticking and play two groups of sixteenths for the first two counts, followed by two quarter notes. Bar 2: RLRL on "1-e&-a," R on 2, L on 3, RLRL on "4-e&-a." Bars 3 and 4: Same as bars 1 and 2, only with RLRL sticking. Repeat and do the exercise again using Sticking 2.

See the long bracket over the first two measures? This indicates that this is a two-bar phrase. Remember what a phrase is? No? OK, I'll tell you once more—a series of measures that makes or expands a musical statement or idea—but from now on, whenever you're not sure of a term, use that glossary I gave you in chapter 11.

Exercise 4: This one's interesting because it contains five bars. Up until now we've only had exercises with an even number of bars, so I decided to throw in a little variation.

More Sixteenth Notes with Quarters

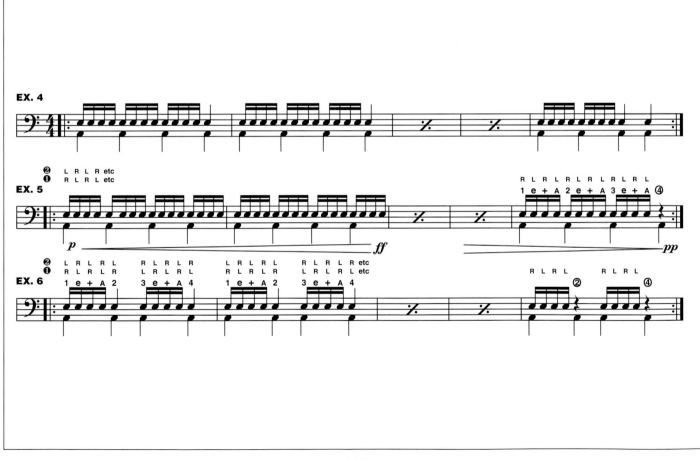

SIXTEENTHS/QUARTER NOTE RESTS

Becoming more familiar with sixteenth notes and combining them with quarter notes and quarter note rests

I hope you've been having fun with these exercises. Even though they're repetitive, playing them with the metronome and seeing yourself getting better and faster should be exciting.

In the following exercises we'll up the challenge a little with some sixteenth, quarter note, and quarter rest combos. As you can see, the sixteenths are proliferating. This means you'll be playing faster and learning more complicated patterns, which is what drumming is all about. Ready? Let's go.

Exercise 1 starts with four sixteenth notes on 1, with RLRL sticking. Next is a quarter note on the count of 2, played with

More Sixteenth and Quarter Note Exercises

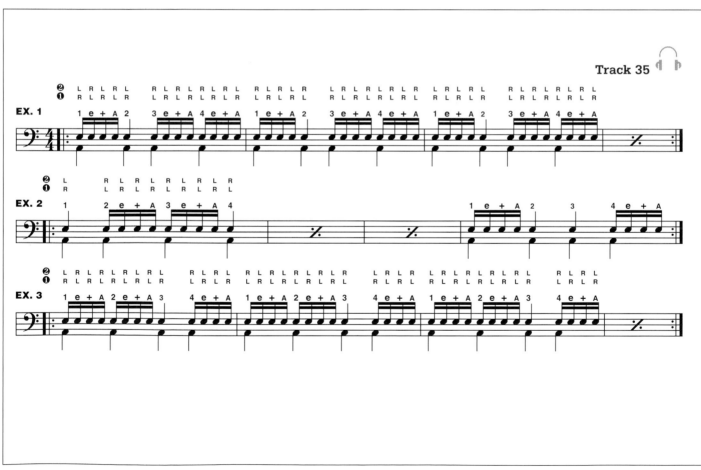

KNACK DRUMS FOR EVERYONE

the RH. Then two sets of sixteenth notes on "3-e&-a, 4-e&-a," with LRLR-LRLR sticking. As usual the BD comes in on 1-2-3-4. This bar is played four times and repeated.

Do Exercises 1-3, following the indicated sticking.

Exercise 4: This is another 12-bar exercise with a different pattern in each bar. Again, the sticking is in the first few bars and alternates. When the sticking is not written out, just keep alternating it. You will find that some of the bars have quarter note rests with sixteenth notes, a new pattern. But from what you know now about notation, this shouldn't give you any trouble. Get going, and I'll see you on the next page!

P.S. Listen to the audio track!

Sixteenth and Quarter Note 12-Bar Exercises

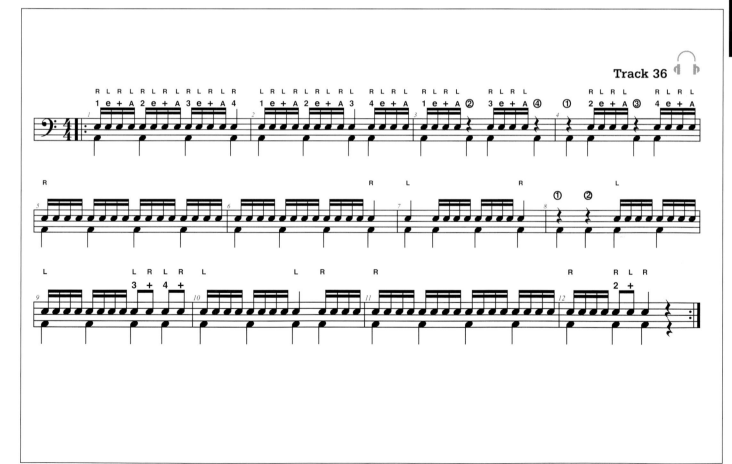

Track 36

SIXTEENTHS WITH EIGHTH NOTES
Learning the sixteenth note pulse and playing it with the eighth note pulse and rests

We're getting to the good stuff now. Mixing up sixteenth and eighth notes, and then adding eighth note rests, makes for some real rhythmic fun.

When playing these kinds of exercises, you'll notice that each beat or fraction thereof may have a different pulse. It

could be faster or slower, depending on where you start. This can be confusing at first. So you really have to examine each exercise carefully before trying it. Remember to practice all the exercises twice using alternate stickings.

Exercise 1: This pattern has two sets of sixteenths and two

Sixteenth Notes with Eighth Notes

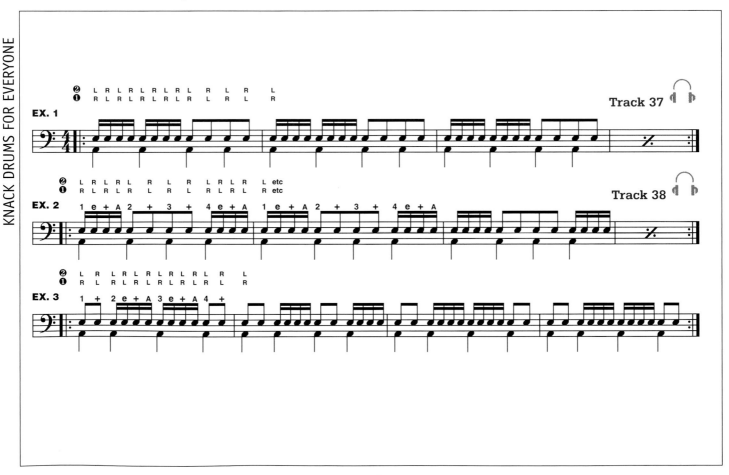

sets of eighths, played LRLR-LRLR on 1-2 and LR -LR on 3-4. There are two pulses going on here. The count is "1-e&-a-2-e&-a-3-+-4-+."

Exercise 2: The pulses are the same except that the eighth notes come in on the "2-+-3-+" and the sixteenths are on the fourth beat.

Exercise 3: I've broken up the pattern here, so that the eighth notes are on the 1 and 4 beats and the sixteenths on 2 and 3.

Exercise 4: Here we start using the eighth note rests to create some real musical patterns. By having the rest on the first half of the beat, the second eighth note is played on the "and," or off beat. So in this exercise, the four sixteenth notes are counted "1-e&-a-2-e&-a" and played with the RLRL sticking; there's an eighth rest on 2; the RH plays on the "and" of the second beat; and the pattern repeats for the third and fourth counts, with LRLR sticking on "3-e&-a." Look over Exercises 1-6 and have a go at them. If you want to play along to a slow rock song, try "Strangle Hold," by Ted Nugent!

Sixteenth Notes, Eighth Notes, and Eighth Rests

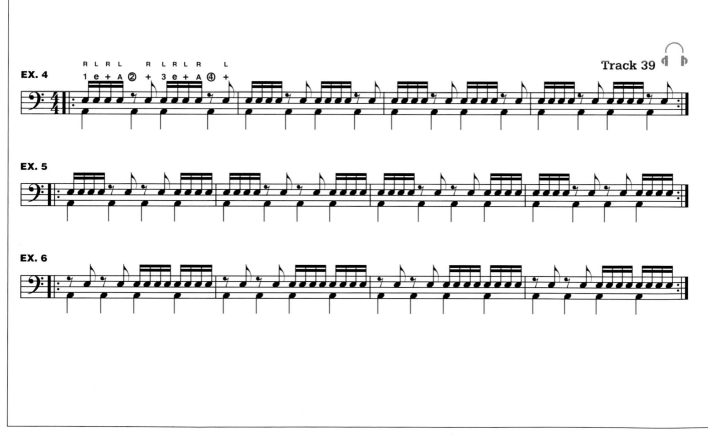

SIXTEENTH/EIGHTH NOTE RESTS

In this section we deal with sixteenth note rests along with eighth note rests

What? You're getting bored? You want some really interesting combinations of notes? OK—you asked for it. The following patterns get into some complicated rhythms. When you throw sixteenth note rests into the picture, you've got to be prepared, because they go by fast! You'll find that it pays to

take time to read these exercises very carefully and count them out loud before you attempt them.

Exercise 1: The first beat is in sixteenths, with the sixteenth note rest coming in on the "1" and RLR sticking on the "e&-a."

I've put the sixteenth note rest in different places in the

More Sixteenth/Eighth Rests

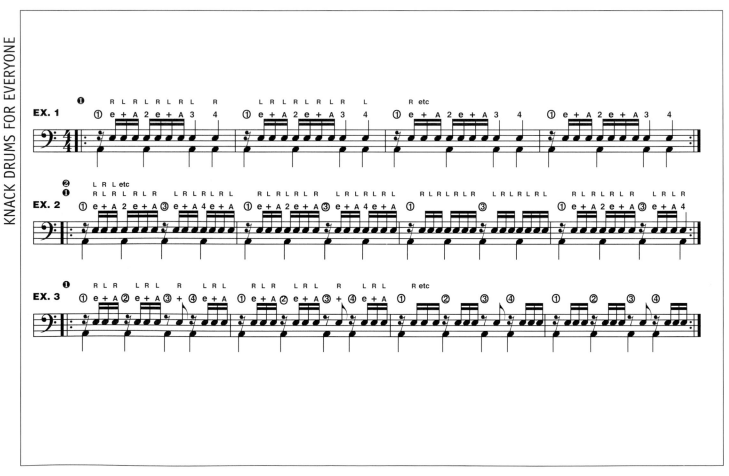

KNACK DRUMS FOR EVERYONE

other exercises. The rhythmic combinations can be tricky, so practice them particularly slowly, over and over, until you can see those little sixteenth rests coming!

Be aware of the pulse changes these rests create, and the difference in the rhythm as you go from sixteenth to eighth notes.

12-Bar Exercises with More Sixteenth/Eighth Rests

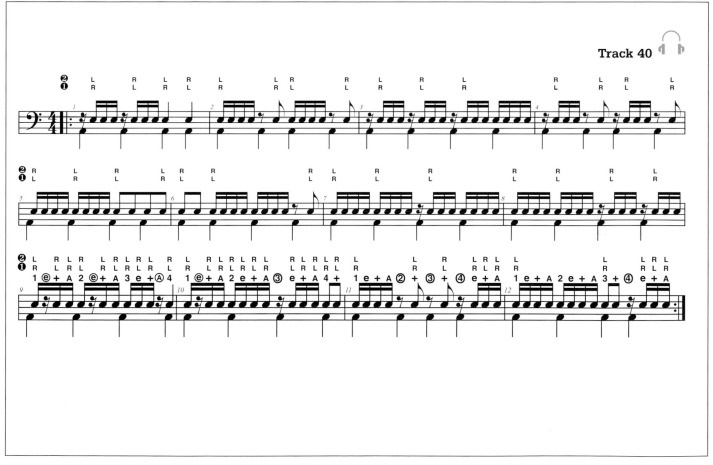

145

THE NEXT LEVEL

Your work is cut out for you with new note-rest patterns in extended exercises

How does that saying go, there's no rest for the wicked? Yeah, I know, that's the title of an Ozzy Osbourne album. But where was I going with this? Oh yeah, in music, there's plenty of rests for the wicked. Although as you're practicing them, they might not give you any rest!

In this section I've decided to give you a real workout. So, instead of the usual six exercises, you get twelve. I've added more repeat marks to save space, so you'll be playing the first bar of each exercise and repeating it three times, and then repeating the whole exercise again as usual.

Sixteenth/Eighth Notes—Next Level

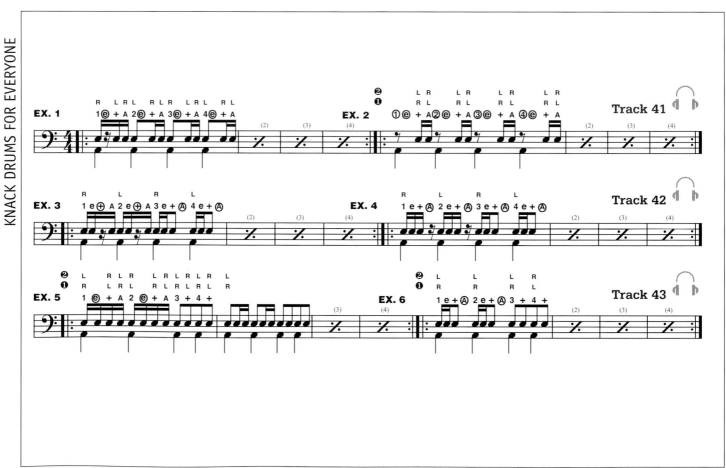

You'll notice some new note-rest patterns. In Exercise 1 the first beat is in sixteenths, with the rest coming on the "A" of the "1-e&-a. In the second beat there's an eighth note instead of two sixteenths, counted "2-A," so it's like having a rest without actually writing it. You then play on the "and-a." Study this pattern and learn to recognize it, because you're going to be seeing it a lot.

Exercise 2 begins with an actual eighth note rest. So you'll count the first beat as follows: Rest on "1-e," play on "&-a."

Exercise 3 contains a nice little pattern. The rest is on the "and," so you'd play it "1-e-rest-a." Play this over and over, and enjoy the cool bounce feel of it.

Note that in all the exercises, the bass drum is playing quarter notes on 1-2-3-4.

Combination Sixteenth/Eighth Notes with Rests

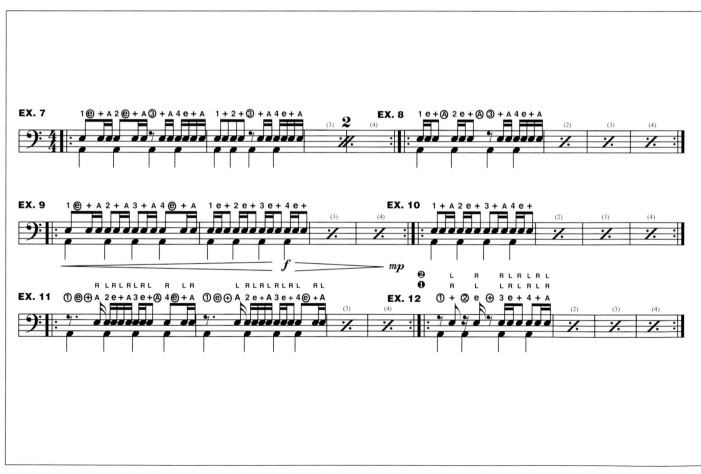

147

SIXTEENTH/EIGHTH COMBINATIONS

Learning new sixteenth and eighth note groupings and figuring out some exercises on your own

By now you should be having a ball with those sixteenth and eighth note combos. So get ready for some more fun. In this section there are a few new notes that you can figure out yourself with your new musical knowledge. I'll explain a couple of them to you, and then you'll be on your own.

First let's look at Exercise 2, which is a sixteenth note grouping in which you play on the "1-e" and rest on the "&-a." This rhythm creates what we call a "bounce" feel. The whole exercise goes like this:

Beat 1: Set of sixteenths counted "1e-&-a."

More Sixteenth and Eighth Note Combinations with Rests

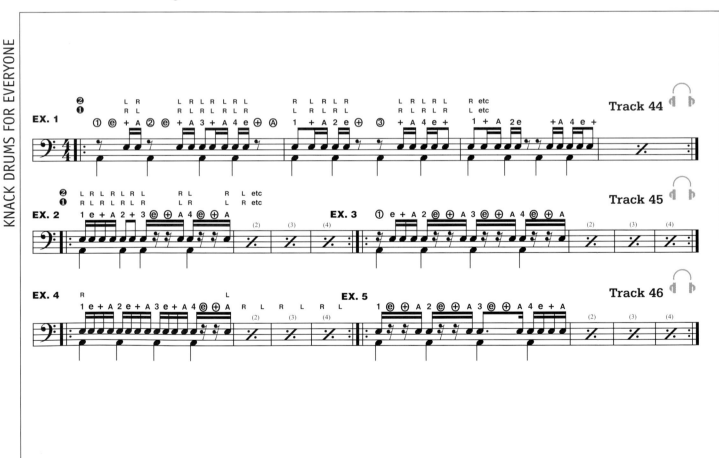

KNACK DRUMS FOR EVERYONE

148

Beat 2: Two eighth notes counted "2-and."

Beat 3: Play on 3, rest on "e&," play on "a."

Beat 4: Repeat the last pattern. When you play beats 3 and 4 properly, you should feel the bounce. Check the audio track to hear what it should sound like.

Exercise 3 has the first sixteenth note grouping counted "rest-e&-a."

Beat 2: A sixteenth note, a sixteenth rest, and an eighth note. Play on 2, rest on "e," play and count the "&-a." It's just like math fractions. Figure it out with values.

In Exercise 5 you'll see the dotted eighth note on the 3 beat. Read the definition of the dot and figure out the note value. Then play the bar.

OK—this is how it goes. Play on 1, rest on "e&" and play on "a." Did you get it right?

12-Bar Exercise with Sixteenth and Eighth Notes

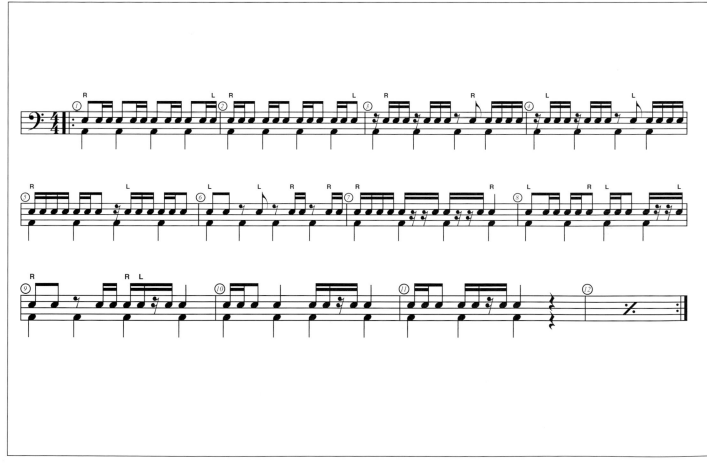

DOTTED EIGHTHS & SIXTEENTHS

The rock musician's best friend—the shuffle feel—and how to create it

In a shuffle rhythm each beat is divided in two, with the first beat being long and "heavy," and the second short and "light." In swing the rhythmic division is less exact and more a matter of "feel."

The basic "unit" of the shuffle is a dotted eighth note and a sixteenth note. As we established earlier, the dot equals half the value of the note preceding it. So a dotted eighth note is the equivalent of three sixteenth notes. You count the dotted eighth "1-A-and," holding it for a count of three sixteenths, and finish up the beat playing the sixteenth note on the "a."

Dotted Eighth and Sixteenth Notes

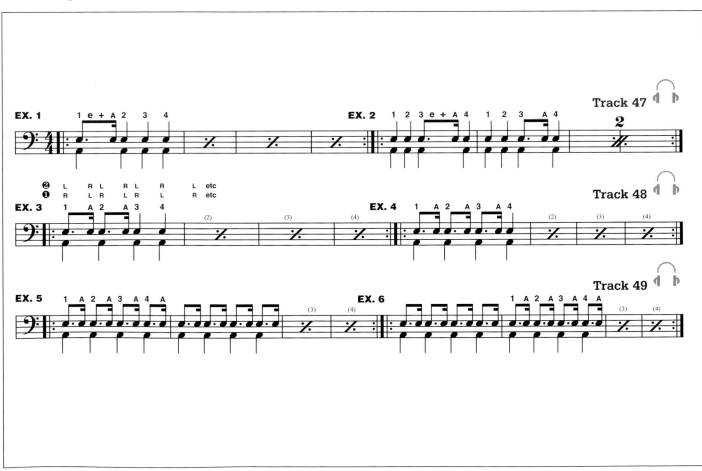

Once you get it going fast, you'll just count it "1A, 2A, 3A, 4A."

Take a look at Exercise 1. There's the dotted eighth and sixteenth note on the first beat, followed by quarter notes on 2-3-4. In Exercise 7 I've got you mixing up the dotted eighth and sixteenths with regular sixteenth note groupings. And in Exercise 11 you've got sixteenth note rests on the "1-A-and" counts, playing only on the "a" count of each beat.

•••••••••••••• GREEN ● LIGHT ••••••••••••
Memorize the shuffle pattern! It's basic to rock and will often appear without warning, changing the entire feel of the piece.

More Dotted Eighths and Sixteenths

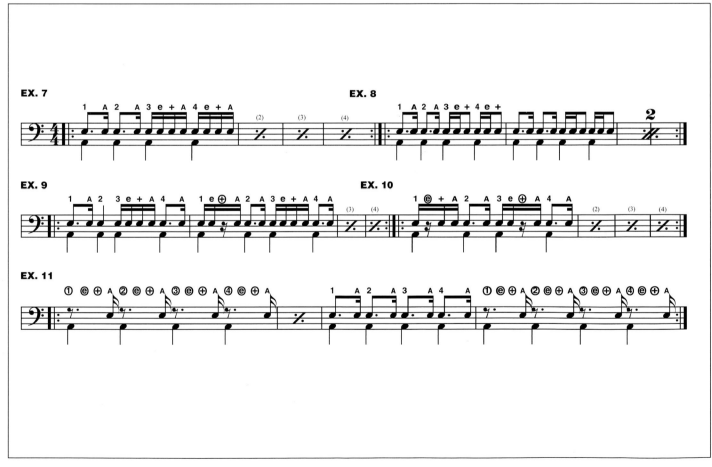

MORE DOTTED EIGHTHS/SIXTEENTHS

Further exploration of the shuffle feel using dotted eighth and sixteenth notes and rests

In this section, we'll get further into the shuffle pattern using dotted eighth rests.

Exercise 1 contains two groupings of dotted eighths. On beat 1, play on the "1," count out "e&," play on "a." Beat 2 is the same as beat 1. Beat 3 is a dotted eighth rest, counted "3-e&,"

and a sixteenth note. So you'll sit out "3-e&" and play on "a." Beat 4 is the same as beat 3.

When you get this pattern down and can play it quickly, you'll find it goes too fast to count out all the sixteenth note values. So you'll count it "1-e, 2-e, rest-e, rest-e."

More Dotted Eighths and Sixteenths

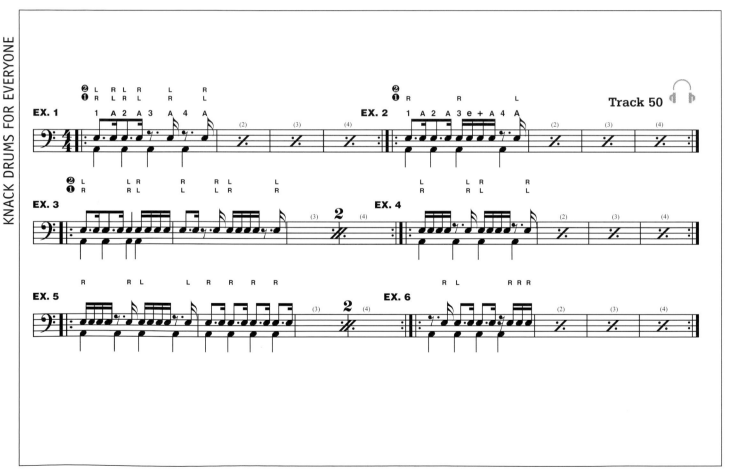

In the 12-bar exercise, bars 2, 3, and 4 are very challenging. You've got the shuffle—dotted eighths and sixteenths, the regular sixteenth note groupings with dotted eighth rests, and a bar with dotted eighth rests and sixteenths, in which you'll be playing on the off beats. Remember to alternate your sticking,

This exercise is a tricky one, so read it over carefully, play it very slowly, and listen to the audio track to hear how it should be played.

······· **RED ● LIGHT** ··············

Make sure you don't start counting the dotted eighth notes like eighth notes.

·········· **GREEN ● LIGHT** ···············

It is a good idea to play them back-to-back.
1&2&3&4& -1-e, 2-e, 3-e, 4-e.

12-Bar Exercise with Dotted Eighths and Sixteenths

Track 51

AN EXERCISE REVIEW

A review of all the notes learned so far; then, on to first and second endings

In this section I'll also be talking about something called "first and second endings," and introducing some dynamics. Look at Exercise 1. See the brackets or beams over bars 11 and 12? They're marked "1st" and "2nd." What this is telling you is that you'll play through the bar marked "1st" and then follow

the repeat marks, going back to the beginning of the piece and playing it over again until you get to that first ending. Then you skip that bar and play the second ending, which concludes the piece.

I've also introduced accent marks, which were in your

Review Exercise with 1ˢᵗ and 2ⁿᵈ Endings

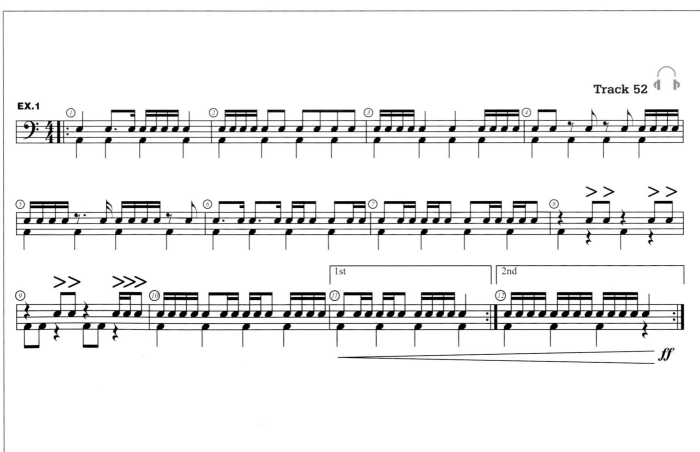

Track 52

glossary of musical terms. They look like this: >. When you see a > over a note, hit that note harder.

Let's also look at bar 4 of the second 12-bar exercise. There's a half note, which equals two quarter notes. And with the dotted eighth rest, it forms an interesting pattern, which goes like this: "Rest-A, play on 2, rest on 3 (because of the half note) and play on 4." As usual, the BD comes in on the quarter notes, 1-2-3-4.

•••••••••••• GREEN ● LIGHT ••••••••••••

Before playing these exercises, look at the 1 and 2 endings, which have a lot of sixteenth notes. Because there's no pause between the last note of ending 1 and the first note of bar 1, you'll have to jump back up to the beginning quickly. Going back and forth several times from the 1 ending to the beginning bar is the way to get used to this transition.

Another Review Exercise

SIXTEENTHS & EIGHTHS

EIGHTH NOTE TRIPLETS
Learning what a triplet is and how to play some really cool triplet groupings

The triplet is a group of three notes with a time value equal to two notes of the same kind. In other words with eighth note triplets, you'd be playing three eighth notes to the quarter beat instead of two. So if we count eighth notes "1-+" to a beat, the triplet is counted as "1-and-A." A full bar of triplets is counted "1-+-A, 2-+-A, 3-+-A, 4-+-A," with the bass drum foot playing on 1-2-3-4. (See Exercise 1, for example.)

You'll find triplets in many musical styles, including blues, jazz, and country. The triplet grouping creates a shuffle feel when the middle note of each triplet is a rest.

Triplets and Eighths

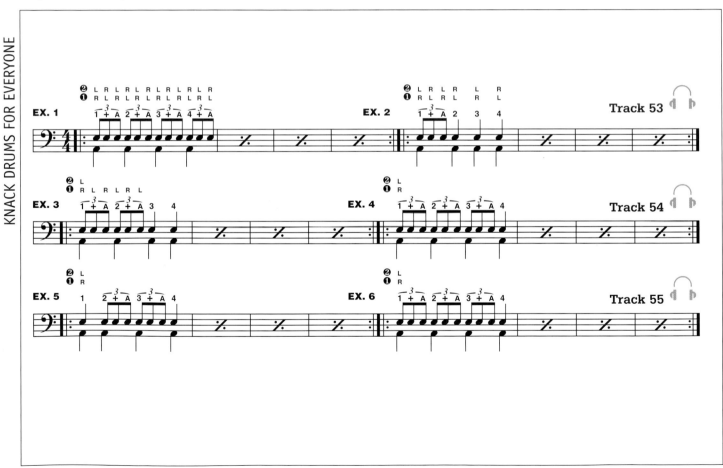

The triplet is simple in concept, but it can be hard to play. Practice Exercise 1 until you get used to the triplet feel, using alternate sticking. And play them without any accents.

In Exercise 2 you're playing the triplet with the two stickings indicated. Then you play quarter notes on 2-3-4. Listen to the audio track to make sure you've got the correct pulses. In Exercise 5 the first beat is a quarter note, the second and third are triplets, and the fourth is a quarter. So the count is "1, 2-+-A, 3-+-A, 4."

············· RED ● LIGHT ···············

Make sure you understand the rhythmic difference between playing three sixteenths and resting on the fourth and playing a triplet. The sixteenths are four beats to a quarter note, while the triplets are three beats to the quarter, which is a totally different feel. The MP3 track will show you how triplets should sound.

More Triplets

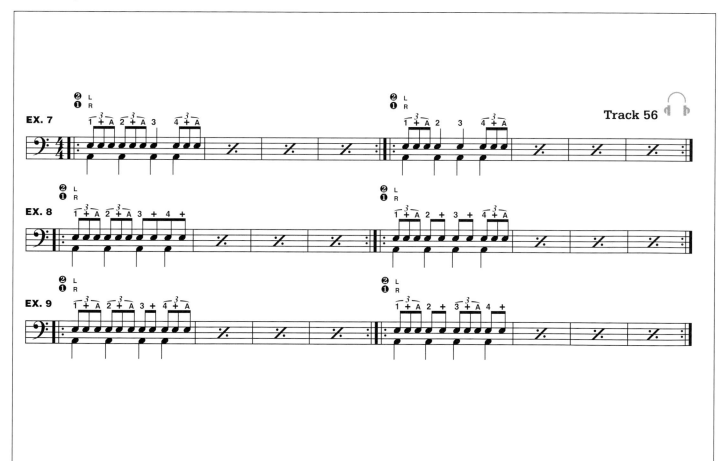

CONTINUING THE TRIPLET TRIP

Triplets with rests and other types of note combinations and the importance of sight reading

In this section we'll be playing eighth note triplets with eighth note rests. The trick here is to keep the triplet pulse with the rests.

In Exercise 1 the first two beats are two triplets, counted "1-and-A, 2-and-A." On the third beat we have a rest in place of the first note of the triplet. So you'll rest on "3" and play the "and- A." Beat 4 is two eighths. The full count is "1-and-A, 2-and-A, rest-and-A, 4-and."

In Exercise 2 note the eighth rests on the 1 and 3 beats. In Exercise 3, the rests are on the 3 and 4 beats.

Triplets and Rests

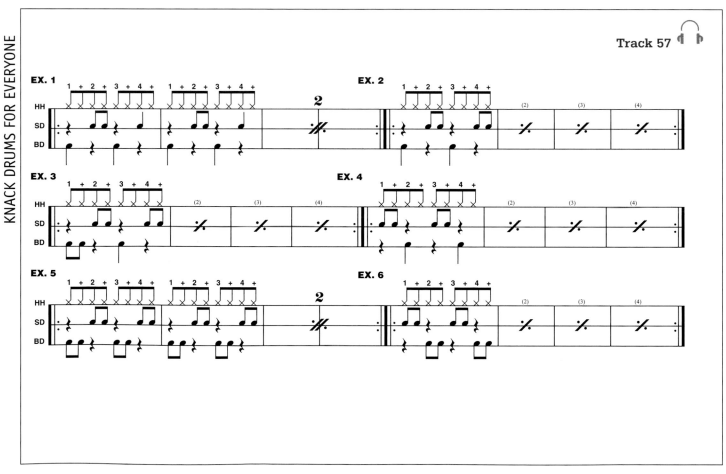

Track 57

In Exercise 5, the BD foot plays on 1-2-3-4, while the hands rest and then play the "+A" on all of those beats. Be sure to use the alternate sticking.

Exercises 7 to 12 have more triplet/sixteenth note combinations. You must get used to playing these different pulses together. Look at exercise 12. Here you're playing three strokes on both the sixteenth and triplet groupings, but in different pulses. Practice these two patterns side by side, over and over, until you really feel the difference.

••••••••••• GREEN●LIGHT •••••••••••

In music, sight reading—being able to play a new piece on sight—is very important. The better you are at sight reading, the more music you can learn and the larger your repertoire will become. Conversely, the more music you read, the better a sight reader you'll be. When you're reading these exercises, you can avoid surprises by memorizing the first bar so that you can look ahead a couple of measures to see what's coming.

More Triplets with Sixteenth Notes

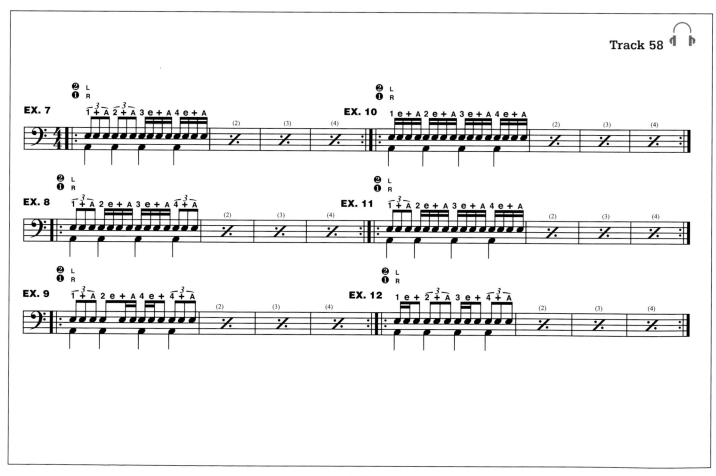

Track 58

159

PLAYING EIGHTH NOTE TRIPLETS

SIXTEENTH NOTES & TRIPLETS

Learning sixteenth and triplet groups that make great drum fills— and improve your chance to shine

Every drummer has to be able to play drum fills. A fill is your chance to shine and improvise. A fill doesn't have any specific length; it can be as simple as a few beats on the toms, or it can be a veritable explosion of sound and speed.

In this section I've chosen groupings that can be used as

fills. Pick any one or two bars and listen to how good they sound on your drum set. You can play the sixteenth notes on the snare and the triplets on the toms, or vice versa.

We've already gone over the similarity between the "1-e&" triplet count and the "1-e&-rest" count of the sixteenths, as

Sixteenth Notes and Triplets

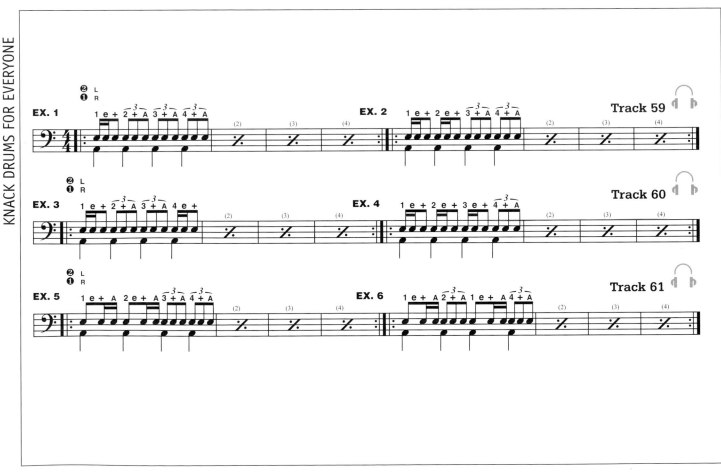

well as the difference in pulses between these two note formations. There's also an alternate way to count triplets: "1-trip-let, 2-trip-let," and so on. You may find this method simpler; I think it eliminates confusion between the triplets and the sixteenth/eighth counts. You'll also notice two different ways I've written the sixteenth note count of "1-rest-+-A." The first consists all sixteenth notes with a rest on the "A." The second is written as an eighth note and two sixteenths. Because the eighth note is worth two sixteenths, you rest on

the second beat of the eighth note. So the pattern will be played "1-rest-+-A."

Now read over the 12-bar exercise. Are there any bars in particular that look menacing? Did you pick bar 8? Yeah, those eighth rests and dotted eighth notes can be intimidating. But we've already gone over all that stuff, so count the bar out slowly and listen to the audio track before trying to playing it.

12-Bar Exercise with Sixteenth Notes and Triplets

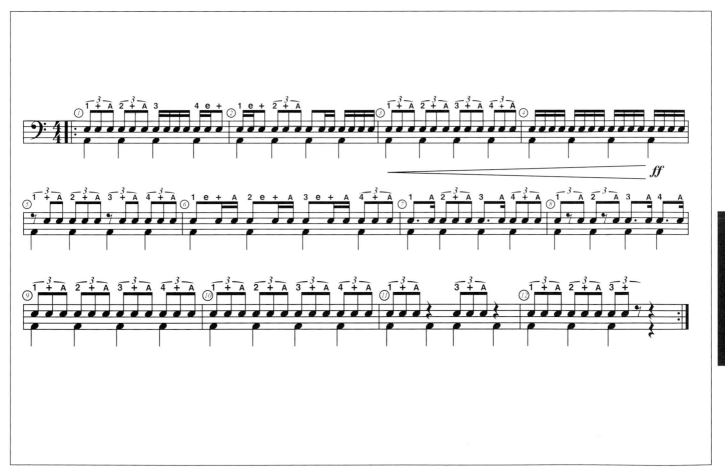

SOME MORE REVIEW EXERCISES

Twelve-bar exercises incorporating everything you've learned so far—watch out for trouble spots

Let's take another review time-out. The two 12-bar exercises in this section include everything you've learned up to this point.

Exercise 1 kicks off with quarter notes. They're easy enough, but you don't want to play them too fast or you'll trip yourself

up when you get to the triplets and sixteenths. So set your metronome at a speed that's comfortable for the fastest notes—the sixteenths.

Scan the exercise for any potential trouble spots—like bars 7 and 8. Bar 7 has the dotted eighth rest that's worth how

Review Exercise 1

many sixteenth notes? Right—three. Bar 8 has triplets on the first two beats, a dotted eighth rest and a sixteenth on the third beat, and four sixteenths on the fourth beat. That's three different pulses in one bar. If you find these or any other bars problematic, practice them alone before going through the whole exercise.

Bars 5-7 of Exercise 2 are also tricky. Bars 5 and 6 have the dotted eighth rest and a sixteenth note, for two whole bars. You'll be playing on every "A" of the counts of "1+2+3+4." Bar

7 contains three different pulsations of sixteenth notes and one triplet on the 3 count.

Go over these two exercises very carefully, referring to the audio track whenever you need to.

Review Exercise 2

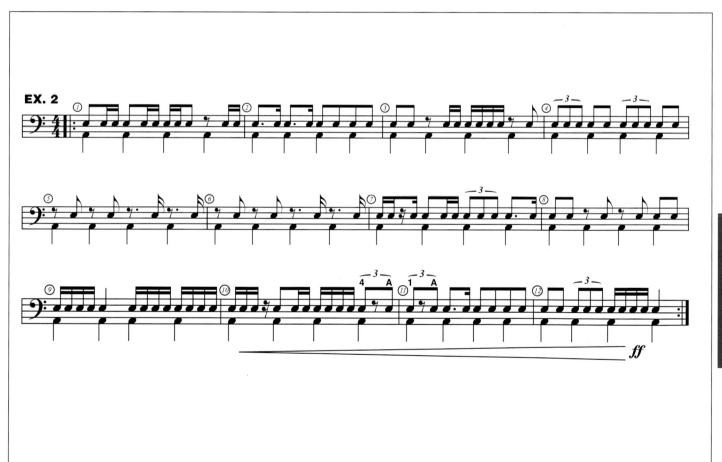

SIXTEENTH NOTE TRIPLETS

If you're feeling comfortable with eighth note triplets, sixteenth note triplets will pick up the pace

Thought those eighth note triplets were fast? Well they were just preparing you for the sixteenth note triplets! By now it shouldn't be hard to figure out that if an eighth note triplet contains three eighth notes, a sixteenth note triplet will contain twice as many notes—six. And because there are two

sixteenth notes to every eighth, they're played twice as fast.

How do you count a sixteenth note triplet? I do it like this: "One-ti-ta+ti-ta." If you were playing a 4/4 bar of all sixteenth note triplets, you'd count it: "One-ti-ta-and-ti-ta, two-ti-ta-and-ti-ta, three-ti-ta-and-ti-ta, four-ti-ta-and-ti-ta."

Sixteenth Note Triplets

KNACK DRUMS FOR EVERYONE

Look at Exercise 1. You've got the sixteenth note triplet on the first beat and two eighths on the second, third, and fourth beats. You'll be counting this "1-ti-ta+ti-ta, 2+, 3+4+." At first it's a bit tricky jumping from the faster triplets to the slower eighth notes, so count out this exercise several times before you play it.

Let's go on to Exercise 6. The sixteenth note triplets are played on the counts of 1 and 3, while 2 and 4 have the dotted eighth and sixteenth notes. When you play the sixteenth after the dotted eighth, it jumps into the triplets with a bounce! This pattern makes a cool drum fill.

And of course, in all these exercises the bass drum plays on the quarter beat.

More Sixteenth Note Triplets

165

MORE SIXTEENTH NOTE TRIPLETS

Learning to play sixteenth note triplets with various note values and rests

In these next exercises I've combined sixteenth note triplets with quarter notes, eighth notes, sixteenth notes, and sixteenth note rests. Let's check out a few of the more interesting bars.

Look over Exercise 1. See the two sixteenth note triplets on beats 1 and 2, followed by regular sixteenths on beats 3

and 4? Even though each beat is in sixteenths, the triplets are faster than the groups of four sixteenths, because you play more of them to the beat.

In Exercise 4, note the sixteenth note rest on the "+" of "2". Exercise 5 is a little different. Here the sixteenth note triplet is

Sixteenth Note Triplets and Rests

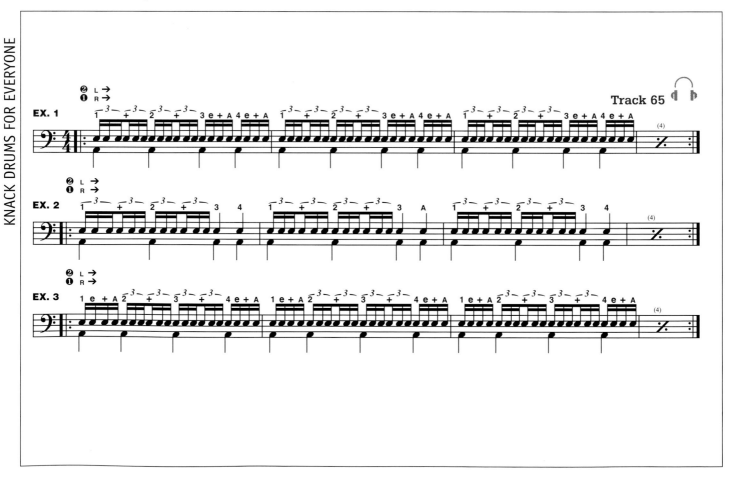

played on the "1-ti-ta-." The "+ti-ta" is the eighth note. Usually an eighth note is worth two sixteenth notes. But in a sixteenth note triplet, where there are six sixteenths instead of four to the beat, an eighth note within the triplet—indicated by the connecting beam—will equal three sixteenths. Beat 2 is the opposite. Here, you play on the 2, count out "ti-ta," and play the rest of the triplet on "+-ti-ta." Beat 3 is the same as beat 1, and beat 4 is the same as 2. The entire bar is played: "One-ti-ta-and (ti-ta), two (ti-ta) and-ti-ta, three-ti-ta-and (ti-ta), four (ti-ta) and-ti-ta."

•••••••••••• GREEN●LIGHT ••••••••••••

We're getting into complicated rhythms here, so the audio track and your metronome are your trusty guides in this new territory. The metronome in particular is essential to your being able to stay in time.

More Sixteenth Note Triplets and Rests

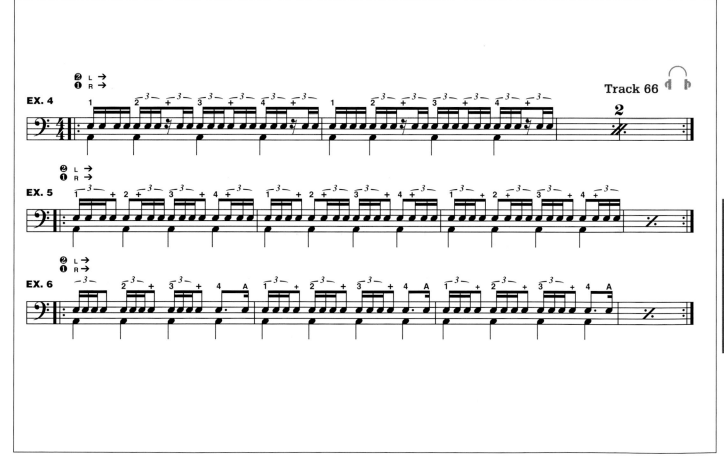

Track 66

PLAYING EIGHTH NOTE TRIPLETS

EIGHTH/SIXTEENTH NOTE TRIPLETS

Two types of triplets, two different pulses—learning to play eighth and sixteenth note triplets together

I can't overstress the importance of triplets. They're in practically every drumming application I do. As I've said many times in this book, triplets are the basis of rock. So you've got to get used to them and know how to play them in different groupings.

The eighth note and sixteenth note triplets are really fun to play together. Think of them as primary building blocks in your rhythmic vocabulary.

First, a good thing to do, as you can see in the exercises, is to just go back and forth from the sixteenth note triplets to the

Eighth Note and Sixteenth Note Triplets

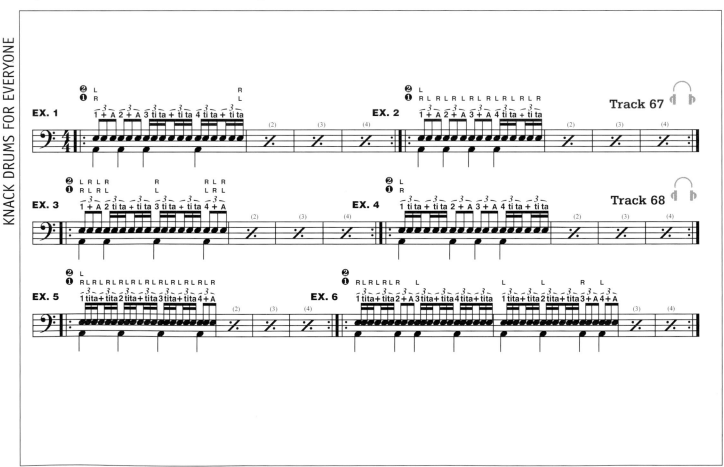

eighth note triplets. Spend as much time on each pulsation as you want. This will help you to get the feel of these two groupings together.

Exercise 3 is a good example of segueing between the two triplet groupings. Beat 1 is an eighth note triplet. Beats 2 and 3 are sixteenth note triplets, and beat 4 returns to the eighth note triplet.

Exercise 7 is a little harder. Beat 1 is an eighth note triplet. Beat 2 is another eighth note triplet with a rest on the "2." Beat

3 is a sixteenth note triplet with a rest on the "3." And beat 4 is a sixteenth note triplet. Try and play it. Getting tripped up? Set that metronome *slow!* Count! There. You're getting it.

Remember to alternate the sticking and to read through the exercises first to familiarize yourself with where the rests appear. In exercises 7 to 12 there are some intricate rests sequences going on. Practice these bars very slowly, only increasing the tempo when you feel you've got them down. Then pick up speed.

Eighth Note and Sixteenth Note Triplets with Rests

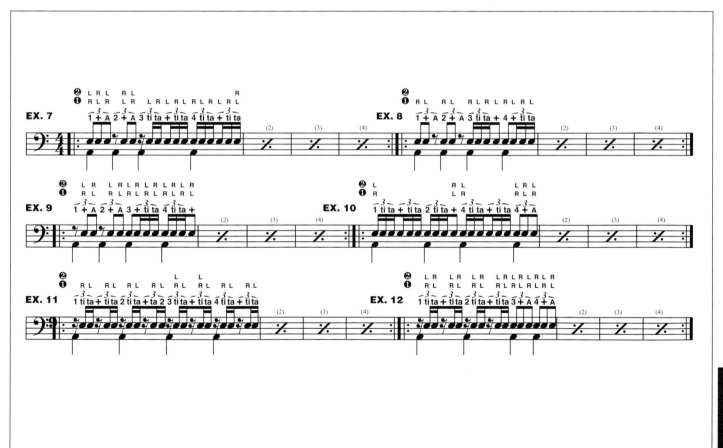

TRIPLETS: TWELVE-BAR EXERCISES

Practice these extended eighth and sixteenth note triplet exercises with and without rests

Getting more comfortable with those triplets? How about some 12-bar exercises? These will really test your rhythmic accuracy because every bar has different pulses within it and the two triplet forms have to be spot on.

Let's look at some individual bars. In Exercise 1, bar 6, there's

an eighth note rest on the first count of the fourth beat, so that the beat is counted "rest-+-A." In Exercise 2, bar 1, the rests appear on the first beat of the sixteenth note triplets. Then the "+-ti-tai" is played on beat "3." The "+-ti-ta" is played then into another pulsation, the "4+."

Twelve-Bar Exercise 1—Sixteenth and Eighth Note Triplets

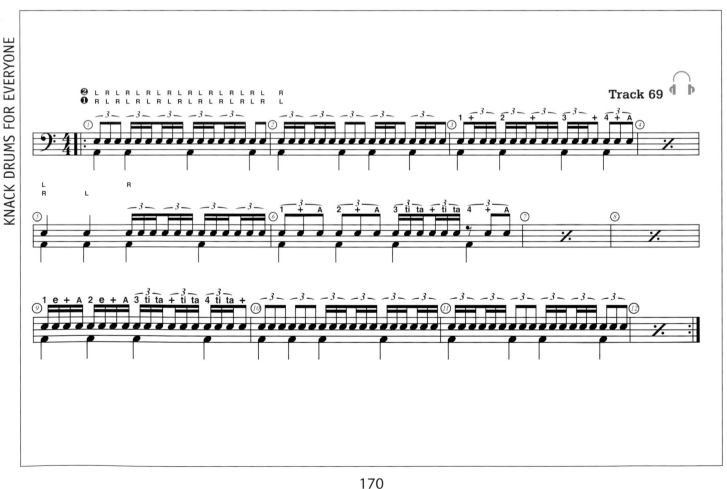

KNACK DRUMS FOR EVERYONE

GREEN ● LIGHT

Again, any two bars of these exercises would make good drum fills. Pick a few that sound good to you and practice them until you've developed the speed and accuracy to transform them into fills.

Twelve-Bar Exercise 2—Sixteenth and Eighth Note Triplets

EIGHTH NOTE TRIPLET ACCENTS

Moving from straight even playing to accented playing, a more animated, energetic approach

Eighth note triplet accents are really fun to play. In fact they're truly one of my favorite things about drumming. Accents define a piece of music and give it energy and personality. It's like the difference between talking in a monotone and being articulate and animated.

Up to this point we've been playing triplets with no accents because our goal was simply to try and keep them even. When you add accents to them, they establish a real beat, emphasize an idea, and turn into real music.

We'll go from two to four and five accents per bar. Before

Eighth Note Triplet Accents

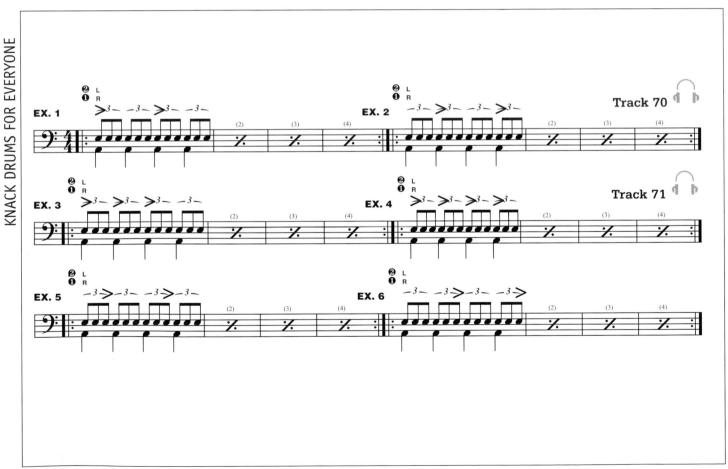

you try these exercises, figure out the accents in relation to the alternate sticking. The accent on the snare drum is actually played as a rim shot, giving it much more power and bite.

Follow the accents in Exercise 1 on the first and third beats; Exercise 2 on the second and fourth beats; and Exercise 3 on the first, second, and third beats. In Exercise 5 you'll be playing on the off beats or "A" counts of 1 and 3; and in Exercise 9, on every off beat. Don't they sound fine?

ZOOM

Great drummers like Gene Krupa, Buddy Rich, and Jimi Hendrix's Mitch Mitchell, jazz fusion pioneer, often used these accented eighth note triplets in their solos. I like them too.

········· GREEN●LIGHT ·········

These riffs can have a really great flow to them if they are in the right tempo. Another tip: It's a good idea to wear some ear protection when hitting the rim shots, as they're a little like rifle shots, with the noise and backfire.

More Eighth Note Triplet Accents

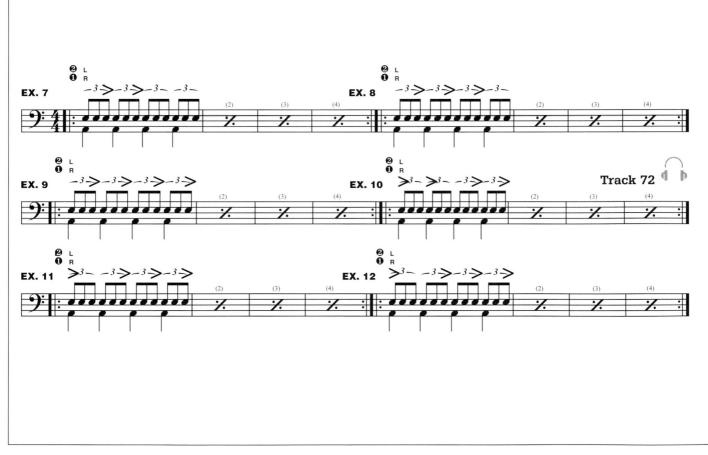

173

MORE ACCENTED TRIPLETS
Building up your triplet accent vocabulary and adding melodic accents to your playing

That's right—these triplets will add quite a bit of vocabulary to your rhythmic arsenal. Exercises 1 to 8 have the sticking written above. When the accents are on the "1" and "A" of the count, they're played with the same hand. In Exercise 1 you have two right-hand rim shots on "1" and "A." The more you

play this, the more you'll notice how melodic it sounds. I love these.

In Exercise 2 the left hand plays the accents on "2" and "A." In Exercise 3 the same hand plays "3+." In Exercise 4 the accents are on the "+-A" of the fourth beat—and so on.

Eighth Note Accented Triplets

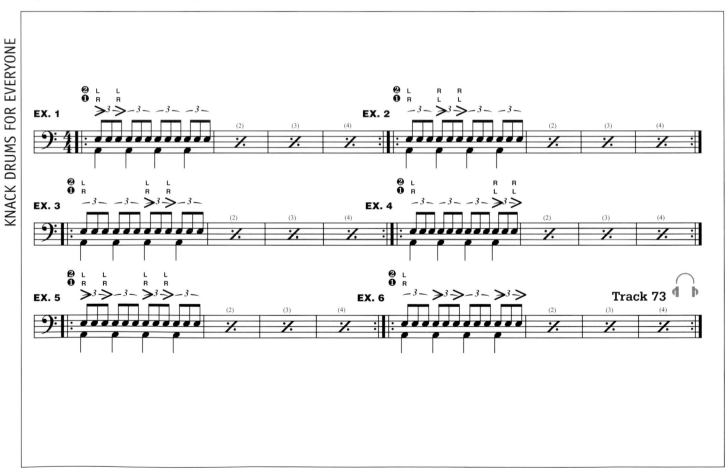

KNACK DRUMS FOR EVERYONE

By Exercise 7 things start getting interesting. In beat 1, the accents are on "1-rest-A." In beat 2 the accent is on the "A" off beat. Played repeatedly, this exercise is so cool! This pattern is seen again in Exercise 8.

Exercise 11 is a two-bar phrase. In bar 1 the accents come on all the off beats. In bar 2 they're on the beat. Play this exercise over and over, and you'll really be groovin', as us old timers used to say way back in the Groovin' Sixties.

More Eighth Note Accented Triplets

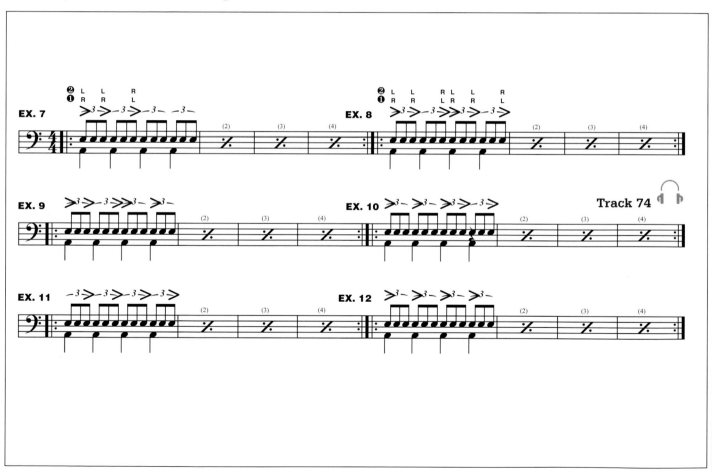

TRIPLET ACCENTS: THE NEXT LEVEL
Some new accent patterns, including a middle accent that you can use for solos and breaks

The exercises in this section contain some really cool patterns. These are the kinds of patterns that you'll use when you start playing solos, four-bar breaks, and two-bar fills. Memorize them!

Watch the repeat signs. Some exercises have the "repeat the last two bars" sign, while other just repeat the preceding bar. While you should learn these exercises at a slow speed, your goal is to get them up to 120 BPM on the metronome.

Exercise 10 is the most difficult. Here I've introduced a new accent, in the middle of the triplet. Play this very slowly. Make

Eighth Note Triplet Accents—Next Level

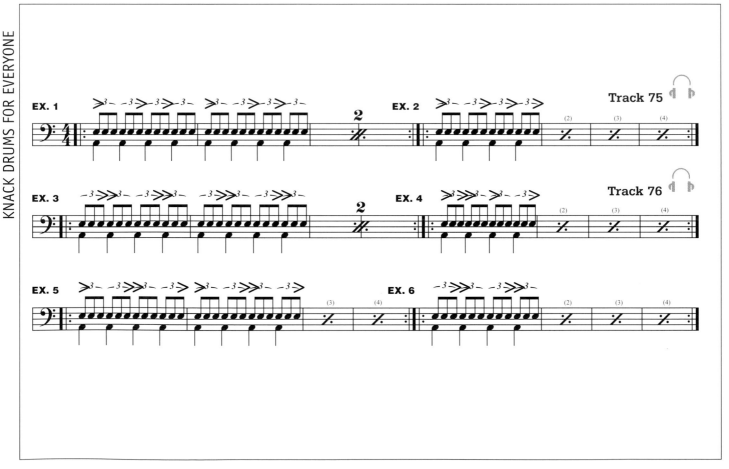

sure your BD foot comes in on 1. Then play the accents on the "+" of all four beats. Once you get this pattern down, speed it up until you can knock it off at 120 BPM. Want to try and go faster? Do it! That's how all the great drummers got up to lightning speed—practice and patience! Exercises 11 and 12 have middle accents combined with other accents to create some interesting patterns.

··········· GREEN ● LIGHT ··········

Just for fun, and to make these exercises more melodic, experiment with playing the accents on different drums. For instance play the main triplet on the snare drum and the accent on the toms. Go from the rack toms to floor toms. This will get you more adept at moving around the drum set and will also give the accents different tones.

Eighth Note Triplet Accents Continued

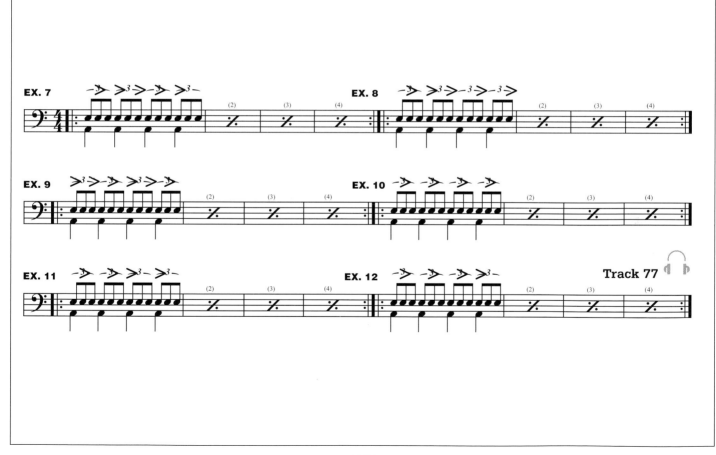

Track 77

HIGH LEVEL TRIPLETS

TWELVE-BAR TRIPLET ACCENTS
Some fun and easy patterns that sound great, especially when playing on the whole drum set

I think it's time to get used to playing on the whole drum set. In the last spread I suggested playing accents on the toms. Let's do that with the following exercises.

Up until now we've played exercise after exercise of the same pattern. As these patterns change in the 12-bar exercises, they create melodies, using the accents and different toms.

Let's start by alternating between the snare drum and the toms. Get in position. Is your seat comfortable? At the right height? OK. Let's begin with Exercise 1. Play bar 1 over and

Twelve-Bar Accented Triplets—Exercise 1

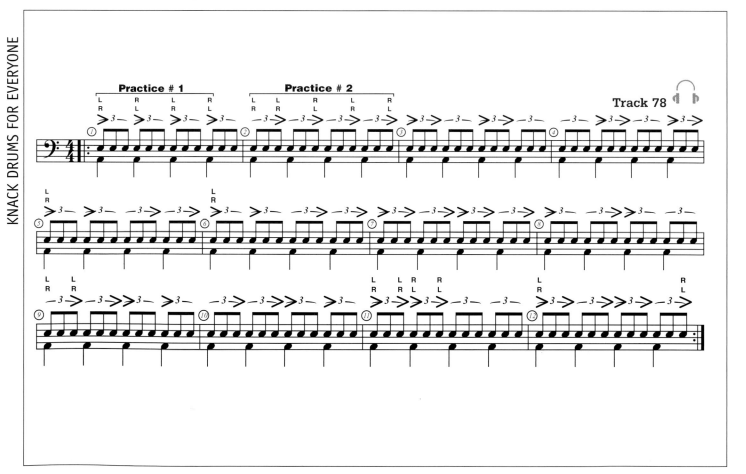

178

over with the accents on the snare. When you've got this down, start moving your hands onto the toms. Hit the "1" accent on the floor tom, the "2" accent on the rack tom (either tom if you have two), the "3" accent back on the floor tom, and the "4" accent back on the rack tom. Follow the sticking and go as slowly as necessary to get used to the coordination. Now, reverse the sticking so that you're starting with the left hand.

Play bar 2 the same way. Here the accents are on the "A" of

the beats. Start again with your right hand on the snare. Then hit the accent of the first beat on the floor tom, the accent of the second beat on the rack tom, and repeat that pattern for the third and fourth beats.

Start with a metronome setting of around 80 BPM and gradually increase your speed until you can really move around on the drums.

Twelve-Bar Accented Triplets—Exercise 2

RUDIMENTARY WORKOUT
Time for some more hand development: learning rudimentary hand accents coordinated with the bass drum foot

This section is about hand development and hand-foot coordination. The exercises have a lot of "RRRR" and "LLLL" sticking. On all of the patterns, your BD foot comes in on the first beat. Practice each exercise for about three minutes. I decided to be nice to you—you won't have to concern yourself with too

much reading. It's the accents and hand-foot coordination that are important here.

Practice each pattern with the right hand, repeating it with the left hand. Exercise 1 is a quarter note exercise with the accent coming in on the fourth beat. Notice the BD coming

Rudimentary Workout

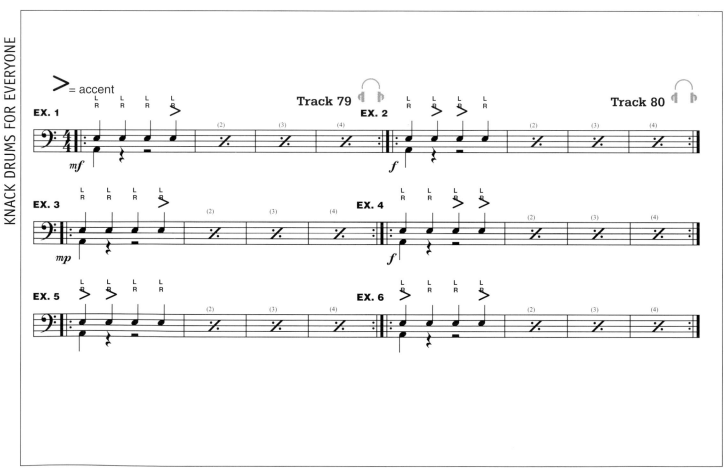

in on 1, followed by a quarter rest—equal to one beat—and a half rest, equal to two beats.

In Exercise 8 the accents are on beats 3 and 4. Here the accents are on "3-4," with the right hand taking the first bar and the left hand taking the second. In Exercise 11 the accents are played on 1, 3, and 4. This is both an interesting pattern and a nice workout for your hands.

· · · · · · · · · · · · GREEN ● LIGHT · · · · · · · · · · · · ·

Once you've gotten all the exercises down, pick a tempo, and start at the top and play the entire page as one piece. Then do it again with the other hand. If you really want to get a good workout, go back and practice each bar with alternate sticking. Play bar 1 with the right hand, then with the left; bar 2, right hand, then left, and so on. This will really help both your reading and your playing.

Rudimentary Workout Continued

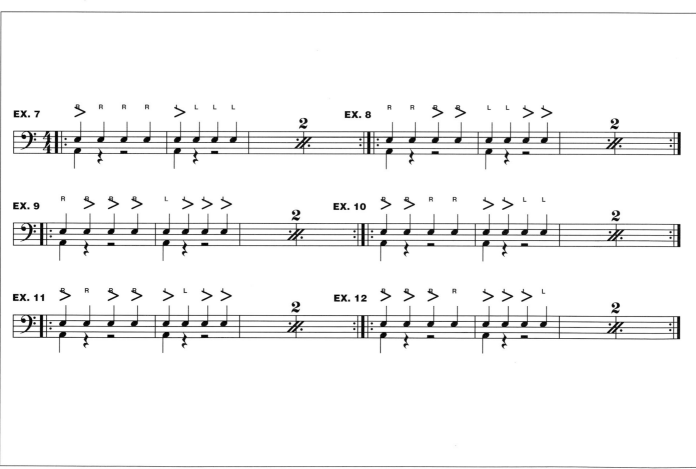

181

THE THREE STROKE RUFF
Here are some core patterns every drummer needs to know

Currently, there are forty International Drum Rudiments recognized by the National Society of Rudimental Drummers and the Percussive Arts Society. In short a rudiment is nothing more than a basic pattern. So don't sweat the big definitions. Just learn them! I'm just going to introduce you to some of the core patterns every drummer needs to know.

In Exercise 1 we have three quarter notes on 1-2-3 and a rest on 4. These exercises have 3 sets of sticking. The repeating "Rights," the repeating "Lefts," and the alternating sticking. You must play each exercise with all three stickings. The accent in exercise 1 is on the "1" count as well as the foot to build coordination.

Three Stroke Ruff

Exercise 2 has the same sticking except that the accent is on beat 3. All the exercises are slightly different, so look at each one carefully before playing it.

In the second part of this section, each line is an 8-bar exercise. There are quite a few repeat marks in these exercises. When you get to the end of bar 8, there's a repeat sign telling you to repeat the entire line. So you'll actually be playing 16 bars. As usual the bass drum foot comes in on the first beat of the measure, with different rest patterns on 2-3-4.

Your goal here is to develop evenness and precision, and then speed.

Eight-Bar Exercise with Three Stroke Ruff

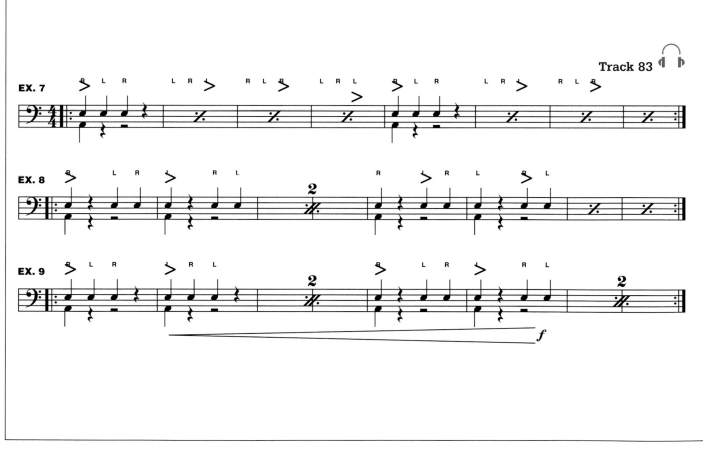

THE FOUR STROKE RUFF

Practicing the four stroke ruff, which is based on triplets, and learning 6/8 time

The four stroke ruff will be useful once you start gaining speed. It consists of three grace notes and a prime note—four strokes in all. All four strokes are alternated—RLRL or LRLR. The four stroke ruff is based on triplets—the grace notes—and in the first set of exercises, I've got triplets followed by quarter notes

(the prime note).

In Exercise 1 the hard part is the accent being on the first beat of the triplet. Use the RLR-R sticking, counting "1-+-A-2 (rest-A), followed by LRL-R sticking on "three-+-A-4 (rest-A)." For a change the BD foot plays on the 1 and 3 of each bar.

Four Stroke Ruff in 4/4 Time

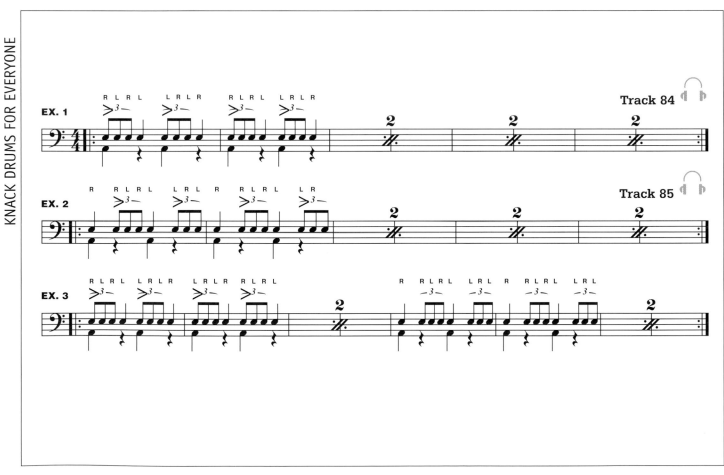

Exercise 2 uses RLR-L sticking and starts with a quarter note on 1. The triplet is played on the "2-+-A," with the accent on the 2. Then there's another quarter note on 3, and the triplet on 4, with the accented first beat. Sticking alternates R-RLR, L-LRL.

In Exercise 5 we move from 4/4 time to 6/8 time. In 6/8 time there are six beats to a measure, with the eighth note receiving one beat. Instead of counting a measure "1-2-3-4," you'll count "1-2-3-4-5-6." So you'll count the triplet in bar 1 "1-2-3," the eighth note "4," and the eighth rests "5-6."

The three stickings for these patterns will give your hands a really good workout while you're learning to count in 6/8 time. At first you'll probably find yourself reverting to the more familiar 4/4 time, but keep counting those six beats to the measure.

The BD foot is back to playing just on the first beat of the measure. Notice the dotted quarter rest, which equals three eighth notes.

Four Stroke Ruff in 4/4 and 6/8 Time

THE FIVE STROKE RUFF

The five stroke ruff is another great rudiment that you can use in your arsenal of rhythm patterns

The five stroke ruff is a great sounding rudiment. It's used a lot in marching bands and modern drumming. In order to give you more practice in reading and playing in 6/8 time, all of the exercises in this section are in 6/8.

In Exercise 1 the count is "1+2+3 (and), 4+5+6 (rest)," with the accents on the 1 and 4 counts. The BD foot also comes in on the 1 and 4. In 6/8 time the sixteenth notes are counted the way eighth notes are counted in 4/4 time: "1+2+ . . ." The sticking alternates RLRLR, LRLRL.

Exercise 2 is played and counted the same way as Exercise 1.

Five Stroke Ruff

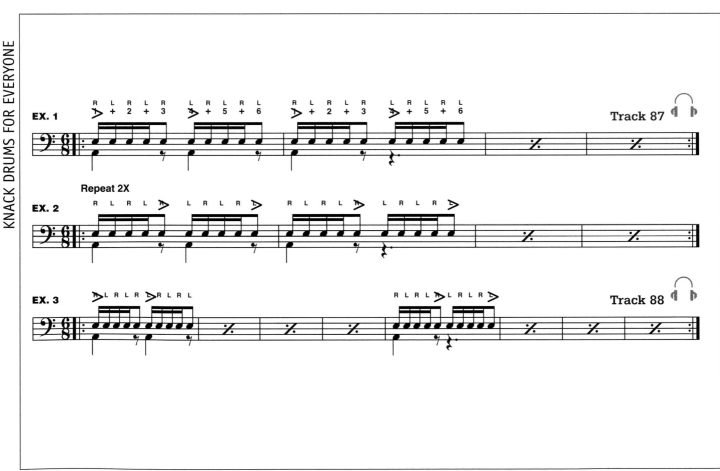

KNACK DRUMS FOR EVERYONE

But this time the accents are on the 3 and 6 counts. With the foot on the 1 and 4 counts, the accents feel like off beats.

Exercise 5 has a bit of a different pattern. The count is "1+2+3 (rest), 4+5+6 (and)" with the accents on the 1 and 4 counts. Exercise 6 begins like Exercise 5, but in bar 6 the accents change, coming on the 2 and 5 counts. This also gives you the feel of off beats.

Ready for the five stroke roll? Let's add RR-LL sticking to the patterns. In Exercise 7 you're playing RRLL-R on "1+2+3,"

and LLRR-L on "4+5+6," with the accents on 3 and 6. The BD now comes in on the 1 and 4 beats. Exercise 8 has the same pattern, but this time the accents are on 1 and 4. To get the accent on the first beat with the RR-LL sticking, do the first practice exercise at the bottom of the page, playing it slowly and building up speed.

Five Stroke Ruff and Roll

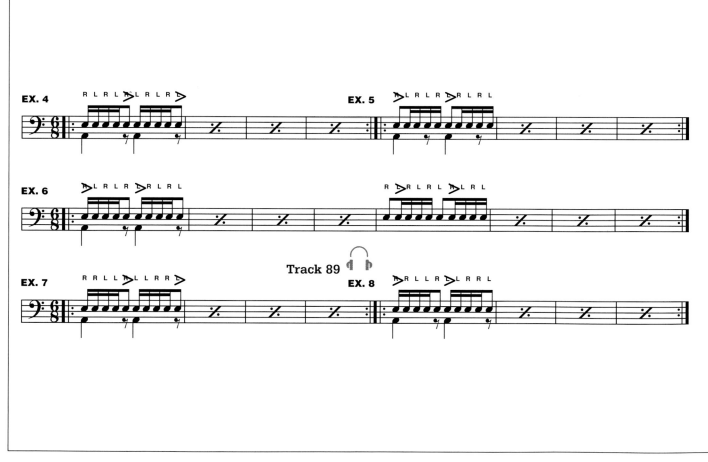

Track 89

THE FIVE STROKE ROLL

Five stroke roll exercises with different rhythms and accents; combining the five stroke roll and five stroke ruff

The five stroke rolls in this section have different note groupings and accent placement. Some of the groupings will be familiar to you, but I've also included some new ones.

In Exercise 1 the eighth note is played on beat 1 with the accent. The count for this bar is "1 (rest)-2+3+, 4 (rest)-5+6+."

The BD foot comes in on 1 and 4. The sticking is RLLRR-LRRLL. This is an incredibly handy pattern that can be used over and over in your drumming. Notice that bar 1 is repeated for eight bars. I recommend playing it longer than that to really get it down and develop some aggression.

More Five Stroke Rolls

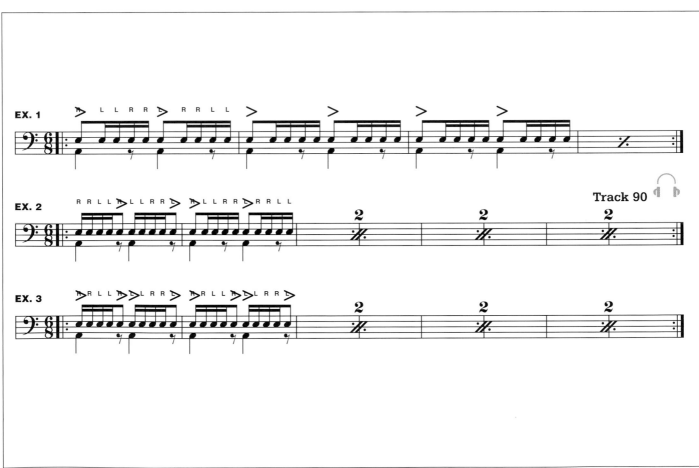

KNACK DRUMS FOR EVERYONE

Once you've gotten Exercise 1 up to speed, go on to Exercise 2. Here I've combined Exercises 1 and 2 from the last section. Again practice this for five minutes until you can play it fast. But don't get ahead of yourself. These patterns require a lot of time and effort to play well. If you start out too fast, or increase your tempo too quickly, you'll never achieve your goal, which is to be able to play evenly and rapidly.

Exercise 4 combines the five stroke ruff and the five stroke roll. It's like a tongue twister for your hands. You've really got to concentrate on which rudiment you're playing. Exercise 5 has a cool new accent counted like Exercise 1 but played with RL single alternate sticking like the ruff. Then it goes to the roll with the same accents. It's really difficult to go back and forth between these bars, so listen to the MP3 track and practice counting it out aloud with the accents before playing it.

Five Stroke Rolls and Ruffs

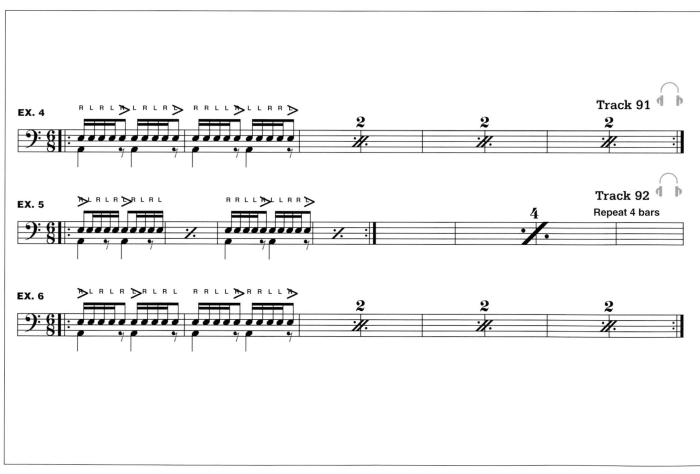

189

PARADIDDLES & MIXED STICKING

Learning the paradiddles—single, double, and triple—in 3/4 and 4/4 time

The paradiddle is a four-note pattern with RLRR or LRLL sticking. When you play multiple paradiddles in succession, the first note always alternates between right and left.

In this section you'll learn to play single, double, and triple paradidles. The single paradiddle sticking is RLRR-LRLL with

accents on the 1 and 3 counts.

In the double paradiddle the sticking is in 3/4 time: RLRLRR-LRLRL. The accents are on the 1 and 2 counts. The triple paradiddle is in 4/4 time: RLRLRLRR-LRLRLRLL. The 1-2-3 counts have the accents.

Paradiddles and Mixed Sticking

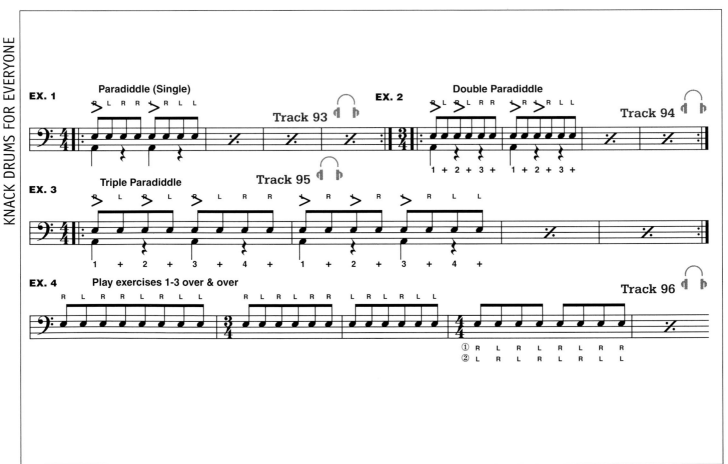

Practice the paradiddles in Exercise 4 one after the other without stopping, to work up speed. In Exercise 5 notice the RR-LL and LL-RR sticking. Build it up from a slow tempo into a long roll, checking in with the audio track to hear how it sounds. Play the mixed sticking in the rest of Exercise 4 and Exercise 5 slowly at first, as eighth notes, with your BD foot on the 1 and 3, gradually building up speed.

•••••••••• YELLOW●LIGHT ••••••••••••

If you don't master these paradiddles at a fast speed, you'll be missing the boat. It's going to take time; you might stay on this page for a couple of weeks before you get the exercises up to speed. But stick (no pun intended) with it and soon you'll be paradiddling away.

Mixed Sticking

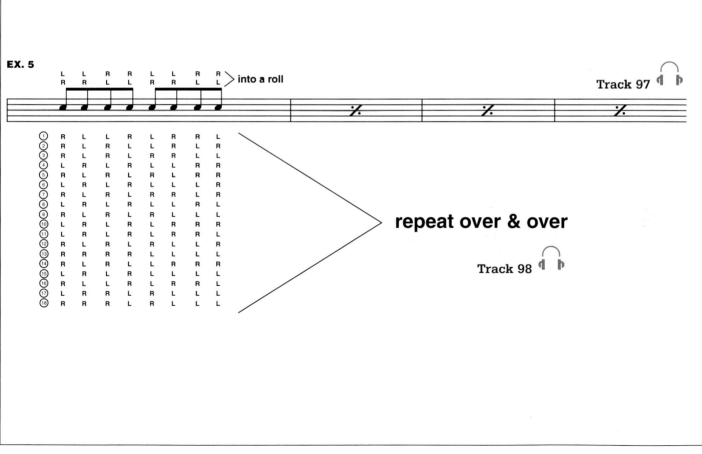

191

GETTING IN THE GROOVE

Learning how to play rock grooves in 4/4 time, adding hi-hat cymbals

Finally! You're ready to play some rock. Let's try some grooves in 4/4 time. By the end of this chapter, you'll be able to play rock songs on drums. It's payoff time!

In Exercise 1 the first thing you'll see is that instead of the two lines of music you've been playing, there are now three.

That's because we're adding the cymbals. The lines are marked "HH" (hi-hat), SD (snare drum) and BD (bass drum). Notice the eighth notes for the hi-hat, played "1+2-and-3+4+." The drums sit this one out, with half and quarter note rests.

In Exercise 2 we've added the snare on 2 and 4. Now you're

Line Rock 1—Quarters

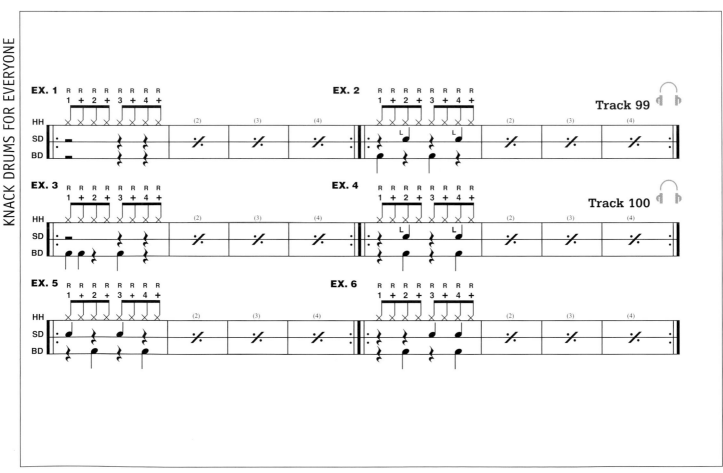

playing with both hands—right on the hi-hat and left on the snare.

The snare sits out Exercise 3 with rests, while you continue playing the HH on the eighth notes, and the BD now comes in on 1 and 3.

Put them all together and you have Exercise 4, your basic rock beat: HH on the eighths, snare on 2 and 4, and BD on 1 and 3.

Play these exercises through first just on the HH, reading down the lines to see where the drums come in.

HH=Hi-Hat
SD=Snare Drum
BD=Bass Drum

Line Rock 2

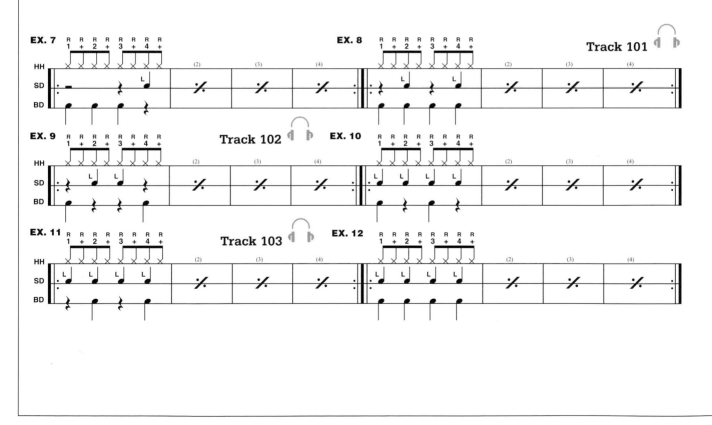

EIGHTH & QUARTERS

The eighth note-quarter note combo with cymbals, snare, and bass drum

The next step in building up your rock chops is combining the cymbals, snare, and bass drum with eighth and quarter notes.

In Exercise 1 the HH still has the full eighth note count, but the SD plays eighths on "2-+" and the quarter note on 4. The BD still has quarters on 1 and 3. In Exercise 2 I've added an eighth note for the SD, so it now comes in on "2+" and "4+."

The exercises become a little more difficult as you go along, but I'm basically only adding one note at a time, so it shouldn't take long for you to get the hang of playing three lines. And these are the patterns you can use from the get go.

Three-Line Rock—Quarters and Eighths

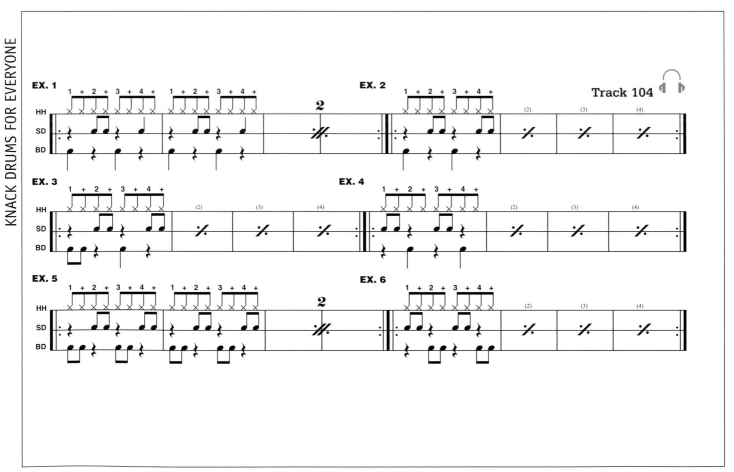

In Exercise 5 the BD and SD alternate on each beat. In Exercise 6 the hands and feet reverse roles, with the SD on 1 and 3 and the BD on 2 and 4. And Exercises 7 to 12 are 2-bar phrases. All these patterns sound really nice when you've got them up to speed. They've been the basis of many a great rock song. Do you recognize any famous songs from these beats?

Always refer to the audio track to hear how these patterns should sound.

••••••••••••••••••• RED ● LIGHT •••••••••••••••

It's easy to get a little discombobulated when you're playing eighth notes on all three lines at the same time. Be careful to make sure that you're hitting all the instruments exactly on the beat. You don't want the BD or the SD and the HH coming in one after the other. That's sloppy playing.

Three-Line Rock—Quarters and Eighths—2-Bar Phrase

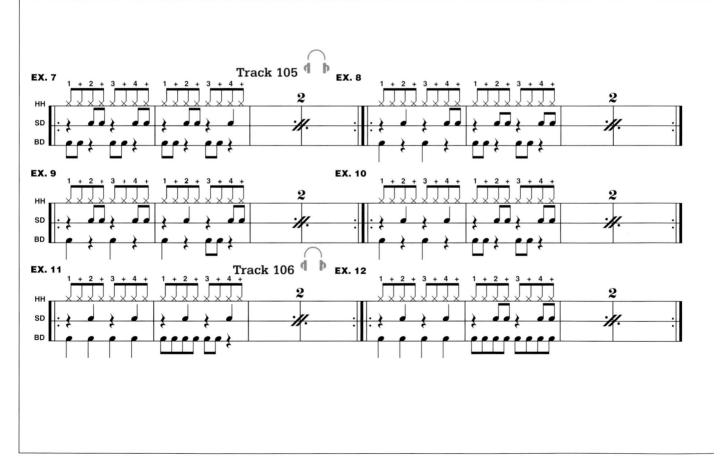

195

THREE-LINE RESTS

Some interesting combinations of eighth note and quarter note rests for cymbals, snare, and bass

The next set of exercises contains many eighth note rests, which means you'll have a lot of off beat patterns.

In Exercise 1 you've got the HH on the "1+2+3+4+," the BD on "1+" and 3, and the SD on 2 and 4. Note the quarter rests on the snare line and the quarter and eighth rests on the bass

line. In Exercise 2 this changes slightly, with the BD on the "+" of the "1+" and "3+" counts. This broken off beat pattern creates a really cool rock groove.

In Exercise 3 the SD pattern changes, playing on the "2+" and "4+." Exercise 4 has the SD playing on 2 and "4+" with the BD

Three-Line Rock Eighth and Quarter Rests

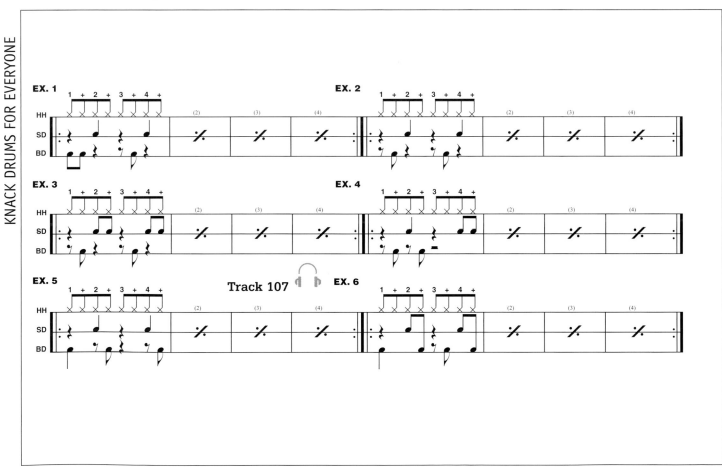

KNACK DRUMS FOR EVERYONE

coming in on the and of "1+" and "2+." Exercise 5 is actually the verse section of Bruce Springsteen's "Hungry Heart." We'll go all the way through that song later in the book.

The 12-bar exercise is a lot of fun to play. Bar 10 has the SD playing on the 1-2-3-4 beats and the BD playing on the "and" of "1+2+3+4+." This is known as an SD-BD "question-and-answer" pattern, or a musical "conversation." Bar 12 repeats this, except that it ends on the count of 3, resting on 4. The rests are written differently in this bar, so refer to the audio track for help.

• • • • • • • • • • • GREEN ● LIGHT • • • • • • • • • • • •

Before playing these exercises, remember to read down all three lines in every bar first to see which notes hit together and when. Then scan left to right to see the note counts on all the lines.

Twelve-Bar Exercise with Three-Line Rock Eighth and Quarter Rests

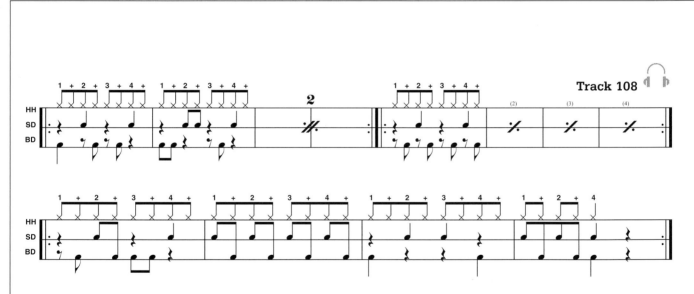

Track 108

This 12-bar exercise was intentionally written differently than the other 12-bar exercises you've seen.

ROCK PATTERNS REVIEW EXERCISE

Twelve-bar exercises recapping the three-line rock patterns, adding the ride cymbal

By now you should be getting the "knack" of rock drumming. Let's take a moment to review the three line patterns you've learned so far.

In bar 1 of the first 12-bar exercise, the pattern should be very familiar: HH on all the eighth notes, BD on 1 and 3, SD

on 2 and 4. In bar 2 the hands and foot again play on quarter notes, but the rest pattern changes. Continue by yourself with bars 3 to 8.

Moving ahead to bars 9 to12: Watch for the off-beat patterns and count carefully. Also play the first and second endings.

Twelve-Bar Exercise 1—Three-Line Rock Review

In the second 12-bar exercise, I've added a new color to the mix—the ride cymbal. When you see the abbreviation RC instead of HH, shift to the ride. You'll want to practice this new positioning and listen to the audio track to hear the difference in sound.

.... GREEN ● LIGHT ....

Practice going straight from bar 11 back up to bar 1 until you get used to the "long jump" of the first ending.

Twelve-Bar Exercise 2—Three-Line Rock Review

RC = Ride Cymbal

MORE THREE-LINE ROCK

Eighth note and sixteenth note combinations for three lines—complicating the rhythms and speed

Up until now we've been going for coordination and precision in three-line reading.

First we're going to take those dotted eighth and sixteenth notes and put them into a drum groove. In Exercise 1 the BD has the dotted sixteenth on 1 and 3—playing it like this

"1-(e&)-a . . . 3 (e&)-a." The SD comes in with the accent on 2 and 4. Look down beat 1 and see where the HH and BD come in together, where the HH and SD come in together, and where the off beats are.

Exercise 2 has the SD taking the dotted sixteenth on the 2

Three-Line Rock—Eighths and Sixteenths

and 4 beats, with the BD taking it on 1. The HH and BD both come in on 1 and 3, and the HH and SD are hit simultaneously on 2 and 4. The best way to tackle these exercises is to 1) practice each line separately, 2) practice the beats where two lines are played together, and 3) put it all together.

Check out the four sixteenth grouping in Exercise 4. You'll be going from the BD on 1 to the SD on "A" and back to the BD on "+a." This takes more coordination at the faster speed. By Exercise 11 you'll really be bouncing back and forth.

ZOOM

Notice that in all these exercises the SD has an accent mark, >. Make sure to play those notes harder or with rim shots. And don't forget your ear protection. Check with the audio track for patterns.

Three-Line Rock—More Eighths and Sixteenths

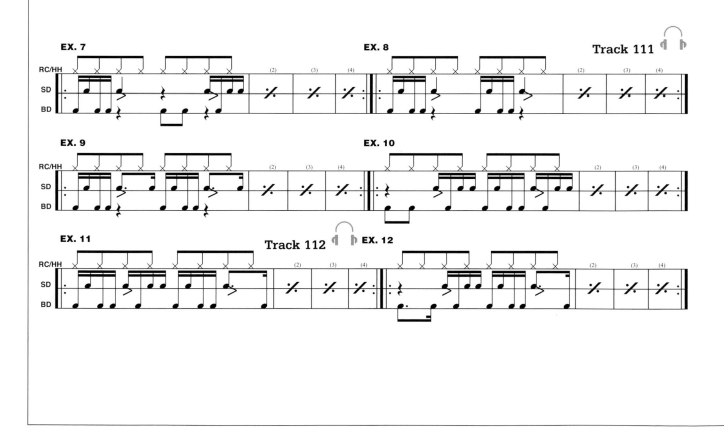

MORE SIXTEENTH/EIGHTH GROOVES
Taking it to the next level—adding more complicated rhythms and picking up speed

The following exercises make more demands on your eye-hand-foot coordination, as well as your rhythmic talents. Look through Exercise 1. This is a great pattern, with a lot going on. Listen to the audio track first. Next read through and count each line. Then play the lines separately until you feel you've

got the individual rhythms down. Finally play through the entire exercise. Now do it again, over and over, until it sounds like the audio track. Exercise 2 is a toughie, so give yourself plenty of time to master it. The dotted eighths on the BD and SD on beats 1 and 2 follow each other fast, and then you've

More Sixteenth and Eighth Note Grooves

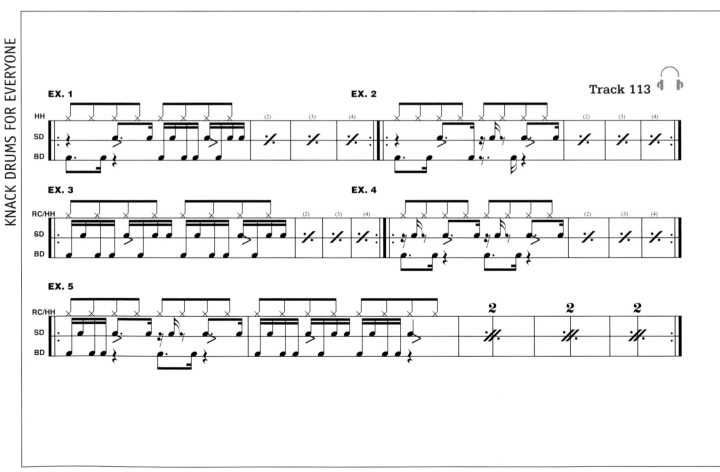

got that sixteenth on the "A" of beat 2, followed by the sixteenth on the "A" of beat 3 on the BD, and the SD taking the dotted sixteenth on 4A. Do it slowly, counting each line separately as many times as you have to. Thought Exercise 2 was a bee-itch? You ain't seen nothin' yet! Exercise 3 has four sets of sixteenth notes going between the hands and feet.

Let's move down to the 12-bar exercise. There are some new patterns in bars 6 and 7 that have that bounce feel you'll hear a lot in hip hop.

············· YELLOW ● LIGHT ··············

Don't forget those accents on the 2 and 4 beats on the SD. As if you didn't have enough to worry about!

Twelve-Bar Exercise with Sixteenth and Eighth Note Grooves

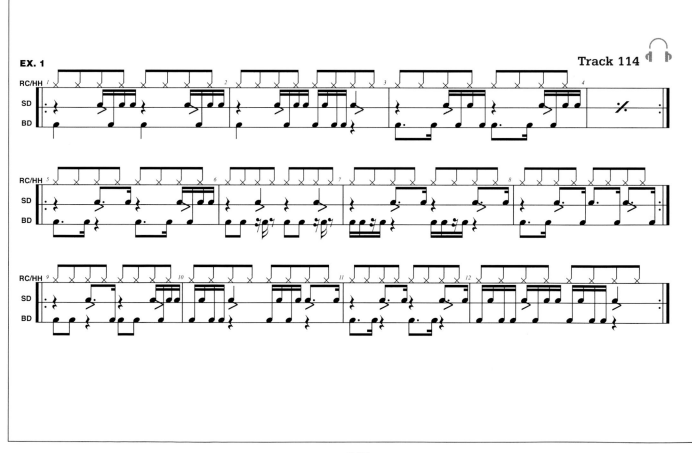

DOTTED EIGHTH/SIXTEENTH SHUFFLE

Moving from the eighth note feel to the dotted eighth and sixteenth shuffle feel

All the grooves and patterns we've been playing so far have been based on the eighth note feel. In this section we'll do a change up to the dotted eighth and sixteenth feel—the shuffle.

Exercise 1 has the HH playing the basic shuffle rhythm ("1A,

2A, 3A, 4A"). The BD has the dotted eighth and sixteenth on 1A and the quarter note on 3. The SD plays accented beats on 2 and 4.

In Exercise 5 the HH and SD play the same pattern, (1A, 2A, 3A, 4A") except the SD is also playing the accents (>) on 2

Dotted Eighth and Sixteenth Shuffle Grooves

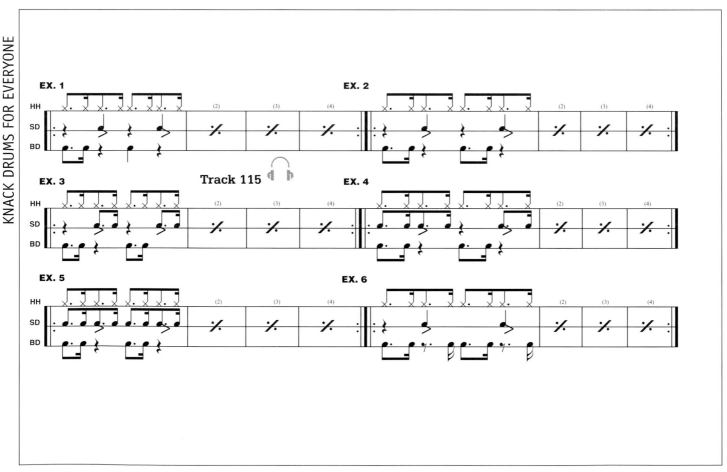

Track 115

KNACK DRUMS FOR EVERYONE

and 4. The BD comes in on "1-A" and "3-A." The hardest part of Exercise 7 is the dotted eighth rest with the sixteenth note. This exercise is a 2-bar phrase.

Exercises 8 to11 have quarter note patterns on the HH that make these shuffle rhythms easier. Whew! You needed to slow down a little, didn't you?

······· RED ● LIGHT ·············

You may need to practice playing the SD on the "2-A" and "4-A" beats with the accent (>) on the 2 and 4. This takes awhile to perfect.

More Dotted Eighth and Sixteenth Shuffle Grooves

DOTTED EIGHTH SHUFFLES

Shuffle grooves with the hi-hat on quarter—and some short shuffle fills

In today's music the most popular way to play the shuffle is with the cymbals on quarter notes and the hands and feet contributing the dotted eighth and sixteenth shuffle feel. The following 12-bar exercise is a good example of this.

In bar 2 the HH plays the quarter notes, while the BD comes in on the "1-A" and on the "A" of 2, where the stem of the sixteenth note comes down from the SD line to the BD line. In this case the note starts on the count of "2" on the SD and the BD takes it on the "A." It's the same for beat 4. Bars 5 and 6 are tricky. Here the BD plays on the "A" of each beat for two bars.

Twelve-Bar Exercise—Dotted Eighth Shuffle with HH on Quarters

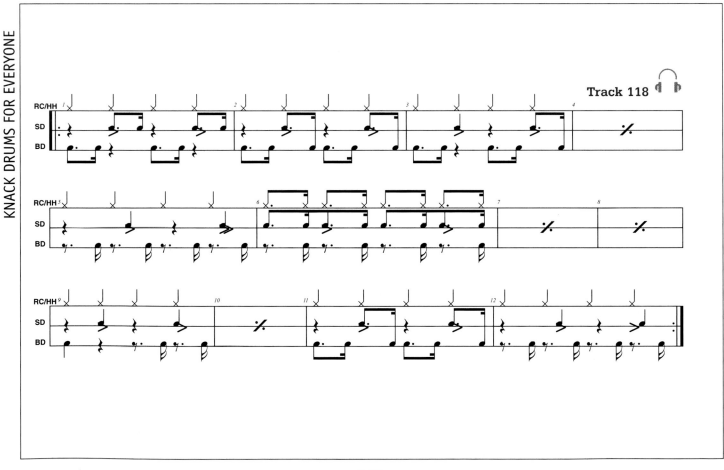

Track 118

KNACK DRUMS FOR EVERYONE

The SD in bar 5 comes in on 2 and 4, and on "1A, 2A, 3A, 4 A" in bar 6, with the accents on 2 and 4.

The next exercises are essentially short drum fills done with triplets. Exercise 1 uses alternate sticking starting with the RH. The BD plays on 1-2-3-4. Then on to a simple shuffle pattern for seven bars, repeating the whole sequence. Exercises 2 and 3 have the same fill, with the SD and a new feature, the rack toms. Listen to the audio track to hear this new sound.

Short Shuffle Fills

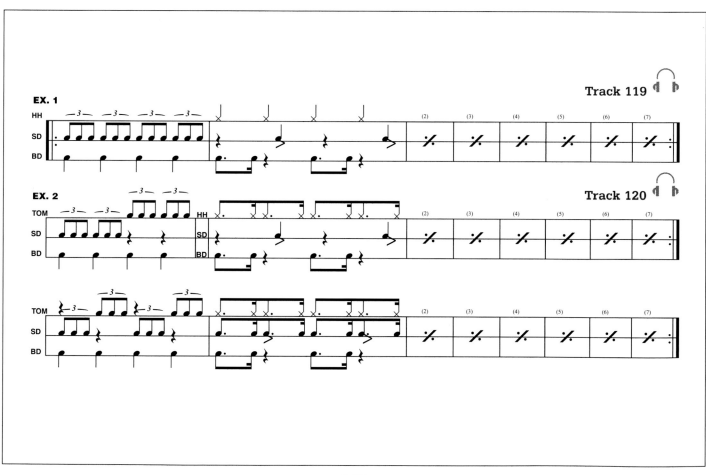

GROOVIN'

FILLING IN
Beefing up your drum fills vocabulary and making up some fills of your own

Every great drummer is known for his fills. In this section you'll be expanding your drum fill vocabulary. There'll be a fill exercise, followed by "playing time." Time is the same thing as a groove. In Exercises 1 to 4, I'll give you the grooves. After that you'll put in your own time.

Exercise 1 is a sixteenth note fill on the SD. The first count of each beat is a rest; you play on the "e&a." Watch the alternate sticking. The BD plays quarter notes on 1-2-3-4. Then play the "time" bar three times. Finally repeat the fill. The fill is the same in Exercise 2, except that I've added the toms. Exercise 3 is an

Drum Fills

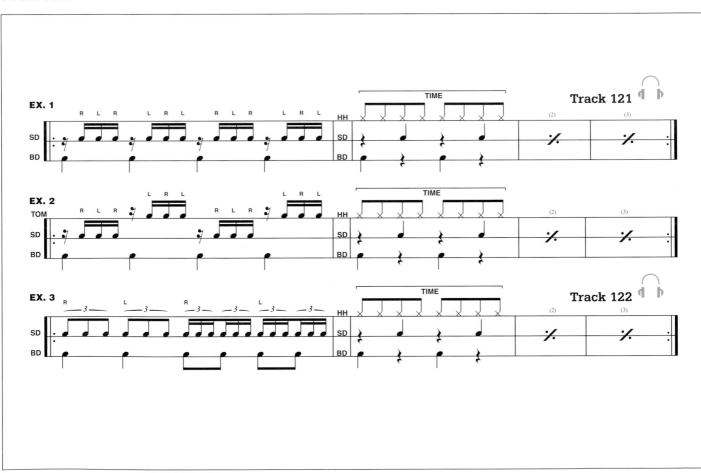

eighth and sixteenth note triplet fill. Watch for two different triplet pulses. After the fill go to the groove, playing it three times. Exercise 4 is the same, but the triplets alternate between the snare and tom, with the BD playing quarter note on 1-2 and eighth notes on "3+, 4+." Exercise 6 is a sixteenth note fill played with both hands alternating on the SD and tom at the same time, with the BD foot answering both hands and playing the quarter note on 4. The SD hits are accented, and it goes into three bars of time. Make up your own time here.

GREEN ● LIGHT

Practice as many fills as you can while going from the SD to the toms. Make up some of your own fills as well.

More Drum Fills

209

ADVANCED SIXTEENTH NOTES ROCK

Some tough but essential sixteenth note grooves to continue to develop your rhythmic sense

Oh, those tricky sixteenths. They're a challenge in and of themselves, but when you're playing them on the whole drum set at the same time, you're really forced to develop your sense of rhythm. So here are some cool grooves with sixteenths.

In Exercise 1 the HH/RC have the basic eighth note beat. The SD and BD alternate on the sixteenths in beats 1 and 3, with the SD on the quarter notes of 2 and 4.

Take a look at Exercise 5. This is a great pattern. The BD plays on the "A-and-a" of every beat and the SD comes in on 1-2-

Advanced Sixteenth Note Grooves

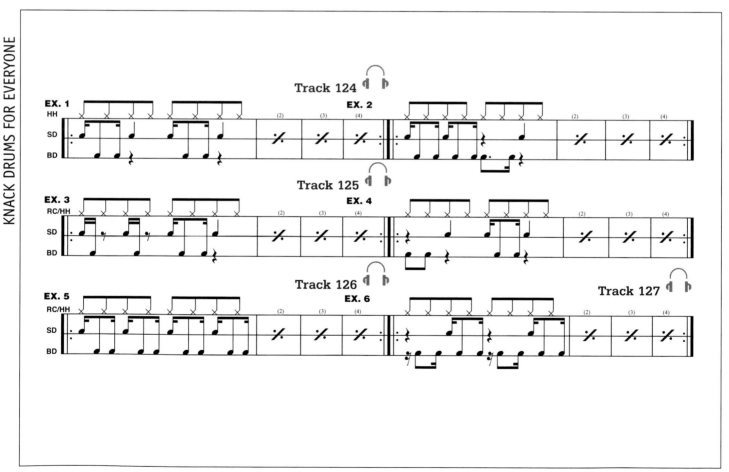

KNACK DRUMS FOR EVERYONE

3-4. After you play this exercise, go straight into Exercise 6, playing it as a single exercise.

I put bars 10 and 12 of the 12-bar exercise in to surprise you. Just a reminder to read the whole exercise over first, getting familiar with every bar, so that when you play it, you won't have any rude awakenings.

ZOOM

These types of patterns were used frequently by groups like Sly and the Family Stone and Tower of Power, putting them in a funk category.

Twelve-Bar Exercise with Advanced Sixteenth Note Grooves

GROOVIN'

PLAYING SONGS
Reading and playing rock songs, starting with Rod Stewart's "Hot Legs"

It's time to start playing real rock songs. So, grab your iPOD or CD player and earphones and get ready for some fun. I'll give you the basic outline of the song, and you can add or subtract drum fills at your own discretion. We'll start with "Hot Legs" by Rod Stewart, with yours truly on the drums.

The song begins with an 8-bar intro groove. In the first bar the BD, SD, and tom come in simultaneously on the 4 beat. Notice how the HH line changes for a second to the tom line. The HH then takes the eighth notes, with the snare on 2 and 4 and the BD on 1 and 3, the "+" of "2+" and the "+" of "4+."

"Hot Legs"—Introduction and Verse

212

In bar 8, we play a fill.

The verse is the same groove as the intro and in the 12-bar sequence there's a fill on the SD leading into the chorus.

In the chorus the BD comes in on 1 and 3 and the "and" of "4+," with a cymbal CRASH (note different cymbal symbol) and the HH on "4+."

In the next bar there's a SD fill on "4-e&a." This two-bar sequence continues until bar 6 of the chorus, where the SD fill goes into the break. In bar 7 the hands hit the "1" on the snare and tom together. Bar 7 continues with the SD on the "e&A" of "4" (this is where Rod sings, "I love you, Honey"). In bar 8 the snare plays on "1+2+," rests on 3, and plays on "+4+" with the HH, while the BD plays on the "1" of the first beat and the "and" of the second.

It seems complicated, but once you get a few songs down, you'll be able to anticipate patterns and it will get easier.

"Hot Legs"—Chorus

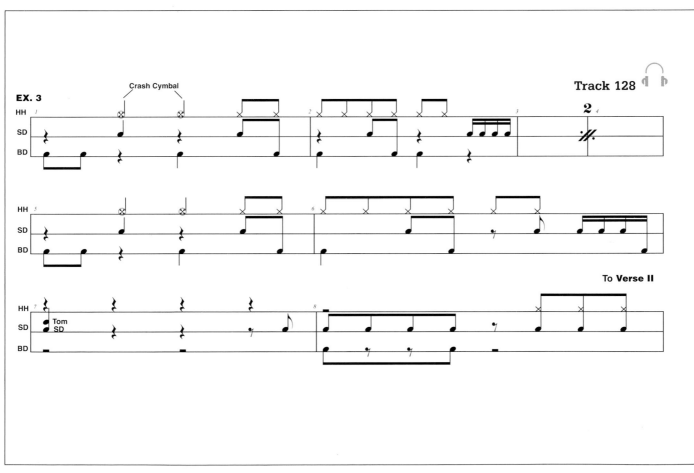

213

"CRAZY IN LOVE"—BEYONCE

Playing advanced sixteenth note patterns in a song—then try improvising your own

The song "Crazy in Love" by Beyonce has some unique patterns, one of which you just learned in the advanced sixteenth note section. Let's start with Exercise 1. The intro has both the BD and HH on the eighth notes—unusual for the BD. The groove in bar 1 lasts for seven bars before the

breakdown, which is where the advanced sixteenth note pattern comes in.

Take a look at bar 7, where BD plays on the first beat and the E of "2" and "4." Play this over and over to get it down. In bar 8 the BD comes in on the "1+" and on the "A" of 2-A and 4." This

"Crazy in Love"—Introduction and Chorus

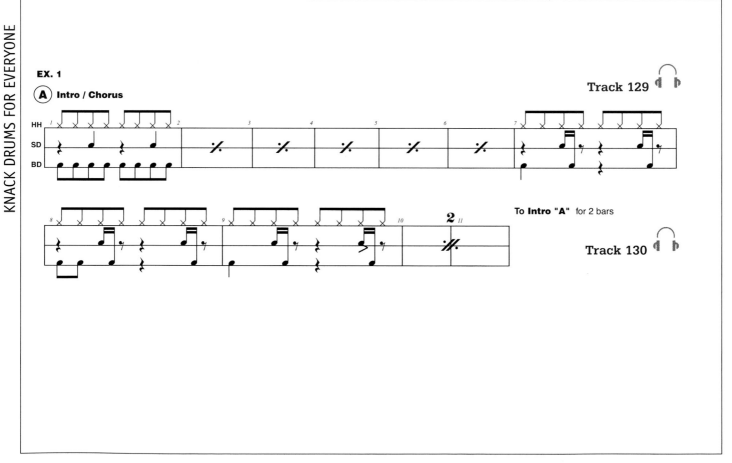

is followed by a two-bar repeat of bar 7. Listen to the song and see how these patterns fit in. Try and play along. The verse is nearly the same as the breakdown section. The drum has a four-bar sequence. Here's the way the song reads: Intro—twelve full bars, Verse—eight bars. Chorus. Back to verse; play along.In Exercise 3 the repeated bar has the BD on 1 and the "A" of "2-A-and-a" and "4-a-and-A," and the SD on "2-and" and 4. The hard part is the HH on the sixteenths. Practice this bar until you get it down. Then try and play it in the song.

··········· GREEN ● LIGHT ·············

Try playing these songs with your own beat and grooves. You should start out with the written music, of course, but doing your own thing, aka improvising, is what being a rock musician is all about.

"Crazy in Love"—Verse and Verse Exercise

EX. 2

EX. 3

Verse Practice   **Track 131** 🎧

Repeat over & over

Follow along with the song while playing the grooves above (bars 1-4).
At the end of the song, fade out at the Chorus "A" groove.

GROOVIN'

"REVOLUTION"—A BEATLES SHUFFLE
The Beatles turned out this fun-loving shuffle with some cool changes

The Beatles song "Revolution" has a pounding shuffle groove that is a lot of fun to play with.

The intro is easy enough to figure out, so we'll go straight to the verse. The basic groove of this song has a great bounce, with the HH playing the dotted eighth and sixteenth note shuffle. The SD part is on the "2A-4A" and the "1a-2A-3a-4A,"

with a heavy accent on the 2 and 4. The BD plays on the 1-2-3-4 quarter beats.

In bar 4 of the intro, you play a four stroke ruff with sixteenth note triplets starting on the "+-ti-ta" of beat 3, into beat 4, and on to the verse groove in Exercise 2, bar 1. Exercise 2, bar 2 introduces a new rhythm in 6/4 time. In this bar the HH and

"Revolution"—Verse/Introduction

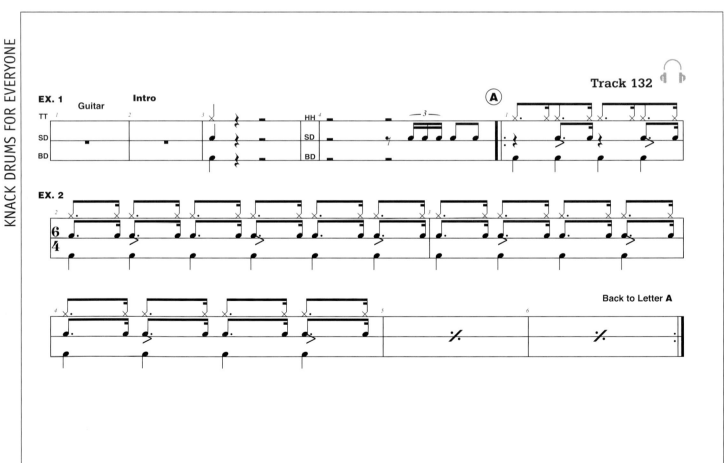

SD play "1A, 2A, 3A, 4A, 5A, 6A," with the BD on the quarter notes. The six-bar verse repeats, so it's actually twelve bars.

Next we go to the pre-chorus. Here the rhythm breaks up with the SD and tom hitting on the first beat of Exercise 3, bar 1, and then on the "2A-4A" for the next two bars. The time signature then changes again to 2/4, with accents played on a cymbal crash together with the BD. In bar 5 only the BD plays. The SD plays triplets in bar 6, with the BD on quarters into the chorus.

The chorus is the same as the verse, except that the BD plays on the "1A-rest on 2" play the "a of 2 and the 3A" and play the "a of 4". Like the intro, Exercise 4, bar 7 has the breakdown, and then it all repeats. Enjoy!

"Revolution"—Pre-Chorus/Chorus

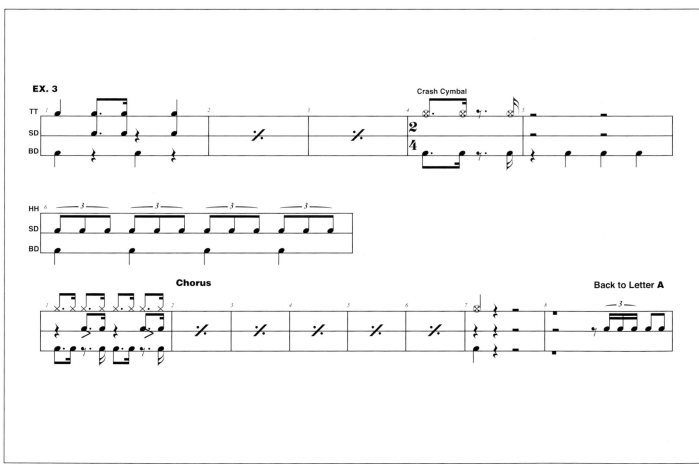

217

"HARDER TO BREATHE"—MAROON 5

This Maroon 5 slow rocker has some of the advanced sixteenth note grooves

"Harder to Breathe" is a slow rocker. Starting with the SD on "3e&-a-4e&-a," the cymbals and BD take over, slamming right into the song. Exercise 1, bar 2 has the HH on the eighth notes. The SD is on 2 and 4 throughout. The BD has the changes. In bar 1 it comes in on "1e," "3e," and 4. In bar 3 the BD plays on

"1E-3E," rests on "+," plays on "A," and plays on the "E+" of 4. Bar 4 repeats bar 2. Note the first and second endings.

In bar 1 of the chorus, the SD plays on 2 and 4 and the HH is on the eighth notes. The BD line is a little more difficult. It plays the "1A", and the "A" on 2, and the "E" and "A" of 3. Bar 2 is

"Harder to Breathe"—Verse

KNACK DRUMS FOR EVERYONE

the same, except that the BD comes in on the "+A" of 4. This repeats for six bars and then goes to a 4-bar breakdown that has the same groove as bar 1 in the chorus. After the breakdown go back to the verse and follow the song.

•••••••••••••• RED ● LIGHT ••••••••••••••

Playing a number like this can get tricky. Because it's a rock song at a slow tempo, each bar is fairly long.

•••••••••• GREEN ● LIGHT ••••••••••••

Experiment with playing this song your own way. I want you to get used to doing your own thing!

"Harder to Breathe"—Chorus/End

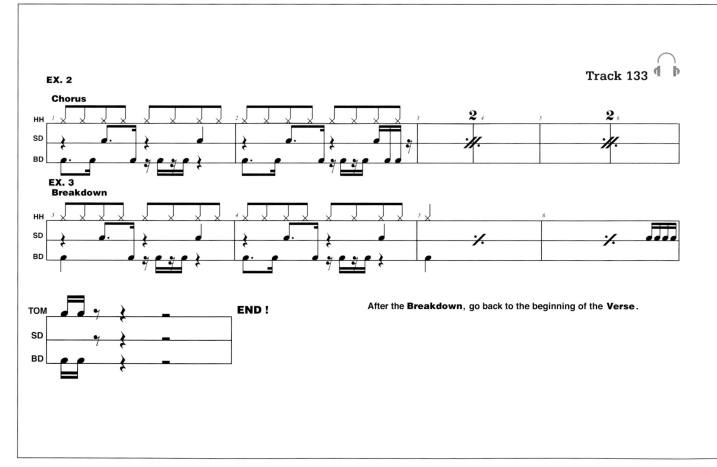

"HEY YA"—OUTKAST

An up-tempo rock song with a great beat; the beat was part of the selling point of this song

Like "My Sharona," "Hey Ya" is one of those songs that can be identified by the fantastic beat and sound of the drums. It also has a very creative rhythm—after every three bars in 4/4 time, there's a bar in 2/4, which makes it really interesting to play.

Let's look at this song. The groove has the HH on the 1-2-3-4 quarter notes—different and cool. The snare is on 2 and 4. Practice the SD and HD parts first before adding the BD.

The groove continues for three bars. Then in bar 4 the time signature changes from 4/4 to 2/4. Now the HH plays on 1-2,

"Hey Ya"—Verse

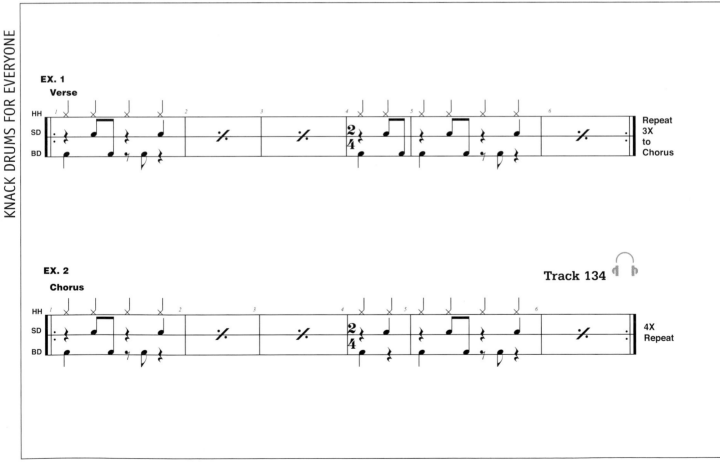

the SD is on the 2, and the BD comes in on 1 and the "+" of "2+."

The chorus is the same, except for the 2/4 bar. Here the BD only plays on 1 and the SD on 2.

The last sequence has a break on the first beat of bar 23 of the verse.

ZOOM

"Hey Ya" has some of the coolest drum sounds ever recorded. In fact the drums are so fantastic that they were the reason people loved it. Like me—when this song came out, I couldn't stop listening to it. It just shows you how powerfully drums can move people.

"Hey Ya"—Breakdown

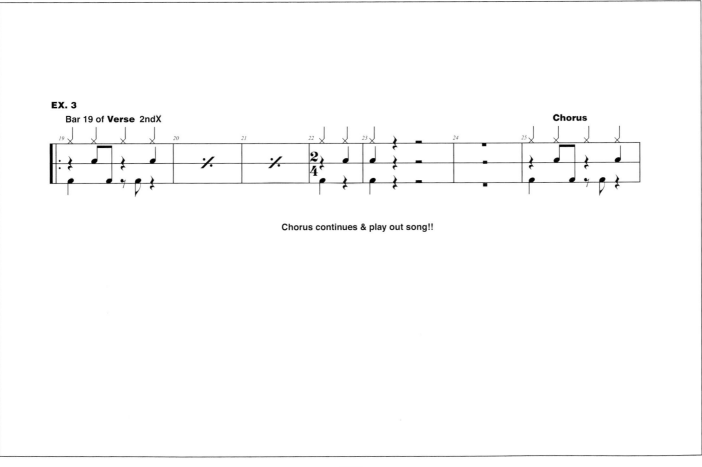

EX. 3

Bar 19 of **Verse** 2ndX

Chorus

Chorus continues & play out song!!

"HUNGRY HEART"—SPRINGSTEEN

This song has a really fine hypnotic groove, with catchy, simple fills at the end

"Hungry Heart" basically consists of one groove with a super drum sound, played by Max Weinberg, the drummer on "Tonight Show with Conan O'Brien," who is with Springsteen's E Street Band. "Hungry Heart" was Springsteen's first Top Ten single and Weinberg's favorite Springsteen song. It

gave this fine drummer a chance to use what critics called his "inexorable kick."

In Exercise 1, bar 1, Max rests for two beats and then comes in with a drum fill on the SD (counted "1+A" "2+"), moving into the pattern with the HH on eighth notes and the SD on 2

"Hungry Heart"—Introduction/Verse

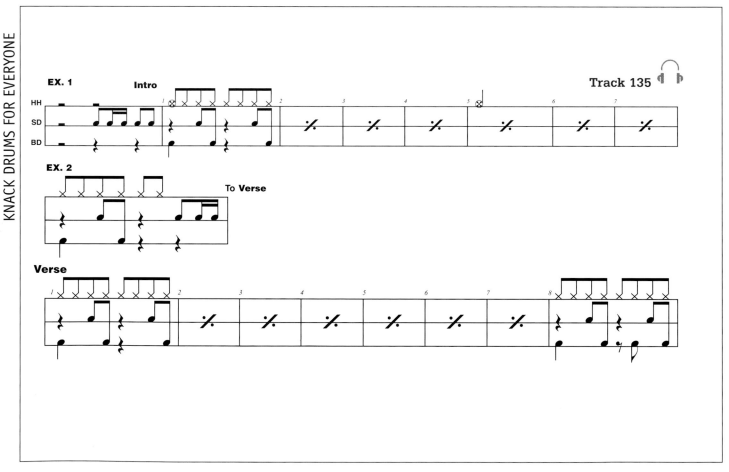

KNACK DRUMS FOR EVERYONE

and 4. What makes this groove come to life is the BD, playing on the 1 and the "+" of 2 together with the bass guitar. When played repeatedly, this pattern creates a hypnotic feel.

At the end of the eight-bar intro, in bar 8, Max does another simple fill on the SD, going right into the verse on the "4-+-a." It's a perfect example of a "less is more" drum part. It's really easy, but it's all in the execution.

On the eighth bar of each verse, Max adds one BD beat on the "1", the "+" of 2, the "+" of 3, and the "+" of 4. He does this every time without fail. He also plays this same pattern in bar 8 of the chorus, and in the last bar of the chorus, he plays another fill on the "+" of "3-+" and "4-+-A."

Some of the fills at the end of the song are simple and really fun to play. Listen to them and play along. And don't be afraid to create your own fills too.

"Hungry Heart"—Chorus/Fills

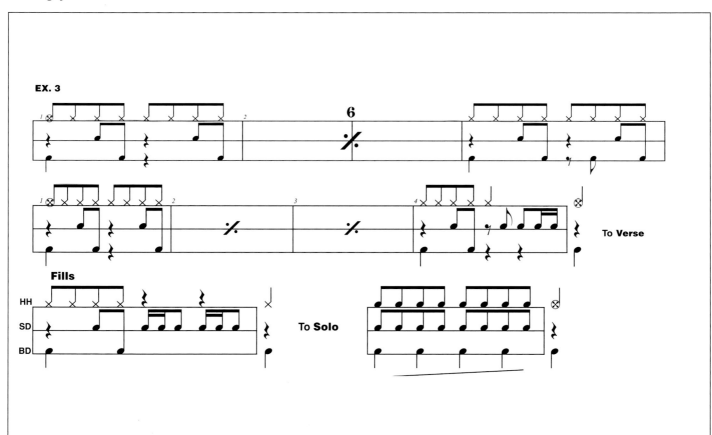

223

"HONKY TONK WOMAN"

This is a classic song with a classic drum groove, played by a classic drummer—Charlie Watts

As soon as the drum groove starts, you know what's coming. "I met a gin soaked bar room queen in Memphis . . ." This 1969 Stones hit has in-your-face lyrics; a seductive, relentless beat; and the one, the only Mick Jagger. Plus, the great drumming of Charlie Watts.

"Honky Tonk Woman" is a classic groove. It all starts in Exercise 1, with the SD and the tom establishing the beat. Then on to the intro and that classic pattern of eighth notes on the HH, with the SD on the 2 and 4 and the BD on the 1 and the "+" of "3-and-4." This groove plays through the entire song. The intro

"Honky Tonk Woman"—Introduction/Verse

KNACK DRUMS FOR EVERYONE

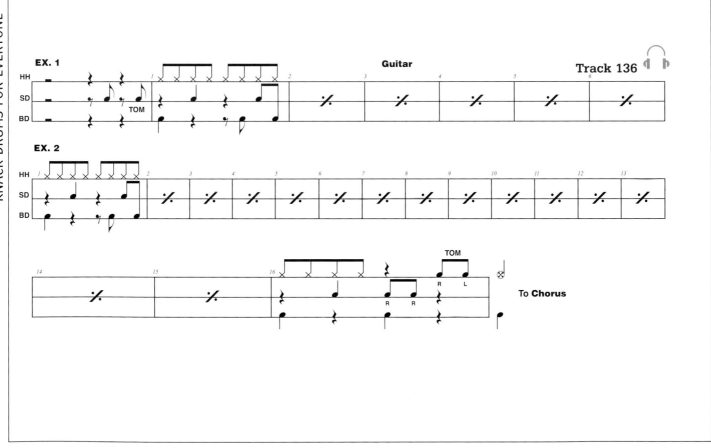

with the guitar goes for six bars, and then the verse begins.

The 16-bar verse (Exercise 2) has a fill with the SD on "3+" and the tom on "4+" leading into the chorus.

Bar 1 of the chorus is different from the same bar of the verse. The HH and SD are the same, but the BD plays on the 1 and the "+" of "2+," the 3, and the "+" of "4+." Bar 2 is the same, except that the BD plays on the "3+." Bar 3 is the same as bar 1. The BD part changes every two bars, but it keeps to a similar pattern. Practice the verse and chorus separately, and then together.

Check out the drum fills at the end of the song. The SD and tom play the same eighth note pattern on 1-2-3-4, with the BD on the "+" counts. This is a powerful fill.

By the way, that sound you hear at the beginning is a cowbell. But Charlie Watts isn't playing it. It's an overdub that provides a counterrhythm to the drums.

Practice along with the actual song. How does it feel to be playing with the Rolling Stones?

"Honky Tonk Woman"—Chorus/Fills

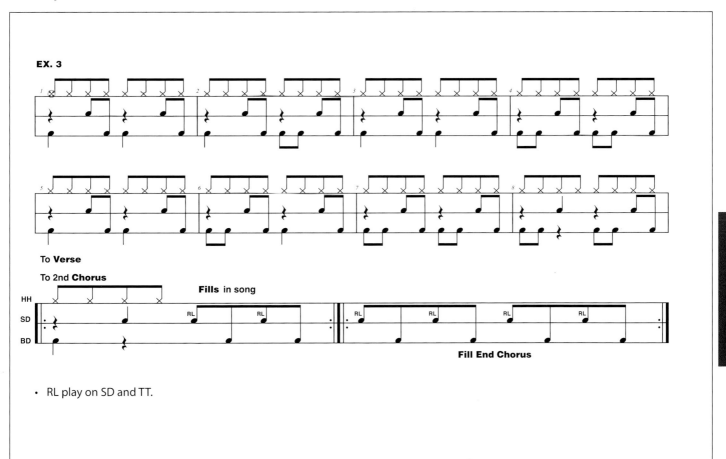

- RL play on SD and TT.

"PAPER PLANES"—MIA

Playing to a remix with a drum machine can be fun and good for you

This song uses a drum machine and is a great practice tool because it's like playing with a metronome. The first thing you must practice is playing the HH on eighth notes and opening the HH pedal a little on the "+" of "4" in each bar. This something we haven't done, but you should learn it. The "o"

notation stands for "open HH." So, play your BD on the quarter notes and the HH with the "o" on the "and" of 4." Do this for three minutes.

Let's move on to playing the song. Here you'll be playing the HH, SD, and BD to all these different programmed rhythm

"Paper Planes"—Introduction/Verse

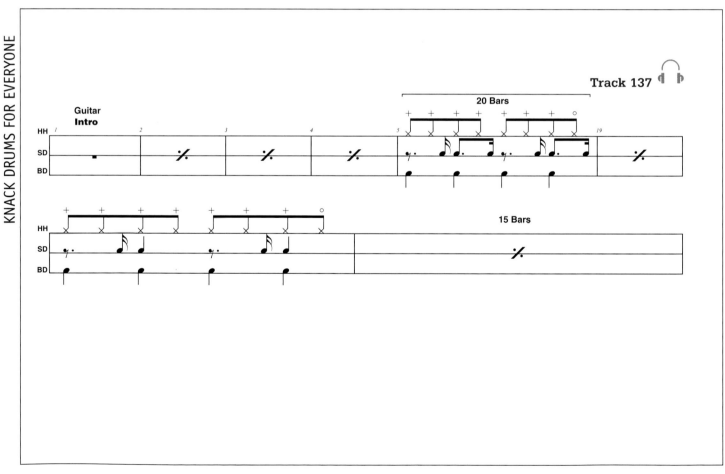

parts. After a 4-bar intro with a riff, you go into the groove. While the BD comes in on 1-2-3-4, the SD plays on the "A" of "1," the "2," the A of "3" and "4-A." This creates a cool pattern against the BD. The HH plays its part against this.

It's pretty much this way for the whole song. There are some fills on the toms in bar 4 of the chorus, and a snare fill in bar 8. Then, back to the groove on 3-4.

"Paper Planes"—Chorus/Fills

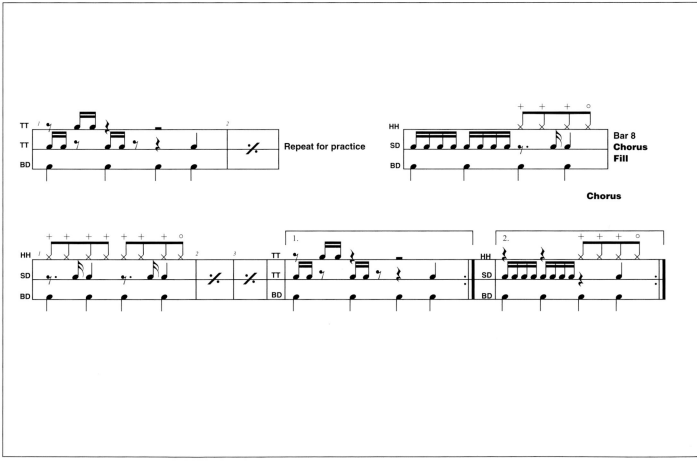

A FINAL WORD

Well, there it is. You've come to the end of this book, and you should really be starting to enjoy your newfound talent. I hope you get as much joy and fulfillment out of the drums as I have.

And I hope someday you get to the point where you're playing gigs—for love as well as money. That's where the real magic comes in. There's nothing like those moments when you've got the crowd with you, the place is pulsating with energy, and you seem to go somewhere else—out of your body, into the stratosphere, becoming one with everything and everyone. I call those "magic nights."

I've had many magic nights, but one in particular stands out. Vanilla Fudge was playing in Central Park, to a crowd of fifty thousand people. When we did the organ/gospel number "People Get Ready," I actually sang it. The audience was so quiet you could hear the buses on Fifth Avenue. It was no longer a song; it became a prayer, and Central Park was the church. The memory still gives me goose bumps. That's the power of music.

Good luck, and remember: No matter how frustrated you might get, if you love the drums, never give up. The best is always yet to come!

DRUM GEAR

Cymbal Companies

Bosphorus Cymbals
- Bosphorus is a new, smaller company that makes very good cymbals. If you're looking for that classic vintage cymbal sound, try one.

- www.bosphoruscymbals.com

Istanbul Cymbals
- These Turkish cymbals are handmade. They sound quite good.

- www.istanbulcymbals.com

Mienl Cymbals
- Meinl is a newer cymbal company out of Germany and ranks next in line after Paiste. They make a large variety of cymbals at good prices.

- www.meinlcymbals.com

Paiste Cymbals
- Paiste is number three in the world of cymbals. For over forty years, they've been Switzerland's premiere manufacturers of cymbals and gongs, at very reasonable prices.

- www.paistecymbals.com

Sabian Cymbals
- In the early 1980s Robert Zildjian left the Zildjian Cymbal Company, a family business for generations, and started his own company, Sabian. Like Zildjian, Sabian manufactures the highest quality cymbals in the world.

- www.sabian.com

Zildjian Cymbals
- Zildjian is the oldest cymbal company in the United States. They've been in business since the early 1900s and have supplied cymbals to all the great drummers. Along with Sabian, they're the largest cymbal company in the world.

- www.zildjian.com

Note: Most of the big companies have both high-end and cheap lines of cymbals. The smaller companies usually have more expensive lines and not as much to choose from.

Drum Companies

DDRUM
- A new state-of-the-art drum company based in Tampa, Florida. They make great products at great prices.

- www.ddrum.com

DW
- This drum company based in the Los Angeles area features a lot of choices for drummers.

- www.dwdrums.com

Ludwig Drums
- Ludwig's slogan is, "The Most Famous Name in Drums," and nobody can argue with that. Ringo played Ludwigs, and that was enough to secure their immortality. Today they are well-made, reasonably priced drums.

- www.ludwig-drums.com

Mapex Drums
- These drums are made in Taiwan. They're good quality and their prices are reasonable. Mapex has been around for twenty years or so.

- www.mapexdrums.com

Sonor
- Sonor is a German drum company that's been around for many years. Their drums are higher priced, but they're very well made.

- www.sonor.com

Tama Drums
- Tama is another famous Japanese drum company. They make very good drums and have been a successful operation for over thirty years.

- www.tama.com

Taye Drums
- Taye is based in China and offers good prices and good quality for the money.

- www.tayedrums.com

Yamaha Drums
- Yamaha has been around since 1967. They're most famous for their pianos, but they make good-sounding drums.

- www.yamaha.com/drums/home.html

Drumheads
Aquarian Drumheads
- Aquarian was the brainchild of famed jazz drummer Roy Burns. Aquarians have to be the strongest, longest lasting drumheads on the market. They offer great value for the money.

- www.aquariandrumheads.com

Attack Drumheads
- Attack is a newer company. They have quite a few heads to choose from, and they're distributed by Universal Percussion.

- www.universalpercussion.com

Peace Drums
- Peace Drums is another Chinese company. Their prices are low, but they're not as professional as some of the other drum companies.

- www.peacedrum.com

Pearl Drums
- Pearl has been around for over thirty years. The company originated in Japan and has been the number one seller of drums and kits for years.

- www.pearldrum.com

Remo Drums
- A spin off of Remo, the biggest drumhead company in the world. Remo drums are good, but not outstanding.

- www.remo.com

Evans Heads

- These heads have been around for some time now and are very popular. There's a good line to choose from, with a wide price range. Evans also sells accessories like drum pads, drum mutes, and snare wires.

- www.evansdrumheads.com

Remo Drumheads

- Remo is the oldest drum headdrumhead company around. They were the first ones to come out with the plastic drum headdrumheads in the 1960s. Almost every drum company features Remo heads on their sets. Remo is also known for their world percussion products.

- www.remo.com

Sticks/Mallets

Ahead Drumsticks

- These sticks are made out of space age material, not wood. They're supposed to last longer than their wood counterparts, but to me, they don't feel the same. Of course, if your first pair of sticks are Aheads, you won't know the difference. Aheads are generally black in color.

- www.bigbangdist.com

Pro-Mark

- Pro-Mark's been around for decades as well. They have many types of good quality sticks.

- wwwpromark-stix.com

Regal Tip by Caloto

- Regal sticks are top quality and have been around for decades. I had Regals when I was a teenager. Regal was the first to put the plastic tip on the drumstick.

- www.regaltip.com

3 Drum Drumsticks

- 3 Drum is a DW company. Their gimmick is "buy two, get one free." In other words they give you three sticks when you buy a pair. 3 Drumsticks are labeled for weight and type of sound and are guaranteed to be straight.

- www.3drumsticks.com

Vic Firth Sticks

- Vic Firth is probably the most popular line of sticks in the world. In addition to their large choice of sticks, they make mallets, brushes, and pretty much everything else for the drummer, including headphones, practice pads, and more.

- www.vicfirth.com

Vater Drumsticks

- Vater is a newer company, no more than ten years old. But they've made a good name for themselves in a short time and have a cool image among the younger drum set (pun intended!).

- www.vater.com

Zildjian Drumsticks

- Zildjian only used to make cymbals, but they now offer an assortment of wood sticks as well.

- www.zildjian.com

To peek in on the mallet world, go online to any of the following sites:

- www.vicfirth.com

- www.regaltip.com

- www.promark.com

DRUMMER WEB SITES

If you do an online search for "drummer Web sites," a whole slew of them will come up. Here are some to start with:

www.drummagazine.com
www.drummersweb.com
www.drummerworld.com
www.drummerzone.com
www.moderndrummer.com

MUSIC PUBLISHERS

Alfred Music
- Alfred Music carries many, many drum instruction books and DVDs and has one of the biggest drum instruction catalogs In the industry. My book, *Realistic Rock,* has been a big seller for Alfred, and you might want to get it if you're going to continue your studies. Other excellent Alfred books are Ted Reed's *Syncopation* and Jim Chapin's *Advanced Studies for the Modern Drummer.*

- www.alfred.com

Carl Fisher
- While not as big as Alfred or Hal Leonard, Carl Fisher is a well-known publisher with a sizeable catalog of instructional books and DVDs. They also publish a lot of piano, band, and orchestra books.

- www.carlfisher.com

Hal Leonard
- Hal Leonard is another big publisher of instruction books, with an excellent catalogue.

- www.halleonard.com

Hot Licks-EMI
- Hot Licks is a video company currently owned by EMI. Their heyday was the1980s, and they have some good older titles. All of their videos are now on DVD.

- www.emimusicpub.com

Hudson Music
- Hudson is primarily an instructional DVD company. Their specialty is percussion. They do have books by some great names in drumming, but they're mainly known for their impressive DVD catalogue, which features the best artists. And the production value of their DVDs is great.

- www.hudsonmusic.com

Power Rock
- This is the video-DVD company I'm involved in. We've got DVDs of me with my brother, Vinny Appice, drummer for Dio's Black Sabbath and Heaven and Hell, plus other artists like Tris Imbodine (Chicago), Slim Jim Phantom (Stray Cats), and more. Check out the Web site.

- www.powerrock.com

MUSIC SCHOOLS

RESOURCES

Drummers Collective (Collective School of Music), New York City

- This is a great school for drummers. They have many famous drummers on their faculty; what better atmosphere for learning than the greatest city in the world, New York?

- www.drummerscollective.com

The following are some famous schools for drumming. Look in your local yellow pages or go online to see what drum schools are available in your area.

LA Music Academy, Los Angeles

- Founded by big session drummer Ralph Humphreys, this school offers a good drum instruction curriculum. It's a great place to learn and have fun.

- www.lamusicacademy.com/

Musicians Institute, Los Angeles

- Musicians Institute features a complete array of instrumental and vocal courses, as well as courses in recording, the music business, and other related areas. It offers degrees in these different subjects.

- www.usjournal.com/en/students/campuses/mi.html

ONLINE CHAIN MUSIC STORES

Most local music stores have Web sites that allow you to buy online. So, before you purchase anything, see what your local store has in stock before going to the big online shops. You'll save money on shipping. When buying online, it's best to try a site with a store in your area first, so you can deal with them in person if there's a problem with your purchase. It can be a real drawback if there's no store in your area and you need to return or exchange an item.

5 Star Drum Shops
- These drum shops have an affiliation and offer five-star services to their customers. Unfortunately, they're not in every city.

- www.fivestardrumshops.com

Guitar Center
- GC has more stores than any other chain. They generally offer pretty good discounts.

- www.guitarcenter.com

Musician.com
- This Web site has plenty of good deals on all kinds of equipment. The down side is, you're paying the shipping cost and if there is a problem, there's no store to go to.

- www.musician.com

Musician's Friend
- This is one of the hottest music gear sites, with the lowest prices since 1983. A great online store that has everything you need.

- www.musicansfriend.com

Sam Ash Music Stores
- Sam Ash is not quite as big as Guitar Center, but they have stores all around the country, with a large selection and good discounts.

- www.samash.com

PUBLICATIONS

Drum Magazines

Drum Magazine

- This magazine is geared toward a younger drumming audience, featuring drummers like Travis Barker from BLINK 182 and newer bands.

Drumhead

- This is a new magazine appealing to the *Modern Drummer* audience.

Modern Drummer

- This is the oldest and largest drum magazine in the United States. It covers all kinds of drumming and also has a good online presence.

Traps

- Traps concentrates more on classic or legendary artists. It's more interested in the art form of drumming than the flavor of the month.

INDEX

INDEX